T0265235

EAGLES AND EARWIGS

First published in 2018
by Eyewear Publishing Ltd
Suite 38, 19-21 Crawford Street
London, W1H 1PJ
United Kingdom

Graphic design by Edwin Smet
Printed in England by TJ International Ltd, Padstow, Cornwall

Set in Bembo 13 / 16 pt
ISBN 978-1-912477-16-6

WWW.EYEWEARPUBLISHING.COM

COLIN WILSON
EAGLES AND EARWIGS: ESSAYS ON BOOKS AND WRITERS

WITH A PUBLISHER'S STATEMENT BY **TODD SWIFT**
WITH A PREFACE BY **GARY LACHMAN**
AND EDITORIAL NOTES BY **COLIN STANLEY**

CONTENTS

PART TWO INDIVIDUAL WRITERS

PART THREE THE WRITER AND SOCIETY

PUBLISHER'S STATEMENT

Gary Lachman has provided this important reprint with an invaluable preface, so I will be brief. I am very grateful to Joy Wilson, for entrusting me with this manuscript, which very much deserved, and needed, to be back in print.

Colin Wilson has meant a great deal to me for over three decades. I first read him at Marianopolis College in Montreal when I was a teenager, idealistic and questing. My friends Douglas and Chris would sit for hours, smoking, listening to LPs, and drinking tea, while reading battered second-hand paperback editions of the Wilson classics, trading them – and their astonishing insights – back and forth between us.

Later, while living in Paris, I was fortunate to have struck up a correspondence with Colin Wilson through email and the post, though we never met – a sure regret of my life. He was polite and helpful with my poems, while making it diplomatically clear they were not the kind of poems he himself preferred; one of the delights of this present book is that we get to see an existential critic at work; in his demands for writing which does more than serve stylistic or aesthetic ends, he prefigures, perhaps curiously, the current intersectionality debates on campuses. The idea that writing be called to higher purpose is not new.

As I have written elsewhere, I believe Colin Wilson to be a visionary thinker and writer of at least near-genius, whose reputation, like that of a fellow outsider fascinated by extreme states of consciousness, science, and mystery – Poe – has equally been side-lined. He is a competent stylist, capable of writing exceptionally readable books, a brilliant collector of both facts and anecdotal wonders, but also a master analyst, able to distil and refine what he has read and thought about.

It may be the case that Wilson only had a few key insights – but his almost uncanny ability to have foreseen the 21st century fascination with sociopaths, sex criminals, the weird and supernatural, as well as science-fiction and self-help, is remarkable. Wilson's books are almost a preamble to our current age of mindfulness and mayhem.

As readers of this book, too long out of print, and handsomely reprinted with the design of Edwin Smet, will soon see, Wilson even predicted the resurgence of interest in Ayn Rand. More importantly, they will find a very effective and clear way into his main ideas and preoccupations, preparing them to discover, or rediscover his two pivotal (and most popular) books, *The Outsider*, and *The Occult: A History*.

I often reflect upon Wilson's insights into what he termed Faculty X, an ability that allows us to sometimes move beyond the inner robot and grasp, in peak moments, the deeper sharper positive clarity of experience. The world, for Wilson, flashed with Chesterton's 'absurd good news'. Secular it may be, but good news nonetheless. Here in this book is some of it for you.

DR TODD SWIFT
Maida Vale, London
August 2018

PREFACE
EXISTENTIALLY CRITICAL:
INTRODUCING *EAGLES AND EARWIGS*

by Gary Lachman

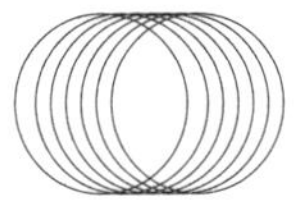

I first read *Eagle and Earwig** many years ago. It was, in fact, in 1983, during the tail-end of a mini European 'search for the miraculous' that had me visiting Chartres Cathedral, Glastonbury Tor, and the site of Gurdjieff's Institute for the Harmonious Development of Man in Fontainebleau, France, among other places. One destination on this itinerary was the small fishing village of Gorran Haven, in Cornwall, England, where I would meet the author of this book, Colin Wilson. There I spent an evening absorbing large helpings of phenomenology and equally generous amounts of red wine, both courtesy of my host.

The next morning found me somewhat worse for wear on a train to London. There I stretched out the last week of my European adventure staying in a youth hostel in Paddington. I spent my days at the old Reading Room of the British Museum, and wandered the streets at night, as I felt all good Outsiders should. The Reading Room had, of course, a romantic attraction for me. Wilson had written about his days there, writing his first novel *Ritu-*

* Publisher's Note: The title has been updated as per Wilson's wishes, as explained later.

al in the Dark, while sleeping on Hampstead Heath. But along with the frisson of echoing my favourite author's early days, my visit had another benefit. At the Reading Room I managed to find a book by Wilson that had so far eluded me. It was *Eagle and Earwig*.

Finding a book at a library may seem a small glory compared to decoding the alchemical façade of Notre-Dame de Paris or meditating on the standing stones of Avebury – two other spots on my itinerary. But for this particular esotourist, it was a high point of the journey. Strangely enough, to refresh my memory before writing this Preface, I recently ordered the book at the new British Library, which took the place of the old, now defunct Reading Room. When it arrived there was the same copy, the one I had first read some thirty-four years ago.

My trail to finding *Eagle and Earwig* at the British Museum started some years earlier in a rather different setting. In 1975 I was nineteen, living in a rundown loft space on New York's Bowery and playing in an underground rock band. Another inhabitant of the building was a flamboyant, eccentric artist who had an interest in Aleister Crowley and the occult. Until then I had had no interest in the occult, but something happened that summer, and I soon found myself fascinated by it. One book that clinched my obsession was Wilson's 1971 'comeback' bestseller *The Occult*. I read it and it is no exaggeration to say that it changed my life.

It certainly made me a dedicated Wilson reader. I spent the next several years tracking down his books and greedily pouncing on any that I could find. As the band became successful, we began to tour, and as we travelled across the country I would head to any used bookstores along the way. I did the same with my own band and with others I performed with. I amassed an extensive Wilson library but there was one book I was never able to locate: the elusive *Eagle and Earwig*.

Although I know copies are available on the internet (usually at exorbitant prices) there is something about finding a much sought after work in a second hand bookshop that carries its own special magic, as rare as that is these days. And although throughout the forty-two years that I have been reading and re-reading Wilson, I have never seen *Eagle and Earwig* in any shop, I still check the literary criticism sections of used bookshops, to see if a copy has by any miracle appeared. It never has. So when Colin Stanley mentioned that he was planning on bringing out a new edition of this rare Wilson collection and asked if I would write a Preface to it, I immediately agreed. I had suggested to Colin several times that he should bring out a new edition of *Eagle and Earwig* and I am happy that he had the good sense to persuade Eyewear publisher Todd Swift to ultimately bring it out. I'm sure the readers of this new edition will feel the same.

Eagle and Earwig is a collection of essays in what Wilson calls 'existential criticism'. The essence of this is outlined in two earlier books, *The Age of Defeat* (1959; called *The Stature of Man* in the US) and *The Strength to Dream* (1962), which make up part of Wilson's 'Outsider Cycle'. And it informs such later works as *The Craft of the Novel*

(1975) and *The Books in My Life* (1998). Not surprisingly it is also the focus of a collection of Wilson's book reviews that Colin Stanley's Paupers' Press publishes, the aptly named *Existential Criticism: Selected Book Reviews* (2009).

What is 'existential criticism'? Wilson himself will tell you in the long essay that opens the book, but the reader will forgive me if I prepare the ground a little here. It is perhaps best if I differentiate existential criticism from ordinary literary criticism, although these days, with the rise of various new critical approaches – deconstructionism, postmodernism, post-colonialism, and others – the kind of literary criticism Wilson was writing against may seem positively prehistoric.

We can say that ordinary literary criticism, the kind academics engage in, concerns itself primarily with *how* a writer says what he has to say, with his technical skill at expressing him or herself with words. It is concerned with style and the influence of one author on another and with comparisons among different writers. Although not every critical school may do this, criticism may also look at *what* an author is saying, the explicit ideas or themes that emerge in his work. Nodding to more recent schools, like those mentioned above, it may also argue that the book or poem or story is a self-contained entity, a reality in itself, and ignore any idea of looking at the writer's life to gain insight into what he or she may have wanted to say (this hardly matters) or the reasons why they said it in precisely *that* way. My own experience of academic literary criticism, endured many years ago, was of teasing out any hint of radical leftist politics in the turbid stream of consciousness making up James Joyce's *Ulysses*. The reader may not be surprised that I did not complete the doctorate.

Existential criticism acknowledges the value of these other approaches – although Wilson has little good to say about deconstructionism or postmodernism – but it is after different game.[1] It is concerned with how a writer *sees* the world, his actual *perception* of it, and with his or her qualifications for making general assessments about that mysterious thing, life. As Wilson writes, for him, it is 'necessary to scrutinize the writer's qualifications for imposing his vision on his contemporaries.' Wilson agrees with William James that 'a man's vision is the great fact about him.' What existential criticism does is to examine that vision, to see how inclusive it is, how much of reality it incorporates. Or conversely, it examines 'how far a writer's attitude toward the world is parochial, based on some temperamental defect of vision.'

Why is this kind of criticism called 'existential' and not some other name? 'Phenomenological criticism' would also be correct, and in some ways perhaps more accurate, if something of a mouthful. This is because Wilson's literary analyses are based on the philosopher Edmund Husserl's – the founder of phenomenology – fundamental insight, that perception is *intentional*. As Wilson wrote in *The Strength to Dream*, man 'has a *will to perceive*, as well as perceptions.' As Wilson has argued in many books, when

1 See Wilson's criticism of deconstructionism and postmodernism, specifically Jacques Derrida and Roland Barthes, in *Below the Iceberg* (San Bernardino, Ca: Borgo Press, 1998), reprinted in *Collected Essays on Philosophers* (Newcastle-upon-Tyne: Cambridge Scholars, 2016).

our intentionality is strong – when our 'will to perceive' is tightly focussed – we may perceive the world as poets like William Blake did, with our 'doors of perception' squeaky clean. But when it is weak and barely working, these doors are fogged over and smeared, and the world they reveal – or rather, obscure – can seem bleak and meaningless. Intentionality, for Husserl, reveals reality. The more we intend, the more it reveals.

Existentialism, which emerged from Husserl's phenomenology, is concerned with questions of meaning and purpose, with our experience of life and our response to its challenges. Wilson appreciates the analyses of 'inauthenticity' and 'bad faith' that Heidegger and Sartre and the philosophers influenced by them apply to everyday life, to our inveterate habit of avoiding complexity and finding safety in doing as everyone else does. But as Wilson's readers will know, he argues that in their final assessment of human existence, which in general they find meaningless, they leave out – purposefully, it often seems – Husserl's fundamental insight. For Wilson, Sartre's 'nausea', which he argues is the bottom-line truth about existence, is really evidence of his weak intentionality. Blake's 'world in a grain of sand', Wilson argues, is much closer to the truth. Yet Sartre's view of life as basically meaningless is presented to his readers, not as a peculiarity of Sartre's temperament, but as a grim but unavoidable fact. He is 'telling it like it is'. For Wilson, Sartre is doing no such thing, merely telling us how *he* sees the world, and performing a literary sleight-of-hand in order to convince us that this is the 'truth'.

Readers will be familiar with how Wilson applies existential criticism to Aldous Huxley, D. H. Lawrence, Graham Greene and his particular bête noire, Samuel Beckett. Here he turns his attention to other writers. Some of these he writes about elsewhere. References to Robert Musil, John Cowper Powys, and Ernest Hemingway can be found in many places in Wilson's oeuvre. Others he has devoted whole books to. David Lindsay, author of the devastating *A Voyage to Arcturus* and other metaphysical fables, is the focus of Wilson's short book *The Haunted Man: The Strange Genius of David Lindsay*.[2]

Lindsay is an interesting subject for the existential critic. *A Voyage to Arcturus*, his early masterpiece, should be much better known as a work of 'gnostic' fiction these days, as it is a much more powerful work of the imagination than anything Philip K. Dick or Thomas Pynchon, two popular 'gnostic' writers, ever wrote. But because Lindsay was a clumsy stylist and lacks the readability of Dick – a pulp professional – or the 'experimental' cachet of Pynchon, he is unknown, except for a band of dedicated readers, many of them brought to him by Wilson. Lindsay's literary technique was, by most critical standards, third-rate, but what he has to *say* is more profound than anything either Dick or Pynchon did – at least to my mind.

Lindsay is an example of Wilson's dictum that one can be a bad novelist but still a writer of genius. All the technique in the world cannot make up for having nothing to say. And what Lindsay says is that the world we take

2 San Bernardino, Ca: Borgo Press, 1979.

for granted, the world that Sartre and Heidegger and the other old-existentialists assume is the only one available to us, is false. There is a 'truer', more vital, more *real* reality under that dull, everyday surface. Lindsay's genius lies in his ability to make the reader *see* that world, to feel its intensity, and so to question what he had so far accepted as 'reality'.

The little read L. H. Myers, who knew Lindsay, is the subject of another essay. It is from Myers' limpid novel of ideas, *The Near and the Far*, that Wilson's gets the phrase with which his readers are no doubt familiar. 'The near and the far' symbolize for Wilson the challenge facing his new existentialists, the task of bringing these two antipodes together. The far is the sunset that young Prince Jali sees, setting the desert and his heart ablaze. He would like to race to the horizon in order to embrace it. But he knows that he would only get sand in his sandals – that is, the near. Race as he might, he will never catch the sunset. And yet he, and Wilson, know that one day, we may all be strong enough to hold both in our hands – our intentionality.

One essay practically worth the price of admission is Wilson's assessment of a writer with whom he shares some common themes, although the conclusions he draws from them are rather different. Ayn Rand, author of *Atlas Shrugged*, was a favourite of Abraham Maslow, the psychologist who introduced Wilson to the notion of 'peak experiences'. Maslow liked Rand's optimism, self-sufficiency, and positive attitude, all traits common to the kind of person Maslow called a 'self-actualiser', someone who approaches life creatively. Yet while Wilson can see her virtues, he is also aware of Rand's shortcomings, one of which was her character as what Wilson would later call a 'Right Man', or in Rand's case, a 'Right Woman'. He also tells an amusing story of his frustrating attempts to correspond with Rand, and the determination of her inner circle to keep his overtures from her.

There is much else to discover in these pages, or to re-discover. And to those, like myself, very familiar with Wilson's work, there is the pleasant delight of spending time with the literary equivalent of an old friend.

London, April 2017

Editor's Note:

In 2001 my Paupers' Press re-issued Colin Wilson's *The Age of Defeat,* in a limited edition of 200, for his 70th birthday. In a new 25-page Introduction he wrote: 'The first version of *AOD* borrowed a phrase from... the hero of [Aldous Huxley's] *Antic Hay* for its title: 'I glory in the name of earwig'. In fact, this early version was later published in a volume of essays which I called *Eagles and Earwigs* (and which, to my irritation, the publisher insisted on changing to *Eagle and Earwig*).' For this reason it has been decided that this re-issue should be published under Colin Wilson's preferred title.

A bold reference in brackets (e.g. (**E89**)) refers to the number of the item as listed in my *The Ultimate Colin Wilson Bibliography, 1956-2015* (Nottingham: Paupers' Press, 2015).

PART ONE
LITERATURE AND PHILOSOPHY

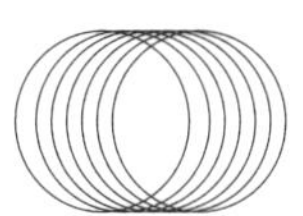

INTRODUCTION
HUMANISM AND THE RELIGIOUS ATTITUDE

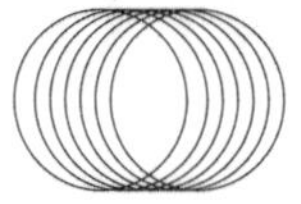

I have deliberately chosen the title of one of T. S. Eliot's best known essays for this introduction because it goes to the heart of the problem of the purpose and value of literature.

Some years ago, I published a book called *The Outsider* whose declared aim was to attack the humanist viewpoint and defend the religious attitude. Today, I would describe myself as a humanist; and yet there has been no *fundamental* change in my outlook. The only change has been in the matter of emphasis. To my mind Eliot and T. E. Hulme were instinctively right; but they over-estimated the strength of the opposition, and so overstated their case, sometimes exaggerating it to the point of nonsense. It seems to me, for example, that Eliot was writing almost pure nonsense when he wrote of Henry James: 'He had a mind so fine that no idea could violate it', and spoke of this imperviousness to ideas as 'perhaps the last test of a superior intelligence'. (I know many people who are impervious to ideas, but this is no sign of superior intelligence; ideas are only intuitions turned into words, and Eliot's essay on James is as full of them as anything by Shaw or Wells – at whom Eliot was swiping.)

Still, I believe that Eliot and Hulme were right on the

central issue. What is this central issue? It can best be defined in terms of literature and art.

In a poem called 'The Circus Animal's Desertion', W. B. Yeats states a view of art that is entirely pessimistic. He speaks of his early work as a mere escape from reality, a 'ladder' that enabled him to climb above the 'mound of refuse' that is the human situation, and ends:

...Now that my ladder's gone,
I must lie down where all the ladders start,
In the foul rag-and-bone shop of the heart.

Admittedly, Yeats has explained earlier in the poem that 'it was the dream itself enchanted me', and said:

Players and painted stage took all my love,
And not those things that they were emblems of.

His meaning may be that, as a consequence of his fixation on the 'painted stage', he has lost the inner reality. But Yeats is always ambiguous, and 'the foul rag-and-bone shop of the heart' is an excellent symbol of the romantic's vision of the human reality. The reality is brutality, stupidity, and weakness – above all, weakness: man's inability to live by his visions, by his imagination. *Man is like a grandfather clock driven by a watch spring; the life in him is inadequate to support the dead weight of his flesh.* This is the 'norm' to which man must return after his brief imaginative escapes.

Now there is an alternative view that might be called 'simple humanism', and that seems to be based on self-delusion and a certain shallow optimism. This can be summarized in various nineteenth-century clichés: 'Man is the master of things', 'I am the master of my fate, I am the captain of my soul', 'Man is born free but is everywhere in chains'. It is the fallacy of simple progress expressed in Tennyson's lines about man rising 'on stepping stones of his dead selves to higher things'. The pessimistic vision certainly sees deeper and truer than this. The other alternative is the religious attitude. This states that although degradation and weakness may be the present human reality, this should not be regarded as a norm in any ultimate sense. Man's present state is the result of original sin – in fact *is* original sin – and imagination gives us a glimpse of a reality which could just conceivably be attained by man. It can be seen that this vision is considerably more optimistic than the one stated by Yeats, and more realistic than simple humanism.

The humanist objection to the idea of original sin is valid enough: that it is nonsense to suppose that the human race is being penalized for having chosen knowledge instead of ignorance and bliss. This is answered by pointing out that original sin can be understood in a broader sense, a sense in which it is applicable to all religions, and not to Christianity alone. All religions recognize that man is in a state from which he requires 'saving', and that salvation is not a matter of material progress alone. Man is 'degraded'; the problem is how he can cease to be so, how he can cease to be stupid, brutal, self-divided, a slave of his impulses: in short, how he can become less of a worm and more of a god.

In this sense, then, it seems to me that the religious attitude is valid and simple humanism is wrong. But when Eliot goes on to declare that 'the life force is a gross superstition', and that the solution of all man's spiritual problems lies in the Church of England, it becomes impossible to take him seriously. His position seems to be based on a series of false antitheses ('poetry' versus 'ideas', science versus belief, religion versus humanism.) But if the problem is simply how man can become less of a worm and more of a god, then Eliot has obviously not covered all the solutions. His own solution – anaesthetizing the critical faculty and then swallowing the Christian superstitions about vicarious atonement – is as obviously shaky as simple humanism. What is needed is a synthesis that transcends both these thoroughly unacceptable antitheses.

Consider again the implications of Yeats's lines about the 'rag-and-bone shop of the heart'. In one of his prefaces, talking about James Joyce, Shaw remarks that 'A certain flippant and futile derision and belittlement that confuses the noble and serious with the base and ludicrous seems to me peculiar to Dublin...' If Yeats is right, then this attitude of 'flippant and futile derision' – that characterizes Dublin's young men – *is only a recognition of reality*. We are back with the controversy about realism and idealism that shook the second half of the nineteenth century. Zola took pride in declaring that he depicted the world 'as it really is', and that the realists were rejecting all the metaphysics and idealism of the romantics, recognizing them to be illusions.

If one compares Joyce with Zola, it becomes apparent that Shaw is being less than fair to *Ulysses*. Forster called *Ulysses* 'a determined attempt to cover the universe with mud', a description that one might apply to many of Zola's novels. But if one can grasp why it is *not* a fair description of *Ulysses*, one has also gone a long way towards solving the 'humanism versus religion' problem. Joyce has recognized that the artist's real problem is to transform reality, not to reject it and create an 'alternative reality'. *Ulysses* must be understood as, to some extent, a counterblast to the early Yeats and to the school of Dublin theosophists. In one of his early stories Yeats had created a character who lived in a velvet-draped room and studied magic, going out only by night. Yeats himself wanted to be such a person. It is apparent from the *Portrait of the Artist as a Young Man* that Joyce felt much the same. *Ulysses* has recognized that such total rejection is no answer. But it is by no means a document of anti-idealism, like certain novels of Zola. It is an attempt to give 'reality' its due, *and still to transform it*.

It is Joyce's various techniques of transforming the reality that are of interest here. It might be said that Joyce studies reality through a telescope, into which he keeps slipping different lenses, each of which gives it a new kind of distortion. First of all, he shows reality as it appears to Stephen Dedalus. Stephen's point of view is almost identical with Shaw's; he is intensely serious minded, and is irritated by the 'flippant and futile derision' of his friends, to whom he refers as a 'brood of mockers'. On the beach on his own, he meditates on Aristotle and Aquinas. Stephen is also suffering from pangs of conscience connected with the death of his mother. Joyce builds him up as a deliberately Byronic figure, the solitary atheist who takes a masochistic pleasure in wallowing in 'sin'. Stephen is not much liked by the Dublin literary set – Yeats, George Moore, Russell ('A.E.'), Lady Gregory, and in one passage Mulligan remarks mockingly, 'He says he will write something in ten years'. The 'something', of course, was *Ulysses*, which gave Joyce a fame that went beyond that of any of the Dublin literary set – which, in fact, made him the most influential novelist of the twentieth century. So the first 'lens' that is used to transform Dublin is Stephen's sense of purpose.

Next there is the Rabelaisian lens. Joyce's attitude towards Buck Mulligan, the 'mocker', is not entirely one of disapproval. Mulligan has a certain gleeful acceptance of the physical realities for which Joyce obviously feels some approval. It would be inaccurate to accuse him of confusing 'the noble and serious with one with the base and ludicrous'; he is a lover of Swinburne and Homer and something of a poet himself; he attempts to be a Dionysian, celebrating life in all its aspects.

Mulligan seems to have acted as a kind of bridge between the young Stephen and everyday physical actuality, as symbolized in Leopold and Molly Bloom. Joyce's portrait of Bloom reveals how far Stephen has come since these early Dublin days. He is a commonplace little man who lacks self-belief; he is a sexual pervert – a masochist, a fetishist and a coprophilist. The chapter of *Ulysses* that is told through Bloom's eyes is told entirely in clichés, and reveals him as intellectually pretentious in an absurd and pathetic way. But he is also shown as a kindly, tolerant, and basically 'decent' little man – in fact, as ultimately admirable. Molly Bloom is treated in the same way. At first she seems spoiled, vain, and commonplace; the last chapter seems also to show that she is petty, materialistic, and a nymphomaniac. And yet at the end of the book Joyce seems to identify her with the earth itself, and with the basic female nature of the universe, generous, impulsive, allowing her body to be used to give men pleasure and bear them children; her nature is pure affirmation : 'Yes I will yes'. Even Bloom acquires dignity and depth as seen through her eyes, when she reflects that she married him because he seemed more sensitive and intelligent than the other men she knew.

I have spoken at length about *Ulysses* because it shows the artistic process in its essence, and refutes Yeats's view of art as a mere escape from the rag-and-bone shop of reality. This problem could have been approached from another angle – through phenomenology. Phenomenology recognizes that we see the world from a 'natural standpoint', but the natural standpoint is not necessarily the truth, even though it may seem self-evident. We may believe that we merely 'see' reality with as little prejudice as a camera, but a little reflection will show that we never 'merely see' anything. In order to see something we must direct attention at it. If you read these words without paying attention, you will, in effect, not have read them at all; the eye has seen, yet has not seen. And the moment we direct attention at anything, we select, filter, and distort. The natural standpoint is as filtered and distorted with prejudices as the vision of a madman. This is not to say that it is all relative, that we can never hope to know reality; phenomenology prescribes a discipline called 'bracketing' or 'filtering' for getting past the distortions we impose on reality. But without such a discipline there can be no 'privileged standpoint' which shows us reality. Yeats may believe that the 'rag-and-bone shop of the heart' is 'truer' than the imaginative vision he tried to impose on reality, but it is not.

This fallacy of the natural standpoint might be called Zola's fallacy: the idea that to see things 'truly' one must see them in as sordid and pessimistic a light as possible. The phenomenologist's objection is that the meaninglessness is as *imposed* as any other meaning. Art cannot therefore be regarded as an escape from reality unless it is a total rejection of the natural standpoint – like Michael Robartes's velvet-lined room.

We can also see that the theory of filters or lenses enables us to define the basic activity of the artist. Art is a war with meaninglessness, with the natural standpoint. The natural standpoint is most itself when man feels tired, exhausted. Then it seems self-evidently true that the material reality is the only reality, and that all man's life is only an attempt to convince himself of something he knows to be untrue – that is, of his own importance. Man wants to believe that his mental processes somehow matter to the universe, and is always realizing that they matter only to himself and his immediate circle of human beings. Art is an enormous confidence trick, because the artist addresses himself to the human race; it is a tradition of self-importance; the human race is already half-way towards the universe, so the artist feels he is addressing the universe. In reality, the artist dies and is forgotten; in any case men never really understood him; they only read their own feelings into his work...

This viewpoint is logically untenable since, as Merleau-Ponty says, human beings are 'condemned to meaning'. There is nothing they can do that is not an affirmation of some meaning; even the act of suicide is meaningful. There is no logical way of living and acting – that is to say, of *being* – in accordance with the 'meaningless' hypothesis; our very existence denies it. We cannot work upon an assumption that man's spirit and will are illusions, that the only reality is matter.

Unfortunately, although our very existence denies the meaningless hypothesis, our very existence does not *affirm* meaning; every act of living demands a certain freedom, a choice. The spirit has an uphill struggle, particularly if it is unwilling to swallow the pre-digested meanings of religion. Art is one of its potent methods of bursting out of the meaninglessness of the natural standpoint; it does this by inserting filters or lenses between the eye and the external world, each one of which subtly alters the world.

It may seem that this argument is self-contradictory; an attempt to prove that in some way the act of imagination brings us closer to reality – when, in common usage, imagination and reality are used as antonyms (i.e., 'He has a strong imagination' may be a polite way of saying, 'He is a liar'). But this is a failure to understand the basic truth of perception: that it is an active process, like grasping something with the hand. There is no such thing as purely passive perception. When man is feeling tired his grip is feeble or non-existent; the next stage is to close his eyes and cease to be aware of the outer world. The more vital his mind is, the more intensely he 'holds' reality. We think of imagination as a tendency to escape into a world of fantasy; but any creative artist will confirm that it is fundamentally a sense of supercharged vitality of mind, when the world is seen to be full of potentiality; creation is then simply the act of selecting from this potentiality. It is identical with the sense of power and affirmation experienced in the sexual orgasm, or when one is carried away by great music. The mind seems to become an immense and powerful hand gripping reality.

The old distinction between imagination and reality vanishes; reality (in Zola's sense) is another name for the natural standpoint. But the natural standpoint is not 'unprejudiced' perception; it is a transaction between a human mind and the external world, when the human mind is in a state of fatigue or defeat. Far from being 'real', its content is a downright lie. The intensity of a Beethoven creating the Fifth Symphony is altogether closer to reality – that is, to the real potential of the human situation.

All this is perhaps the most fundamental statement that could be made about the human situation, and I would hold that this problem is precisely what all art and poetry is about. Once this is clearly seen, it is also seen that the kind of pessimism and defeat expressed in various modern writings is no more than a misunderstanding of the human situation due to vague and confused thinking. An animal facing nature may well feel that life is no more than a continual battle to hold its own. But science and art are more than coloured matches designed to save man from a sense of defeat. They represent victories over the banality of the natural standpoint. The animal world may be a continual struggle against nature, in which the balance of forces remains constant; in the human world the balance of power is slowly changing. Whether we like the idea or not, man is, in a fundamental sense, becoming more godlike.

Now it will be seen why the whole 'humanist versus religion' conflict is old-fashioned, and a new synthesis is needed. As outlined by Eliot, Hulme, Irving Babbitt, and others, the conflict is artificial. Both sides have fundamental insights; both sides have carried them to a point where they cease to be true. Humanism believes in 'progress', but oversimplifies; religion sees deeper into the 'human reality', and is consequently inclined to be pessimistic about man and his future possibilities.

Religion, to begin with, tends to be suspicious towards science. This is a fundamental mistake. Science does not mean merely technological progress. In the ultimate sense it is what distinguishes man from the animals. The animal takes its life and its problems for granted; it uses its mind, its cunning, but for purely defensive purposes.

Man's accidental development of language and of writing revealed altogether new possibilities – the use of mind as an instrument of aggression, for changing the balance of power in the struggle against nature. Man is, above all, the *aggressive* animal. And when man the social animal became man the creator the battle reached an altogether new stage. He learned detachment and impersonality, and in learning these became in a true sense a 'spiritual creature'. Detachment is a characteristic of gods; the animal is too embroiled in the struggle for existence to be able to afford any thoughts or feelings that are not directly related to its immediate welfare. Sculpture, painting, music, poetry, philosophy – these carry man's aggressiveness into a new field. If one considers the work of any of the great philosophers – Plato, Hegel, Nietzsche – it can be seen that they were thinking with a kind of excitement, in the way that an army fights when it can see victory. Their thinking was not an abstract exercise, like drawing patterns in the sand with a stick; there was a feeling that, through thought, man could achieve an altogether new kind of victory over matter *and over himself*. As one reads Nietzsche one feels that his sentences are like sword thrusts or the blows of a hatchet; he is cutting and slashing at the chaos of human existence and trying to introduce into the human field the same kind of order that Newton introduced into the mathematical field. It is not a game or an amusement; he was fighting, in the most real and fundamental sense, for human evolution. That he was defeated is beside the point; the real cause for depression is that so few people have recognized the significance of what he was trying to do, and a shallow, dilettantish pessimism flourishes as though Nietzsche had never existed.

It can be seen now why pessimism is a misunderstanding and an irrelevancy. The pessimist feels that, in a basic sense, man is better off than the animals. Art is lies; religion is mostly superstition; science only affects the surface of life and leaves the inner chaos untouched. This is like the petulance of a rich boy saying that he is bored with money. The pessimist's ability to assert anything so abstract and impersonal is based upon the labour of thousands of generations of men denying that they are mere animals. In the very act of expressing an impersonal thought man is denying pessimism and affirming the reality of his spiritual evolution.

Considering the immense period of time over which man has evolved, it may seem rash to assert that human evolution has passed into a new stage in the past 200 years; and yet I believe that this is so. A new thought, a new idea, is slowly coming to birth, and this thought is the one I have expressed above: of optimism. Ancient philosophers tended to be pessimists; they divided the world into spirit and matter and tended to reject matter, believing that spirit possessed its own realm apart from the material world. Plato and Plotinus, like so many later Christian thinkers, regarded death as a consummation. William Blake was perhaps the first expression of the new spirit: the rejection of the dualism, the assertion that spirit and matter are somehow in this struggle together, and that to separate them is no solution. Plato saw matter as a kind of magnet that has trapped spirit – or as a gigantic octopus; the task of spirit is to kill the octopus and get free. Blake saw the 'consummation' as the final enslavement of the octopus so that it becomes the instrument of spirit. He does not reject matter, but sees it transformed. Blake's idea is the characteristic idea of the new age; but it has not yet permeated into the general consciousness. We are still soaked in the Platonic world-rejection, which is the worst part of our Christian heritage; hence modern pessimism.

It is significant that Blake's first work should be a 'prophetic book' about the French Revolution; for the French Revolution is the beginning of the new age. Man has cast off the old notion of his creaturehood, according to which the desire for knowledge was a form of *hubris*, and begins to work on the assumption that he might use his mind to become godlike. There is a new *spirit* abroad in the nineteenth century, and one can feel it immediately in the poetry of Shelley, Byron, Goethe, or the music of Beethoven or Wagner. The human spirit is on the march to new goals; man wants to know why he is not a god, and how he can become a god. There is greatness in the air. What immediately strikes us in retrospect is that this greatness so persistently misunderstood itself and ended as pessimism. What impresses us most in Schopenhauer is not the pessimism of his solution but the fresh, vital manner of his thinking; the sense of grasping human life through the activity of mind. It has exactly the same kind of confidence that one finds in Blake's *Marriage of Heaven and Hell*, a natural authority that is as different as could be from the prevalent tone of the eighteenth century (as expressed in *The Analogy of Religion* and thousands of volumes of sermons). Man has undoubtedly grown up since Bishop Butler. In the same way, the music of Wagner expresses something that would have been inconceivable to Rameau or Haydn, and its effect seems to have little to do with the pessimism of *Tristan* or the *Ring*. In spite of the 'Magic Fire' music and the 'Liebestod', this is not essentially music of tragedy; it is music of assertion of the spirit of man. Still, the nineteenth century had advanced several stages beyond the pessimism of the Greeks. Even if Schopenhauer and Wagner decided that human life was ultimately tragic, they kept raising the question of the destiny of man. Carlyle expressed it as Everlasting Yes versus Everlasting No. Man sees himself as a suffering Prometheus, not as a mere creature.

Nietzsche was the first to recognize conclusively that a new optimism had been born; but even he failed to grasp its nature of inevitability; he was still too tied to the old Greek modes of thought to see to the depths of his own conclusions, and counter-weighted his idea of the superman with the completely contradictory notion of eternal recurrence. If eternal recurrence is true, then 'nature' is once again a shadow, an appearance, unconnected with spirit, for only a machine repeats itself – like a gramophone record stuck in a groove.

The twentieth century has raised again the question of Everlasting Yes versus Everlasting No. It has now become a central issue in literature and philosophy. Hesse's *Steppenwolf* goes to the heart of the problem; although it is unsatisfactory as literature, it should be regarded as one of the key works of this century. It is again the problem expressed by Yeats in 'The Circus Animal's Desertion'; although Steppenwolf is soaked in great literature and music, he finds his everyday life unsatisfactory – boring and purposeless. He is inclined to suspect that this is the 'reality', and art and philosophy are only an attempt to escape it, or sugar the pill. The tacit question of his existence is: If man is really evolving into godhood, why am I so bored? If Nietzsche and Wagner and the rest are really speaking about realities, why does my spirit remain in a stupor? *Steppenwolf* is about this battle between belief and disbelief, and about how Steppenwolf learns to achieve some degree of the self-control and certainty that he feels to be missing. *Steppenwolf* is a fundamental work because it shows its hero divided between the two states that are experienced by every poet or artist: the boredom of the 'long littleness of life', and the sudden moments of intense insight and illumination. The question is whether the poet will have the strength to spend a lifetime pursuing the insights, sustaining his sense of purpose through sheer will-power, or whether he will give way to discouragement and neurosis. And obviously the fundamental issue is this question of which is the 'reality' – the boredom or the vision. One writer on existentialism has used the revealing phrase: 'the fundamental alienation of beings from the source of power, meaning and purpose'.[3] The basic issue could not be stated more clearly. Does

3 William Kimmel, Introductory essay to *The Search for Being, an anthology of existentialist writings*. Noonday Books, 1962.

that 'source of power, meaning and purpose' really exist objectively in some sense, so that man could rediscover it by searching in the right place? Or is it a purely subjective state, achieved by chance, like the satisfaction of a good meal? If a man is to devote his life to the search, then he must assume that the 'source of power' is a reality, like Piccadilly Circus, purely on the evidence of his occasional experiences of insight. But during the long periods of boredom the chief task is the investigation of the status of the 'peak experiences' (to use Abraham Maslow's expression for these moments of affirmation), which necessarily involves the whole question of human existence – what Heidegger calls the *Seinfrage* (question of being) but which should perhaps be called the *Lebensfrage* (question of life). So the initial impetus of existential philosophy is this basic experience of the poet – the moment of sudden insight, the feeling of vital affirmation.

This, then, raises the religious question. Is life necessarily the rather dreary thing we know most of the time: necessarily, that is, because the reality of the world is basically material, as nineteenth-century science affirmed? Or is religion right in regarding man's present condition, his everyday consciousness and its values, as somehow sub-normal? This is the issue that divides 'simple humanism' from the religious attitude. But I have tried to show that a less superficial humanism arrives at precisely this position: the recognition of the sub-normality of everyday consciousness; it arrives at it through the study of the human mind and its powers. Religion and humanism can agree about the 'fallen-ness' of our everyday consciousness. The difference is that religion attributes this fall-en-ness to some 'original sin', whereas humanism accepts the term figuratively. Man has not fallen; he has climbed a long way; but in relation to his possible existence – a state he catches glimpses of even now – his present reality is certainly a poor second best.

Art has been the chief medium of man's evolution, and literature has perhaps contributed most of all. Religion should also be taken into account here; but here it is necessary to make a distinction. Bergson talked of 'open' and 'closed' religion; open religion is the religion of saints and mystics, that is, of men with a real religious vocation whose religion is a search for God. Closed religion – which is unfortunately what most people mean by religion – is the religion of dogma and superstition; this is 'religion from the natural standpoint'. Open religion and poetry are fundamentally of the same nature, so the above assertion that art has been the chief medium of man's evolution remains broadly true.

All human experience can be approached from either of the two viewpoints I have tried to describe: Yeats's 'rag-and-bone shop' theory, or the 'religious' view. As the Commander's statue remarks in *Man and Superman* when Don Juan asks him the way to heaven: 'Oh, the frontier is only the difference between two ways of looking at things. Any road will take you across it if you really want to get there.' The problem is that the sheer persistency of our everyday consciousness inclines us to choose the materialist view. Sex is of particular interest to the phenomenologist (and phenomenology, of course, is only the science of the different ways of looking at things) because its enormously dynamic nature makes it easier to pass from one point of view to another, and because its distortions (sexual perversion) enable us to see the curious consequences of approaching it persistently from the 'rag-and-bone shop' viewpoint. I have gone into this question at considerable length elsewhere.[4]

This point of view I have outlined above means that all artists, whether they know it or not, possess a fundamental identity of aim. 'Pessimistic art' is a contradiction in terms.

Why, in that case, should it be necessary to make such a statement? If pessimistic art is invalid, then it will vanish of its own accord.

But this is not the point. The real problem is that art today must become conscious of its fundamental nature in order to escape self-defeat. The nineteenth century raised the question of Everlasting Yes versus Everlasting No, and in retrospect it seems that the answer of romanticism was 'No'. On the other hand, the 'No' of Wagner's *Tristan* possesses so much vitality that it impresses us as a 'Yes'. But few twentieth-century artists have possessed a stature comparable to Wagner's, and the 'No' of Beckett or Ionesco certainly does not impress us as a disguised 'Yes'. It honestly believes that it is facing the great problem implied by the nineteenth century, and giving the logical and consistent answer. I have tried to show that 'No' can never be a logical answer. These twenti-

4 See my *Origins of the Sexual Impulse* (London: Arthur Barker, 1963).

eth-century pessimists are junior romantics without the stature to carry their questioning as far as their ancestors of the last century. The problem is to make this so clear that their works will be criticized for their superficiality. These writers of a vaguely pessimistic tinge are regarded by many as the latest development of the twentieth-century spirit. But this is a case where science is a great deal ahead of art. The sciences, particularly psychology, are revising their foundations – usually as a result of phenomenological criticism.[5] The next task is for art to catch up. This will undoubtedly mean the disappearance of *avant garde* formalism in literature and art: of abstract art, of non-tonal music, and of 'experimental' literature of the kind produced by Beckett, Ionesco, the anti-novelists and the rest. Most of this experiment is a sign of complete loss of the inner drive that produced the great art of the past. Much of its 'difficulty' is not the result of genuine complexity in the creative process, but an attempt to produce a substitute for any real sense of artistic purpose.

It will be the achievement of the twentieth century to bring to birth a new optimism, a new sense of purpose that will mark a new stage in human evolution. Until this happens, the blind creative faculty will be insufficient to produce important works of art; it will be necessary for the artist to discipline himself into becoming a thinker.

It will, by this time, be evident that the view of art that I hold is anything but relativist: 'beauty is in the eye of the beholder', etc. Admittedly the question of artistic

5 For a detailed examination of the way in which this is happening, see *Phenomenology and Science in Contemporary European Thought* by Anna-Teresa Tymieniecka. Noonday Books, 1962. My own *Beyond the Outsider* is also devoted to this problem.

merit is so complex that it is never possible to say simply: 'Such a work *should* produce a certain response, and anyone who does not feel this is somehow making a mistake', as if he had made a mistake in a calculation. Vladimir Nabokov says that he detests Dostoevsky; unfortunately, there is no final court of appeal to prove Nabokov wrong. But here is my point – we cannot get round the question by saying that it is purely a matter of individual feelings, *chacun à son goût*. There *are* standards, even if they are extremely difficult to apply. And I believe that Eliot's instincts were right when he felt that it should be possible to supplement 'literary criticism' with another kind that is of a religious or moral nature. But Eliot used the word 'religious' in contrast to simple humanist relativism; for him it was a synonym for real values. I have tried to indicate that Eliot's notion of religion may have been too narrow; either that, or true values may lie outside the field of religion.

In an interesting book *Suicide and Scandinavia*, Herbert Hendin says that if a man could be interviewed in mid-air between the top of a skyscraper and the pavement, his feelings might be very different from those he had a moment before as he prepared to jump. Tolstoy had this same insight in *Anna Karenina* as Anna throws herself under the train. The greatest problem of our everyday human existence is this: that we are all confined by laziness, stupidity, and lack of curiosity to a narrow, personal little world that is soon exhausted by the act of living. The paradox is that the walls of this suffocating world are not made of granite; a firm push will bring them down;

and yet we are incapable of administering that push. This is the phenomenon of the St Neot Margin.[6] Partly because we are spoilt and lazy, partly because we are not yet truly human – we are still 99 per-cent animal, and an animal is a machine – we pant for breath when a single movement could open the windows, a movement that we do not yet know how to make. For the suicide the windows must fly open, revealing what a hopeless miscalculation is the act of self-destruction. For some reason the act of living paralyses this will to *live more*. On the point of being shot, Graham Greene's 'whisky priest' realizes that it would have been very easy to be a saint. Dostoevsky had the same realization as he was about to be executed. *So what is it that paralyses the will?* This is the greatest question that can confront human beings, and its solution, which may well be affected by phenomenological analysis, would be the greatest step forward in the whole of primate evolution.

Now here is what I am contending: a work of art affects gently what a suicide attempt can affect with absurd brutality; the window that divides man from reality is flung open. It sometimes happens that the outer reality itself can affect an entrance without the help of art. In *War and Peace*, for example, one remembers clearly two moments of great insight. One of them happens to Peter when he is on the point of being executed by the French. The other happens to Prince Andrew when he goes through a forest and sees an oak tree shooting its first spring buds. It has precisely the same effect as Peter's

6 See *Editor's Notes* [Ed.]

insight: of waking the sleeping-consciousness; of stirring the mind into a recognition that life is never exhausted *because it is pure potentiality*. But this insight produced in Prince Andrew's mind by the sight of an oak tree – for which, admittedly, he had been prepared by his growing love for Natasha – is in essence the poetic experience itself. Poetry affects our minds in exactly the way that the oak affected Prince Andrew, and that the threat of execution affected Peter or Greene's whisky priest or the young Dostoevsky. Poets differ from other men only in that there are more cracks in their walls, so that the reality keeps filtering through, bringing a sense of joy and release from the trivialities of personality, from the banality of being human.

The purpose of all art, then, is to effect this escape from personality, this vision of the world as pure potentiality. This will make clear why I call literary criticism from this point of view 'existential'. Its standard of value is existence, the opposite of the limiting personality. All art is in its essence evolutionary. Men do not possess their own lives; instead of living they half-live. This is the problem of the St Neot Margin, and to some extent it can be remedied by art. The existentialist instinctively judges all art in this way: how far does it succeed in revealing existence as potentiality, in combating the St Neot Margin?

Judged by this standard we are all despisers of life, even the greatest artists and poets who ever lived. But a book like Beckett's *Molloy* or Hadley Chase's *No Orchids for Miss Blandish* produces on one an active effect of life-denigration, and leaves the mind bored and fatigued. There is a difference, of course; Beckett's book is at least actively pessimistic, and so has an effect of inverted affirmation that could enrich the consciousness of the reader. Chase's novel is far more pessimistic and life-denying in being passively so; it is a step nearer death.

Such works as the novels of Balzac and Stendhal are altogether higher on the ladder of artistic merit; yet if I turn from Lindsay's *Voyage to Arcturus* to *Chartreuse de Parme* I feel that I have descended from a world of enriched meanings to an altogether more banal and commonplace world. But here is a problem: Lindsay is obviously not to be compared with Stendhal as an artist and technician; how, in that case, can my intuition of their relative value be justified?

I would not suggest that it can be justified in any ultimate sense; but it will be something if it can be established that works of art are not to be judged purely by their effectiveness in achieving their own aims. They must also be judged on what they have to say. Although there is much in the quality of Stendhal's mind for me to admire, I cannot sympathize very deeply with his curiously limited and egoistic personality, with its streaks of vanity, self-pity, and impotence. And when I read *Madame Bovary*, I am torn between admiration for the quality of the artistic intelligence revealed, and irritation at the obvious shallowness and immaturity of Flaubert the man. And when Ezra Pound states in *Mauberley* that 'his true Penelope was Flaubert', I know that I need attach very little importance to his judgment of Bernard Shaw as 'an artistic pigmy'. If this is what Pound thinks important about art he is hardly qualified to grasp Shaw's significance.

Art must be judged by other standards than art, as well as by standards of artistic discipline. If works of art were judged by purely existential standards, Constant's *Adolphe* would be non-existent, Jane Austen's novels hardly more important, while Stendhal, Balzac, and Flaubert would rate as very small fry indeed. On the other hand, Ayn Rand would deserve quite a high rating.[7] Such a judgment would be absurd, yet it would be absurd only because we are dealing with the foothills of art, and human civilization has so far produced no mountains. T. E. Lawrence went to the root of the problem in a letter: 'I have looked everywhere in poetry for satisfaction: and haven't found it. Instead I have made that collection of bonbons, chocolate éclairs of the spirit, whereas I wanted a meal. Failing poetry, I chased my fancied meal through prose, and found everywhere good little stuff, and only a few men who had tried honestly to be greater than mankind...'[8]

'Good little stuff' – this describes all that the world has so far characterized as great literature. Seen from this exacting standard of existential criticism, there have been no real mountains, only high foothills – Dante, Goethe, Shakespeare, Dostoevsky. With even the greatest it is necessary to exercise the double standard: to recognize that greatness of vision may be adulterated by failure

7 See Chapter 11 [Ed.]
8 23 October 1922.

of self-discipline and artistic discipline (as in the case of Dostoevsky), or that artistic achievement may conceal a timid and fundamentally bourgeois vision (as in the case of Flaubert, and probably that of Shakespeare). If we can stimulate the imagination for a moment into conceiving Dostoevsky's feelings when facing a firing squad, or Hendin's suicide poised in mid-air half-way down a skyscraper, we can immediately see why all art so far must be considered a failure. Such a crisis would reveal the world as almost infinite potentiality, and all works of art that have ever been created would be seen as dreary libels of existence.

Let me propose, at this point, a notion that may clarify the whole concept of existential criticism. It is this: that literature may be divided into two kinds: one accepts the values and limits of the 'natural standpoint'; the other is always striving to get beyond them, to probe the question of existence itself. For the existential critic, the first kind must always be regarded as of a lower order, even though most of the world's literary masterpieces belong to it.

Let us admit at once that this is a simplification, and that it is as open to objections as most generalizations. Still, there is an important element of truth there. We might first of all consider an extreme example of the first class: the simple adventure story, such as *The Three Musketeers*, *King Solomon's Mines*, or *The Lost World*. The reader who takes up such a book knows precisely what to expect; its values are simply those of changing events, of physical danger and achievement. But now consider novels that are generally admitted to belong to a superior literary hierarchy, for example, Balzac's *Lost Illusions*, Stendhal's *Chartreuse de Parme* or *Lucien Leuwen*, Dickens's *Great Expectations*, Gogol's *Dead Souls*. Is it not true that, judged by this standard, these are no more than 'superior' adventure novels? The literary standards are higher; the psychology is subtler; the picture of the human world is profounder, and usually more realistic. Nevertheless, the values are laid down before we begin to read, and we follow the career of Rastignac or Rubempré or Fabrizio with the same kind of interest that we bring to D'Artagnan. On the other hand, an altogether different kind of curiosity is necessary to make us keep on reading Mann's *Magic Mountain*, Lindsay's *Voyage to Arcturus*, or L. H. Myer's *The Near and the Far*. These novels are somehow more akin to great poetry or music; they continually attempt to transport the mind beyond the human limits, beyond the ordinary values connected with our day-to-day strivings.

The objections are so obvious as to need no elaboration; even the title of *Dead Souls* reveals that Gogol's preoccupation cannot be wholly defined in terms of the merely human. And a book like *War and Peace* simply overlaps the two classes; it is an adventure story and an exploration of the values of human existence. Nevertheless, I would contend that this distinction between a purely 'humanistic' literature (meaning 'simple humanism') and the literature of values – that is, of the ultimate values of human existence – is a useful one, and may one day become a very important one.

This distinction makes clear, I think, my position on the question of humanism versus the religious attitude. The first class of literature might well be labelled 'humanistic', although it sounds a little odd to apply such a label to *The Lost World*, but it would be absurd to speak of *The Magic Mountain*, *The Near and the Far*, and *A Voyage to Arcturus* as religious novels. They are clearly different in their premises from the novels of Stendhal and Balzac; they pose the *Lebensfrage*. Eliot's distinction between humanism and religion is too narrow. The real distinction is between 'set values', limited human values; and 'transcendental values', values that question the meaning of human existence.

For the existential critic, this latter is the *sine qua non* of real literature. The problem that this raises is obvious enough, and I have already mentioned it: the literature of real values forms a very small class when compared with 'humanistic' literature; what is more, most of the masterpieces belong to the latter kind, from the *Iliad* down to *Ulysses*. Judged purely as literature, the works that appeal to the existential critic scarcely bear comparison with the 'humanistic' masterpieces. Admittedly there are *Faust* and the novels of Dostoevsky; but apart from these, very few large 'bodies of work'. The novels of Hesse are fascinating, yet they never rise to greatness. Several of Mann's novels belong to the humanistic camp – *Buddenbrooks* and *Joseph*, for example; *The Magic Mountain* and *Doktor Faustus* are his only real contributions to the literature of the *Lebensfrage*. There are the plays of Shaw; but here again his major contribution, *Back to Methuselah*, is unsatisfactory as a work of literature. Dr Leavis would insist that the novels of George Eliot, Henry James, Joseph Conrad, and D. H. Lawrence should be included in the 'literature of values'; the existential critic would probably judge that, like *War and Peace*, they overlap into both camps. There are also a great number of solitary works that appeal to the existential critic: Jefferies's *Story of My Heart*, Mark Twain's *Mysterious Stranger*, Imre Mádach's *Tragedy of Man*, Myers's *The Near and the Far*, Lindsay's *Voyage to Arcturus*, Granville Barker's *Secret Life*, T. E. Lawrence's *Seven Pillars of Wisdom*, D. H. Lawrence's *Man Who Died*, H. G. Wells's *Croquet Player*, Sartre's *La Nausée*. Few of these works would rate highly judged by the standards of the humanistic masterpieces. In fact, it might be argued that preoccupation with the *Lebensfrage* makes for bad and careless writing, or for the kind of amateurism that one finds in Hesse. Perhaps such writing suffers from its kinship with philosophy, for most philosophy is badly written.

And yet I cannot believe for a moment that this is necessarily so. Man is evolving slowly and painfully towards the truly human; what distinguishes him most clearly from the other animals is that he has evolved through the use of mind. This has developed fairly recently – in the past few thousand years – into an ability to question his own existence, an ability that reached a new phase with the coming of romanticism. Man has still not become truly human; he is still uncomfortable in the realm of pure mind – man's peculiar province – and glad to get back to the solid earth with its animal certainties. This is only to say that man as he exists today is an awkward link between the animal and the truly human. But if the intellectual history of the past 200 years means anything – with its rejection of religion, its questions about the 'stature of man', and its self-divided 'outsiders' – it is surely that a crisis has been reached in the history of human development; man is teetering on the brink of evolutionary change.

In that case it becomes impossible to doubt that all great literature of the future will be in some way actively concerned with values and the *Lebensfrage*. Art has been one of the most important elements in man's evolution beyond the purely animal stage; if the next stage in his evolution involves a new level of self-consciousness, then art must become an instrument of his self-consciousness; it must learn to place the whole of his existence in question.

This point of view forms the background of my approach to literature, and it will be found throughout this book. The essays collected here have been written over a number of years, some of them dating back to 1957. Most of them are literary essays: which is to say that I wrote them out of a purely literary interest, as distinguished from a philosophical interest. Most of the writers dealt with here do not fit into the philosophical scheme that I have outlined in the six books of the 'Outsider Cycle'; otherwise they would probably be found in those books. But there are certain exceptions. 'I Glory in the Name of Earwig' was, in fact, the germ from which I eventually produced *The Age of Defeat*, the third volume of the cycle.

Again, the essay 'Existential Criticism' might easily have been a chapter in *The Strength to Dream* The same is obviously true of the essay on Powys and Hemingway.

I have therefore grouped the essays in this book into three parts. The first contains essays that deal either specifically or by implication with the themes I have outlined in this introductory essay. The second contains essays on writers whose work has interested me. But the third group of essays are altogether more personal; these were written at the request of particular magazines, and their general theme is the problem of being a writer in the twentieth century.

1965

Editor's Notes

The 'Outsider Cycle' is as follows: *The Outsider*. London: Victor Gollancz, 1956 (**A1**); *Religion and the Rebel*. London: Victor Gollancz, 1957 (**A2**); *The Age of Defeat*. London: Victor Gollancz, 1959 (**A3**); *The Strength to Dream*. London: Victor Gollancz, 1962 (**A7**); *Origins of the Sexual Impulse*. London: Arthur Barker, 1963 (**A9**); *Beyond the Outsider*. London: Arthur Barker, 1965 (**A14**). A summary volume *Introduction to the New Existentialism* (London: Hutchinson & Co) appeared in 1966 and was reprinted as *The New Existentialism* in 1980 (London: Wildwood House (**A18**)).

The 'St Neot Margin', sometimes referred to as 'The Indifference Threshold', was a concept conceived by Wilson when hitching a lift in a lorry through the town of St Neots in Cambridgeshire:

> ... it came to me that human beings can lapse into a mood of indifference where pleasure has no power to stimulate, and where only active discomfort or pain can penetrate the boredom... I have found myself returning again and again to the conception of the St Neot margin. Why is human consciousness so narrow? Is this not another name for the concept of original sin? Why are human beings not grateful for the lives they possess? And most of all, how can we achieve control over the mechanism of the St Neot margin, and banish the sense of boredom and lack of purpose from human life?

Voyage to a Beginning: a preliminary autobiography (London: Cecil Woolf, 1969 (**A25**)).

1

'I GLORY IN THE NAME OF EARWIG'

A STUDY OF THE MODERN HERO

In November 1956 I took part in a discussion at the Court Theatre on what is wrong with the modern theatre. It was not a particularly brilliant discussion. Nobody seemed to know quite what *was* wrong. Arthur Miller sucked his pipe and talked about the common man, with the air of a man who feels he has nothing to be ashamed of. Mr John Whiting and Mr Benn Levy argued about the meaning of 'intellectual drama'. Wolf Mankowitz confined his contribution to comments on how much he disliked *The Outsider* and his satisfaction at being an Insider. I was in rather a false position, being the only one present who had never had a play produced, so I talked mainly about Shaw. When the chairman threw the discussion open to the audience, the speakers from the floor very rightly confined their comments to how bored they had been with the whole thing, and we all went home feeling it had been a waste of time. And so it had. It did not occur to anybody to say that what is wrong with the modern theatre is only another aspect of what is wrong with modern literature generally, and that modern literature is only a reflection of modern man. Perhaps this is just as well; the audience might have fallen asleep or started throwing things. As it was, only Mankowitz's sallies and the presence of Marilyn Monroe in the front row kept them from going home. (No one found out what Miss Monroe thought.)

But the evening taught me one lesson about the theatre. I noticed that the audience were least bored when Mankowitz and I came near to blows on the subject of Cockney dialect. The intellectual discussion bored them; the prospect of a fight woke them up.

Shaw's method

This set me thinking. I had already noticed that Shaw seizes his audience's attention by setting two characters at one another's throats. In *Mrs Warren's Profession* it is Vivie and her mother; in *Man and Superman* it is Ramsden and Tanner; in *Major Barbara*, Cusins and Undershaft. In *Good King Charles* he actually has Newton and the future James the Second rolling on the floor. There is intellectual discussion, but he never relies on it to hold the attention of the audience.

I drew this conclusion: The best and most satisfying kind of play is about conflict; preferably the type in which the characters produce swords and try to run one another through. The sophisticated will say that this is true only of a simple-minded audience. I beg to contradict them. The craving for heroic action is universal. If sophisticated intellectuals fail to feel it, this is not a sign of highly developed taste but of a certain self-betrayal of boredom.

The drama is, in essence, heroic. And the problem of the drama is the problem of the hero.

What is a hero?

In the language of the twentieth century the hero has come to mean only the central character in a play or book. Yet this is plainly not the real meaning of the word. In the Middle Ages he was the brave man. In the Arthurian romances he was also the gentle and honourable man. In Greek mythology he was essentially the man loved by the gods, the lucky man. He is usually the undefeatable man in the Ancient mythology of any race.

These meanings have disappeared almost completely in the twentieth century, which is the century of the unheroic. In all twentieth-century literature there is not one true portrait of a hero.

Unlucky heroes

The hero of modern literature is essentially unlucky. The man who possesses most of that ancient sense of the heroic, Ernest Hemingway, has not one lucky hero in his whole gallery, from the castrated journalist of *Fiesta* to the tired old man of *The Old Man and the Sea*. James Joyce's major attempt at a hero, Stephen Dedalus, has no money and no prospects; he dislikes washing and is given to picking his nose. When the modern novelist sets out to be honest, his honesty compels him to show his heroes in defeat: Studs Lonigan of James T. Farrell, Charlie Anderson in Dos Passos's *U.S.A.*, Anthony Adverse in Hervey Allen's novel.

Aldous Huxley makes no bones at all about creating unheroic heroes. 'I glory in the name of earwig', says Gumbril in *Antic Hay*. In some odd way he spoke prophetically for the hero of the twentieth century. The heroes who do not actually glory in it accept it as inevitable.

Maupassant's villainous hero

But the lucky hero turns up again in the oddest places. The hero of Guy de Maupassant's *Bel-Ami* is a rogue and profligate, with the insatiable sexual appetite of a goat. When Tolstoy wrote about the novel he gravely interpreted Maupassant's message as: 'All that is pure and good in our society is perishing', but in fact there is no evidence that Maupassant had any such moralistic intentions. Bel-Ami begins the novel as an underpaid clerk and ends it as an immensely rich man decorated with the Legion of Honour, being married to the young and pure daughter of a millionaire in a cathedral. No one but a Calvinist can fail to be delighted by Maupassant's refusal to comply with the convention that dictates that the villain should meet retribution in the last chapter. It took Bernard Shaw to create a man who would have been capable of approving of Bel-Ami's career – Andrew Undershaft, the 'dealer in death and destruction' of *Major Barbara*. Unfortunately, Maupassant has no intellectual pretensions.

Although his novels and stories are full of a sense of the gleeful acceptance of life which is essentially a heroic emotion, his heroes are no more than a series of variations on Don Giovanni. For Maupassant, there is one heroic achievement: seduction. He is not entirely wrong.

Seduction is only the twentieth-century's name for what the nineteenth century masked as 'romance', and all romance is contained in Dryden's heroic line: 'None but the brave deserve the fair'.

But the seducer who lacks self-analysis, the power of reflection, is really a poor sort of creature. In so far as he seduces, he is heroic. In so far as he does it unreflectively, he is a fool. The two are not really compatible.

Wilde's immoral hero

Oscar Wilde produced the prototype of the intelligent seducer in Lord Henry Wotton, in *The Picture of Dorian Gray*. Unfortunately, for all his intelligence, Lord Henry hardly compares with Bel-Ami or Don Giovanni. Possibly this was because Wilde could hardly write a novel about the kind of seduction he had in mind. Yet it is equally probable that, even if the nineteenth century had not objected to an epic of homosexual eroticism, Wilde would not have made Lord Henry an active seducer. Lord Henry is a thinker; he takes pleasure in his Socratic power of persuasion. Libertinism is not really in his blood.

The problem of Hamlet

The incompatibility of thought and action: immediately one thinks of Hamlet – and a new interpretation suggests itself. Shakespeare had spent a lifetime creating stupid heroes: the rhetorical, moralistic bone-headedness of Henry V, the dogmatic self-assertion of Richard II, the high-minded ineffectuality of Brutus. Yet one suspects he was taken in by his own creations, that when the newly crowned Henry V snubs his old comrade Falstaff with moralistic platitudes, Shakespeare looked on with an approving smile. A play by Kyd leads Shakespeare to attempt the most difficult of all creations: the hero made unheroic by intelligence and self-analysis. And the problem of Hamlet was the problem that Shakespeare himself could not answer: Is such a man still a hero?

For his age, Hamlet was one of the most extraordinary heroes ever created. Other heroes of Shakespeare had been condemned to death by their own stupidity, and there were more to come after Hamlet: Othello, Lear, Coriolanus, Antony. Other Elizabethans had treated problematic heroes; Ford's Perkin Warbeck is a pretender who goes to his death staunchly declaring that he is the heir to the throne; and he dies with the sympathy of the audience, who know he is a liar. But Hamlet was the first man condemned by his own intelligence.

To historians of the civilization that replaces ours, it may be that Shakespeare's significance will lie in this: that he was the bridge between the old, unreflective hero of Homer and Malory, and the Faustian hero who came after.

The last hero – Don Quixote

At the time Shakespeare was writing *Hamlet* (about 1600), Cervantes was producing the last monument to the hero of Homer and Malory. The bravery of an Achilles or a Lancelot lies in his undivided mind, his unreflection. Don Quixote is also undivided, because he is insane. He is the final sad comment of the age of Faust on the age of Homer: the unreflective hero is the stupid hero.

Faust – the hero that failed

But the question remained: can the intelligent man be a hero?

Goethe, himself a far more intelligent man than Shakespeare, never got closely to grips with the problem. His Egmont is the old unreflective hero. Werther, the reflective man, commits suicide. Wilhelm Meister is not a hero at all; he is a good-tempered, endlessly curious bourgeois.

Goethe's Faust is his only attempt to take up the problem where Shakespeare and Cervantes set it down. His Faust is Hamlet in another guise. Marlowe's Faustus was an ageing scholar; Gounod's Faust, based on Goethe, is an old man whose first gift from the devil is youth. Goethe does not load the dice against his Faust. He is described as too old for love affairs but too young not to want them – a man approaching middle-age.

Faust is the highest type of man – a man possessed by a pure passion to know truth. His tragedy is to feel that, with half his life gone, truth cannot be known.

Yet the bargain he should have made with Mephistopheles was that he would achieve complete and utter certainty. This was the true way out of his dilemma. Instead, he asks to be made stupid enough to take an undivided pleasure in living, to love and be loved: and the result of his bargain is that he seduces an innocent country girl. He might as well be Sir Lancelot. Goethe could not face the problem of defining certainty; and in spite of his immense attempt in the second part of *Faust* to deepen his approach, the problem remains untouched. Faust has sold his soul for the oblivion of stupidity, and forgotten that what tormented him was a desire for complete certainty.

Dostoevsky – the death of the hero

Dostoevsky dotted the i's and crossed the t's of the Faust dilemma. The hero of his *Notes from Underground* is a kind of Faust. He is resentful, irritable, frustrated, in his basement room. His intelligence has made him quite incapable of action. He envies undivided, stupid people and is contemptuous of them. He thinks of the man of action as a sort of bull who lowers his head and charges. He is capable of action because he is stupid.

Yet this beetle-man with his resentment and frustration, is not simply born unlucky. When he is inspired enough to exercise his power, his incorrigible idealism, he can generate the powers of the hero and the lover. The prostitute on whom he tries his idealism promptly becomes his adoring slave. But he finds her adoration unbearable – an ironic reminder of the uncertainty that torments him – and drives her away. If Goethe had penetrated his Faust theme to its depths he would have made Faust do the same.

The nineteenth century

The nineteenth century saw the birth and death of the romantic hero. The author who wrote romantically identified himself with his hero. The hero was his own huge shadow-image cast on a screen, in Yeats's words:

> ...a superhuman
> Mirror-resembling dream.

Goethe began the fashion with his handsome, pale, sorrowful poet, Werther. Schiller's Karl Moor in *The Robbers* is a passionate, violent young man who speaks of freedom, complete, ultimate freedom from all restraints, and who becomes a robber chief to express his revolt against society. Rousseau, the arch-priest of freedom, went further and made himself the romantic, freedom-seeking hero of his *Confessions*. These were the forerunners. The nineteenth century began with a spate of romantic heroes. Shelley projected his own 'mirror-resembling dream' image of himself in Prince Athanase, Alastor, the Wandering Jew Ahasuerus. The Byronic hero is a Hamlet-like dreamer, irresistibly attractive to women, weighed down with strange sins. Novalis, Jean Paul, and Hoffmann in Germany produced their variations on the freedom-seeking Schiller hero.

But another type of novel began to oust the romantic tradition: the realistic novel. It had, admittedly, existed much earlier – in Fielding and Defoe, for instance – but usually for the purpose of satire. Balzac and Dickens began to use it to make social observations. Stendhal, in *Le Rouge et le Noir*, seems to hesitate between the two traditions, the romantic and the realist. His hero is shown as an intelligent and ambitious young man, and for the first half of the novel, in which Julien Sorel becomes a tutor at the house of the mayor and seduces the mayor's wife, it seems that the author is identifying himself with the hero and intends to show him rising to triumph. Instead he seems to have a sudden change of heart, and has the hero executed in a manner so pointless and arbitrary that one can have no doubt that he simply got tired of writing the book.

But the real turning point of the nineteenth-century novel is certainly Flaubert's *Madame Bovary*. When I first read this, in my teens, I found it impossible to imagine what had prompted Flaubert to write it. There is not a single person in the book with whom the author could conceivably have identified himself. I had and still have a deep-rooted prejudice that all works of art are somehow connected to the author by an umbilical cord of passion, involvement. *Madame Bovary* still seems to me a kind of monster, a purely documentary novel. The novelist has ceased to be the poet, with his secret interest in projecting 'mirror-resembling dreams', and become a spiritual brother of the statistician and the political economist.

The immediate result of Flaubert's influence can be seen in Zola. Admittedly, the umbilical cord connecting creator to creation is again visible here, for Zola's novels (like Maupassant's) are mainly about adultery and rape, with a quantity of physical violence thrown in as seasoning. This comment is not intended as a belittlement of Zola's achievement. But the greatness of his realism does not save him from being strangely barren and disappointing when it comes to laying bare the emotions of his characters.

To try to make my point about Zola clear, it is necessary to go into some detail about his work.

One of his first novels, *Thérèse Raquin*, provides an interesting example of the contradiction inherent in realism. Thérèse is the bored, frustrated wife of an ailing clerk who is also her cousin. She has been brought up with her future husband in an atmosphere of illness that has made her thin, pale-faced, listless. An old schoolfriend of the husband's, Laurent, comes into the home and decides to seduce Thérèse. The seduction proceeds without any hitches and Thérèse, suddenly released from the suffocating, sickly atmosphere in which she has been brought up, becomes a tempest of sensuality. United completely by their physical ecstasy, the lovers decide to murder the husband.

So far, the novel has never once released its grip on the attention. The theme of frustrated energy finding an outlet is one that never fails to exercise fascination. But now Zola's hold seems to relax. The scene of the murder – they drown the husband in the Seine – is worthy of Dostoevsky; and the chapter that describes Laurent's daily visit to the morgue to see his victim has a grisly power that Zola was never to surpass. But having got this far, Zola seems to be uncertain what to do with his characters. The rest of the book describes their torments of conscience; and the final scene, with their attempt to murder one another turning into a suicide pact, is too far-fetched to be dramatic.

My own explanation of what happened is this. Up to the scene of the murder, Zola's imagination was working *inside* his subject, identifying himself with the frustrated woman who makes a bid for freedom. But Zola himself did not know enough about the nature of freedom to know what to do when Thérèse obtained it. His imagination failed at the effort that was demanded of it: to enlarge and widen that freedom.

This is a fact that strikes one again and again in reading Zola's novels. They are epics about wasted lives. The force that carries them forward is the negative force of torment and adultery. But when it becomes a question of free human beings exercising their freedom, Zola fails. Like Shakespeare, he had an immense feeling for life that made him create like a machine, never failing to get the reader to participate in what he was describing. But Shaw's objection to Shakespeare applies to Zola also: he could understand human weakness but not human strength. He understood the obscure lusts and sluggish drives of the human body and emotions but nothing of the greatness of the intellect and the spirit. And perhaps the worst thing that can be said against him is that some of his books read like an anticipation of the sadistic gangster novels of the 1940s. *La Terre*, for instance, has a contrived brutality and sexiness that brings to mind *No Orchids for Miss Blandish*.

The whole difference between nineteenth-century realism and romanticism is pin-pointed in a phrase of Daphne du Maurier's in an introduction to George du Maurier's *The Martian*: 'The book is not a novel. It is, in point of fact, the autobiography of George du Maurier – with one difference. And the difference is that Barry Josselin, the hero, is *the man that George du Maurier, in his secret heart, longed to have been*'. It is, in other words, the 'superhuman, mirror-resembling dream', that Yeats spoke of. It is true that these dream heroes do not convince the reader as completely as the carefully observed realities of Zola. But that is the whole challenge: to write with the realism of a Zola and the imaginative zest and heroic conviction of a Shelley. It is a challenge that the nineteenth century accepted – and then forgot. The twentieth century has not yet dared to take it up.

Shaw

In his Caesar, Shaw made a deliberate attempt to portray the moral greatness of the hero, combining intelligence with courage.

Again, in his Don Juan, Shaw treated the seducer hero in his characteristic way, endowing him with the kind of self-consciousness and intelligence that Zola's heroes lacked. Unfortunately, in the play (*Man and Superman*) Don Juan only talks of seduction, and is thereby less satisfactory than Mozart or Zola, who show it.

Yet Don Juan speaks plainly once again of heroic action: the heroism of the intelligence, the heroic purpose of 'helping life in its struggle upward'. And he also speaks of a purpose: 'that life is a force that has made innumerable experiments in organizing itself; that the mammoth and the man, the mouse and the megatherium, the flies and the fleas and the Fathers of the Church, are all more or less successful attempts to build up that raw force into higher and higher individuals, the ideal individual being omnipotent, omniscient, infallible, and withal, completely un-illudedly self-conscious; in short, a god'.

The last words are the important ones. For the Greeks, the hero was the beloved of the gods. This concept disappeared completely in the age of Faust. Shaw flings out his imagination towards a time when men will become gods. The question of whether this is possible or not is beside the point. The imagination is being used for its real purpose – envisaging the heroic in order to strive to create it.

The twentieth century

Shaw is an odd figure, great and yet out of tune with the twentieth century. Dostoevsky's beetle-man is more typical of the twentieth century than Don Juan.

Why are there no heroes in twentieth-century literature? I have outlined my own answer above. The hero reflects his creator's state of mind. If the creator feels no heroic striving, he will not create characters who feel it.

To some extent the heroic continues to survive in stories for boys and in comic papers – the unreflective heroic. The reflective writers confess themselves beaten.

The 1914-18 war produced its crop of anti-heroic war books, like *All Quiet on the Western Front*; and its crop of anti-heroic poets, like Owen and Isaac Rosenberg. T. S. Eliot produced his twentieth-century Hamlet, Prufrock, who is so certain of his own insignificance that he considers Hamlet a heroic figure and declares: 'I am not Prince Hamlet, nor was meant to be'.

Twenty years later, the hero of Sartre's *La Nausée* suffers from the same problem, the paralysis of action by reflection. The work of Sartre also revolves around the problem of the hero, but in spite of its intelligence it fails to enrich the concept of the hero. Mathieu, the hero of the first volume of *Roads to Freedom*, suffers from the same old inability to believe in himself, to feel himself a solid, positive person. Because he possesses intelligence without principles or discipline, he is the slave of his own laziness and cowardice. The novel shows him subjected to humiliation after humiliation as he seeks to borrow enough money for an abortion for his mistress; too intelligent ever to feel himself a beetle, too weak and negative to feel himself a man, he is a man lost between two worlds. In the play *The Devil and the Good God* he demonstrates how his hero-without-belief is capable of great acts of good and evil, all without conviction – a point Dostoevsky had already made in *Notes from Underground*.

Albert Camus has, in some ways, been more successful than Sartre in creating the new hero. In at least one book, *La Chute*, he shows a man who has passed beyond the self-deception that keeps him comfortable, and has given up his comfort to live in the dives of Amsterdam and talk, like the ancient mariner, to any casual stranger. In passing beyond 'bad faith', in becoming a Hamlet, his hero has not lost heroic stature; on the contrary, he has somehow gained it. It is a kind of parallel to stories of saints of the Middle Ages, except that there are no miracles possible – none of divine origin, anyway.

The problem of nothingness

Having come thus far, it is perhaps time to speak of the problem in slightly more technical terms. Man knows himself as a sort of vacuum in nature, as a nothingness.

Your consciousness of yourself at any moment is your consciousness of your body and of the things around you. This is a perfectly simple concept. Everyone notices that different people make them feel different. If you are a man, talking with a huge, masculine man will make you feel slight and feminine. Talking with a very feminine woman will make you feel masculine. Talking with a dry old man will make you feel young and revolutionary; talking with a brash and self-assertive youth will make you feel mature and very stable.

You are aware of yourself as a subjectivity in a great universe of objects, and you are not aware of yourself as a subject, but only as a kind of gap, a hole in the objects around you. Even your own body is an object like any other. But you, you yourself, are the consciousness that sees and feels these objects; and to be conscious is to be conscious of something. We do not know whether it is possible to be conscious and yet conscious of nothing (although Mr Eliot uses the phrase in *East Coker*); so that, in a perfectly plain sense, your existence is completely dependent on the existence of the universe around you. If man is a soul, then he is never conscious of his soul, or if he is, then so faintly that he hardly ever isolates his consciousness of it enough to be fully aware of it. It would be like a candle flame in a sunlit room. For all practical purposes, man is aware of himself as a vacuum.

This is an embarrassing thing, for Nature abhors a vacuum, mentally as well as physically. Man's consciousness thus has a sort of chameleon quality. Some men are more chameleon than others (like the café proprietor in *La Nausée*, 'When his café empties, his head empties too'). Others have a higher resistance to surroundings, and strive to assert themselves among the objects and circumstances of their lives.

There are occasional moments – very occasional – when man suddenly becomes aware of himself as a somethingness instead of as a vacuum. These happen quite unexpectedly; perhaps in a sexual orgasm, or in the moment when some great project is conceived, or simply because a shaft of spring sunlight produces a leap of the heart and a consciousness of oneself as a living being. To became aware of oneself as a somethingness is to become aware of oneself as a being capable of will. The something one becomes aware of is one's own power.

And here a complication arises. There are two kinds of power: this kind, the interior kind, and the exterior kind.

Bad faith

Exterior power depends completely on circumstances. A completely empty-headed man, like Sartre's café proprietor, would feel it if he was placed in a position of authority. He would act as if he possessed power. But if circumstances reversed his position he would instantly feel weak. The man who is taken in by temporary circumstances, who actively strives to be taken in, to deceive himself, because it is more comfortable to be taken in, is said to be acting with bad faith.

Obviously, all of us live in bad faith all the time. This is automatically implied in the previous statement that we are all, to some degree, aware of ourselves as vacuums. But there is a choice between being taken in fully and partly refusing to be taken in. Thus, for instance, a man who was suddenly placed in a position of authority would, if he were a man of bad faith, feel himself to be a man of power, a leader and ruler. A man who possessed more honesty would exercise the authority that had been thrust upon him without *feeling* like a leader.

In short, the reverse of bad faith is another name for the Christian virtue of humility; not the kind of humility that Nietzsche hated, the humility of spiritual laziness, a form of self-betrayal, but a mere safeguard against self-deception, the fundamental human vice.

Sartre's parable of bad faith

Sartre has illustrated bad faith in an exceptionally clear parable, *The Childhood of a Leader*. His hero is portrayed as an over-sensitive boy, far too self-analytical to make a leader. The height of his self-analysis and the feeling of weakness and humiliation that comes with it occur when he is seduced by a homosexual schoolmaster, who convinces him that he must imitate Rimbaud and 'derange his senses' by paederasty. This brings about a strong reaction, and total capitulation of his intelligence. He joins a group of anti-Semitic young hearties and begins to feel less soiled. One day he is rude to a Jew at a party given by a friend. Afterwards he is filled with remorse; only cowardice and shame prevent his rushing to beg the pardon of his friend and his sister. But the next day, when he meets them, they hasten to beg his pardon. The friend declares how much he admires his courage in sticking so sternly to his principles. The sister looks at him with awed admiration. He goes away drunk with the praise, with the power they have handed to him. In a café he day-dreams of strength and determination. Half an hour later he emerges, a complete anti-Semite and embryonic leader. He has dramatized himself; he is *acting the part* of the leader, the undivided man, and turning away from his sensitivity and self-analysis.

The necessity of bad faith

And yet, as I have pointed out, bad faith is unavoidable, except in extremely rare moments of deep self-awareness. And the obvious alternative, continued humility, a kind of permanent self-scepticism and self-analysis, has immense disadvantages – especially in the bustle of the modern world. The best thing is obviously to choose carefully what form of bad faith to commit oneself to. And the choice will be dictated by certain moral considerations. Most men have a natural preference for being benefactors of the human race rather than its enemies; for being saints rather than murderers; for being kind rather than cruel. A man might be fascinated by, say, the personality and life of Beethoven, and 'act the part' of Beethoven. The result might quite possibly be some great music; at all events the result would certainly be less harmful than if he was fascinated by the achievement of Hitler or Landru. No one knows what forms of 'bad faith' dominated Beethoven's inner life. His music, in so far as it is great, represents a conquest of the bad faith, but it would have been impossible without it. (Some men act the part of themselves-when-young, and this can be observed particularly in writers and artists, when the later work seems like a spurious imitation of the earlier.)

This act of accepting the least harmful form of bad faith is known as 'commitment'. The form of a man's commitment will be determined by what he knows of himself and his inner needs. It may be of any kind, ranging from the communism of Sartre to the lonely individualism of Camus. But it is essentially a decision to act in a certain way.

The existential hero

All that I have just said on the subject of man's nothingness, his bad faith, is only a more psychological way of expressing the problem of the hero in the twentieth century. Hamlet was simply the man who was aware of himself as a vacuum. If he had allowed the ghost to convince him that Claudius should be killed like a dog to avenge his father, he would have committed an act of bad faith. Faust asked Mephistopheles to intoxicate him with life until he no longer hated himself for the bad faith he could not avoid. Dostoevsky's underground hero preferred to withdraw from the human race rather than commit bad faith. This recognition of man's nothingness is the basis of the modern philosophy called Existentialism. And since what we are asking for is a hero *in spite of* too much intelligence, too much self-analysis, this new hero, not yet created, can be called the Existential hero.

Canutism of the humanists

The foregoing analysis has provided at least one possible answer to the question of why there are no heroes in twentieth-century literature. Modern man does not believe in himself enough to think in terms of heroes. A fatal kind of modesty, of self-belittlement, crept into the modern mind at some time between the *Morte d'Arthur* and *Hamlet*, and grew in importance until it became the sole theme of literature.

But, some religious critic might object, it was a wholesome modesty; it was justified by man's increasing bewilderment. Quite. And this is just the problem that confronts us today. Before the existential hero can be created, in fiction or in fact, that bewilderment must be routed and replaced by some kind of certainty.

Some modern writers have urged that the only way to stem the tide of chaos is to propagate a belief in man and in his possibilities. They call this Humanism. Mr Bill Hopkins[9] has invented an admirable word to describe this attitude: he calls it Canutism. The man of goodwill, with his simple faith in human reasonableness, the accessibility of human nature to reason, is like King Canute in the face of the tide of modern chaos. He reminds one of John Stuart Mill's father, who thought that he could reason maniacs back to sanity by talking to them and pointing out the illogicality of their conduct.

9 See *Editor's Notes* to Chapter 14 [Ed]

The immense but limited value of reason

Reason is not, of course, to be dismissed. One must recognize that. But there is an abyss of violence and craving in human nature. The depths of the mind are like the depths of a volcano. The craving for violence, the craving for infinity that coexist there, have no counterpart in the conscious human world. No matter how far he may seem to accept the dull, trivial, rational, civilized world in his conscious life, every human being contains the poles of heaven and hell, and between them an unimaginable tension that is never relaxed. Of all this, reason takes no account. Yet it is not within the power of reason to satisfy human nature, although it can never be dispensed with. To deny the tremendous, irrational tensions within the human being would not be to dignify man, but to devalue him.

The function of religion

These irrational depths in man are inaccessible to reason. And yet they are not inaccessible to symbols. This is the reason that religion is never finally out-dated, no matter how many times agnostic thinkers succeed in demonstrating that its legends and assumptions are an unreasonable farrago of nonsense. To suppose that it can be discredited in this way is rather on a parallel with supposing that Haydn's *Creation* is valueless because the account of creation which he uses has been disproved by Darwin.

The modern decline of religion is a further reason for the decline of the hero. For at least the Church dignified man by supposing him capable of damnation and salvation, thereby conferring a certain heroic stature on him. For this reason, a training and mental conditioning by the Church is infinitely preferable to training and conditioning in, say, an American business college, where the go-getter ethics of Arthur Miller's salesman are taught. All forms of materialism are a slow and deliberate diminution of man's stature.

My own aims and values

Having said this much, I should have made fairly plain what I consider to be my own immediate task. It is, I think, the task of all writers of the future – the creation of the existential hero.

This is, of course, a purely artistic task. It is an imaginative challenge, not a practical one. The problem has been raised by the observation that there are no heroes in twentieth-century literature. It is no answer to say that no honest writer would think it worth his while to create a boys'-magazine hero, and that the lack of heroes is a tribute to the integrity of our writers. Let us agree that it would be pointless for any imaginative writer to create a hero as irresistible and unbelievable as Baron Munchausen. But the hero is, by definition, a man great enough to inspire us with his courage. It goes without saying that his creator must also be capable of convincing us of his reality. It becomes therefore an imaginative challenge. Dudintsev, for instance, has tackled it most interestingly in his *Not By Bread Alone*, where his inventor shows a positively heroic persistence and patience in the face of the government bureaucrats who want to suppress his invention. But the weak plank in the book is the invention itself – a machine for casting iron drainpipes. An English reader might be forgiven for feeling that there are more important things in life than drainpipes. The inventor remains a hero, but his heroism would have been greater if he had spent ten years fighting for a great moral idea and not a mere machine.

In my journal for November 1952 I find the following entry:

> I wonder what it is I resent so intensely about modern novelists? I think it must be their determination to attribute their own weaknesses to all mankind. There seems to be a strong desire among them to prove that human nature is basically weak and neurotic, a constant prey to sexual frustration, inferiority complexes, boredom, and any temptation that drifts in its way. Aldous Huxley tries to prove that all men are either morons (usually good-looking) or weaklings. Charles Jackson, whom I've been trying to read lately, would like to demonstrate how mankind is a helpless prey of its passions – which include booze, homosexuality, and a desire to rape small girls... Even Shaw's later characters tend to make me disgusted with mankind...

The problem of the hero had been occupying my thoughts for a long time before this. I had come to observe that heroism requires a temperament that is violent, passionate, and ambitious (I am speaking now of the born hero, not of the men who show themselves capable of heroic action when some emergency happens to demand it). But when men happen to be born with this temperament they must also have a field to exercise it in.

But there, I noticed, a new problem appears. Some men feel quite at home in the world they are born into. They may dislike certain aspects of it, but that is all the better because they can put their heroic temperament to work to alter it. These men become what Shaw calls 'world betterers'; men like Lenin, William Morris, Jesus, Luther.

But some men are positively not at home in the world. They have no feeling of belonging. They are over-sensitive about the folly and cruelty of life. Their sense of not belonging gives them an unusual and penetrating insight into human life, a remorselessly clear vision of 'truth'. But their clarity of vision is no advantage to them in the world. It may make them great artists, writers, composers, but it also frequently leads them to suicide or the madhouse. They have, however, this important advantage over other men – an occasional insight into some strange glory in the human soul. There are moments when their feeling about man and the world expresses itself in extraordinary phrases like 'life is entirely good', or 'man is a god'. Their attitude to life, which to the 'ordinary man' often seems preposterously pessimistic ('Misery will never end', said Van Gogh), swings to an extreme which seems insanely optimistic.

It was the paradox of these men that led me to write *The Outsider*: the fact that, although they may end in the lunatic asylum, they achieve a deeper vision of truth than most of us ever approach. The book had an instant and surprising success. I was, admittedly, a little surprised and puzzled by some of the interpretations of it. On one occasion I attended a lecture on 'Angry Young Men' by a lady novelist, and heard an explanation of my ideas that startled me. I had written, she told her audience (in which, fortunately, no one knew I was present) to prove that all men of genius are Outsiders – gloomy and tormented geniuses, like Lord Byron. Of course, she could not entirely agree with me; take Mozart and Shakespeare, for instance ... At the first opportunity I slunk out quietly. She was an intelligent woman whose work I admired, and yet she had entirely missed my point. I brooded on this in the pub next door, and decided that I should have invented a far more complex terminology, dividing my Outsiders into weaklings, apocalyptics, existential heroes, saints, and prophets. Later, when I published the second part of *The Outsider*, I bitterly regretted not having done so, for the chief complaint directed at the book was that the word 'Outsider' had become too universal to have any meaning. A more careful classification of various types of Outsider would have avoided this.

Lawrence – the existential hero

In point of fact, there is at least one existential hero in the book – T. E. Lawrence. The most casual reading of *The Seven Pillars of Wisdom* shows a man more riddled with self-doubt than Dostoevsky's underground hero. Yet his achievement was heroic – even if we grant Mr Aldington every reservation he makes in his debunking biography. This was precisely the kind of thing that irritated me into writing *The Outsider*. There may have been a great deal of nonsense about the Lawrence legend, and a great deal of silliness about Lawrence the man; but he was pretty well the only living model of an existential hero we possessed. This cannot be tossed overboard so lightly. Yet all the biographies of him fall into two extremes of incomprehension: either to make him out to be a perfect example of the old 'stupid hero', a cross between Sir Lancelot and Sir Winston Churchill, or to deny that he was a hero at all.

The necessity for belief

Both my Outsider books point to the same conclusion: heroism is impossible for a man without belief. Belief, of course, need not necessarily mean religious belief. Lawrence achieved heroic stature supported by a slowly deflating belief in the Arabs. But sooner or later a man like Lawrence feels the need for a belief that will affect everything he does and thinks. Without it, he is like a tired swimmer without a life-belt.

Let us take a look at some examples of types of belief that have supported various writers. I have already quoted Shaw's Don Juan: the vitalist ideal of 'helping life in its struggle upward'. This is the kind of belief that inspired Shaw's life-work. On the other hand one might consider Chekov, a scientific humanist who believed that science would finally leave mankind no more problems; or Zola, another liberal materialist who pinned his faith in 'the human spirit' (I must confess that these words have always seemed quite meaningless to me: 'human' and 'spirit' seem to be contradictions); or Paul Claudel, who found that he could accept the Roman version of the Christian myth, and cheerfully spent a lifetime propagandizing it.

Or, more interesting than any of these, take Wordsworth, with his lifelong certainty of being a dedicated priest of nature. I say more interesting, because Wordsworth took himself with a seriousness that would seem quite out of place in the twentieth century (except possibly in a politician). The degree to which he committed himself to his mission excites derision in most moderns. It makes some of his less successful poems seem unreadably pompous; and the memory of them stays with us when we read his greater works, *The Excursion* or *The Prelude*, and helps to spoil them. (One remembers Mrs Wordsworth rebuking Keats: 'Mr Wordsworth is *never* interrupted'.)

Yet Wordsworth's greatness springs completely from that sense of dedication. He acted on the assumption that he was born with a mission, and the result was greatness. And the same is true of his neglected contemporary Blake, just as it was true later of Shelley. It is interesting to wonder what would happen to a Wordsworth born in the twentieth century. We can see what happened to the Wordsworth temperament when it was incarnated in Arnold and Tennyson in the nineteenth century: scepticism and self-doubt honeycombed it as effectively as woodworm eats away a beam.

Here, then, is one more facet for the existential hero: a sense of dedication; the ability to take himself seriously.

It is not enough to make a hero; otherwise Joyce's Stephen Dedalus would be an existential hero. But it is a good half-way towards it.

The post-war hero

When we consider the serious writers who have appeared over the past thirty years, the prospect seems unrelievedly gloomy.

Hemingway, after early attempts to create heroes who were not neurotic failures, began to specialize in the Brainless Superman, a species that first appears in *To Have and Have Not* (although he is anticipated to some extent in the self-portrait in *Green Hills of Africa*). Graham Greene produced a series of novels that were brilliant studies in human neurosis, but the element of religious faith that enters into some of the later novels to redeem it, produces an unpleasant impression of faking.

The post-war period has produced at least half a dozen new names in English writing: Angus Wilson, John Wain, Kingsley Amis, Iris Murdoch, John Osborne, Bill Hopkins. The first four named are aggressively anti-hero, rather in the sense of Mr Aldington's book on Lawrence. Mr Amis particularly is responsible for a cult of 'the ordinary chap'. All go in for a negative kind of debunking of their characters.

Osborne's work has special interest for me because, on the appearance of *Look Back in Anger* (his first play), critics tended to classify him with me. In point of fact, I have very little sympathy with his work to date. There is a distinctly Chekhovian air of frustration and dreariness about his plays. This, of course, is acceptable enough; except that, at the end of the plays, the dreariness is still unresolved. When his play *The Entertainer* is compared with, say, Wells's *Mr Polly* (which is also set in a little seaside town, and is about frustration and dreariness) its lack of positive conclusion becomes plainly visible. Mr Polly decides 'If you don't like your life, you can change it', and does so. Archie Rice, like Jimmy Porter, travels on into an unrelievedly gloomy future. If Osborne's intention was to produce an impression that life is futile and pointless, this would be justified; but from his pronouncements on socialism and the middle classes, it is plain that this is not so. His work, so far, strikes me as negative in tone.

Bill Hopkins's novel *The Divine and the Decay* seems to me an attempt at a far more positive statement than these other writers have attempted. The fanatical, power-driven politician, with whom the author obviously feels some sympathy (how much is difficult to say) is a relief after Amis's 'ordinary chaps'. But technically the novel is still a long way below Amis or Angus Wilson, and it is safer to wait to see what Hopkins will produce in the future before attempting to pass judgment on him.[10]

The new villain – the opportunist

So, to date, the problem of the hero is still unsolved. No creator has appeared who can face the political and spiritual chaos of our time and produce a positive, heroic, sympathetic figure who is not swamped by it all.

There is an interesting story by Budd Schulberg

10 See *Editor's Notes* to Chapter 14 [Ed]

that can be regarded as a parable of our creative predicament. In *What Makes Sammy Run?* he contrasts the thick-skinned, ruthless opportunist Sammy Glick with the hero, the gentle, sensitive, good-tempered narrator. Sammy wins every trick when it is a question of competition with the narrator. At the end of the book Sammy is a highly successful film magnate; the narrator is a moderately successful, reasonably happy script-writer. But in spite of its moral – that Sammy's material success does not produce contentment – the book conveys the idea that, in the twentieth century, there are only two types of man: the successful go-getter and the unsuccessful sensitive man. It is still the predicament of *Hamlet* and *Faust*, presented in terms of Hollywood: when it comes to making a success in action, sensitivity and intelligence are a dead loss.

The whole climate of our time is against the creation of the existential hero. Our sensitive and intelligent men have so far come to identify strength and certainty with the Sammy Glicks (or worse still, the Hitlers and Stalins) that there is an active resistance to any attempt to revive the dying concept of the hero.

Yet there is one cheering sign in the world of modern writing. There may still be no concept of the hero, but there is undoubtedly a concept of the villain. The villain – the compromises and futilities of our mass-produced civilization – has been pilloried ever since Eliot's *Waste Land*. Messrs Amis, Wilson, Correlli Barnett, Wain, and others are still attacking vigorously. It is easier to attack than to create new standards; but if the attacks become violent and serious enough, we may hope that something positive will result. While we wait for the existential hero to come to birth – as he will, slowly and inevitably – we can do no better than continue to spotlight and expose the sources of our chaos. Our business is analysis, unending analysis. Pursued relentlessly and continuously enough, it becomes creation.

1957

Editor's Notes:

The 'Second Encore Symposium on British Play Writing' was held at the Royal Court Theatre on November 18, 1956, chaired by Kenneth Tynan. A verbatim transcription of the proceedings appeared as 'Cause Without a Rebel' in *Encore*, no. 9 (June/July, 1957) pp. 13-35 (**C12**). The transcript includes notes of audience comments, laughter and grunts: 'Stick to the theatre, not an attack on Wilson!', directed at Mankowitz, was heard at one point. Near the end of the proceedings, after it had been agreed that there was a dearth of talented contemporary dramatists in England, Tynan asked Wilson 'What contemporary English hero would you like to write a play? Who would he be?' Wilson's reply was: '... since all plays are essentially about oneself, I guess me.'

2
EXISTENTIAL CRITICISM

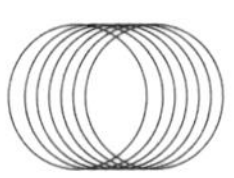

It is my hope that, within the next two decades, the techniques of existential thinking will become a commonplace in England and America. They would undoubtedly provide a solution to many problems which we now regard as peculiar to the mid-twentieth-century: the problems, for instance, set out by David Riesman in *The Lonely Crowd*, or by William H. Whyte in *The Organization Man*. It is true that England and America have so far contributed nothing to the development of existentialism: we trace its origins to Germany, Denmark, and in more recent years, France. And yet 'Continental existentialism' reached a sort of impasse many years ago. Heidegger has contributed nothing since the first part of *Sein und Zeit* in 1927. Sartre and Camus would appear to have 'dried up' in the fifties. The Anglo-American temperament is cautious, experimental, positivistic; better adapted to pursuing and elaborating ideas than to originating them. Yet England had an existential thinker long before Dostoevsky, Nietzsche or Kierkegaard; I refer to William Blake. At least one great classic of existentialism came from America – William James' *The Varieties of Religious Experience* (James actually uses the word 'existentialism'). And the Anglo-American temper may yet find itself able to continue and develop where the continental Europeans have reached a dead end.

In August, 1958, I published in *The London Magazine* an article entitled 'Existential Criticism and the Work of Aldous Huxley'[11]. The next issue of the magazine published a letter from an irritated reader who claimed that, as far as he could see, existential criticism differed from ordinary literary criticism only in its pretentiousness. I hope in the present essay to provide a refutation of this comment.

In my own case, I was an existentialist long before I had ever heard the word. In my Journal for 1950-1, I find the following entry:

> Living is exhaustion of life. It is pleasant to think of atmospheres, the focussing of an imaginative ideal through thought, literature, music. But they all vanish in the immediate ordeal of living... *I can find no system of philosophy that fits, even remotely, the facts of my everyday existence.* All seems untrue in the face of mud and boredom.

I prefer to quote my own journal, rather than some definition by Kierkegaard or Sartre, because existentialism cannot exist without a frankly personal preoccupation. The disease of our time is the diffidence, the sense of personal insignificance, that feels the need to disguise itself as academic objectivity when it attempts to philosophise. I have dealt at length with this 'fallacy of insignificance'

11 Vol. 5, no. 9, 1958, p. 46-59 [**C15**], expanded and reprinted as 'Appendix 1' in *The Strength to Dream: literature and imagination*. London: Victor Gollancz, 1962. [Ed.]

in my book *The Age of Defeat*. It is the diffidence that has made modern American literature so rich in critics, and so poor in novelists and poets. In England, it has led to the domination of Logical Positivism in philosophy.

But this is not to say that existentialism means merely 'daring to be subjective.' The American 'Beat Generation' and the British 'Angry Young Men' are subjective without deserving to be dignified by the label 'existential.'

This leads to a preliminary definition: Existentialism is the attempt to philosophise with no reference to *a priori* intellectual concepts. It is, as it were, the philosophy of intuition. This also helps to mark the boundary between literary criticism and existential criticism. Literary criticism has many standards that are based on technique, and a poem or a novel may be judged as a pleasing exercise in words rather than by its sense of purpose. A literary critic turns without embarrassment from Milton to Dostoevsky, from Jane Austen to Shaw. Such nonchalance may be envied by the existential critic, but he has no desire to imitate it. He cannot consider Jane Austen in relation to Dostoevsky without asking awkward questions: 'What, fundamentally, was she saying?'; 'How mature was her moral vision of the world?'; 'What concepts of human purpose are concealed in the basic assumptions of her novels?'

In the case of Aldous Huxley, I pointed out the 'insignificance premise' that forms the basis of the character of every one of his heroes. In order to enjoy the impressive intellectual and creative achievement in his works, the reader has to 'identify' himself with a weakling, to swallow the premise that he has a great deal in common with a Gumbril, a Denis Stone, a Philip Quarles or Anthony Beavis. I always find such a premise very difficult to accept. It offends my fundamental belief in my own capacities, without which I would find it impossible to write a single line or state a single opinion. In the same way, the heroes of Graham Greene or Thomas Wolfe arouse feelings of mild protest. My protest is not based upon a high opinion of my own powers, but on a more obscure feeling that these writers are somehow not 'playing the game.' If a man began a dart game with me by saying 'I'm afraid I'm absolutely no good; I may or may not hit the board, and I couldn't hope to hit a double,' I'd be inclined to say: 'In that case, let us not play, for I *know* I can hit the board, and am moderately efficient at getting doubles.' If he still insisted on playing, and in fact showed considerable talent as a dart player, I'd be inclined to feel that his original protest had been rather pointless. I experience the same reaction on beginning a novel by Huxley. I feel like saying politely to the hero, 'I'm awfully sorry, but I really can't identify myself with you if you're as weak as you say you are.' I am not, I think, more confident of my capacities than the average man; but I feel that an attempt to achieve something presupposes a certain formality of self-belief. It would seem that the diffidence of many modern novelists has reached a point where even this formality is regarded as self-conceit. One takes it for granted that the hero of a modern novel will prove himself to be an 'ordinary chap.' Just as modern science and technology set out to satisfy the needs of 'the average man,' so modern culture has become a department store whose prices are all within reach of 'the average pocketbook.' Instead of Faust, Hamlet, or Captain Ahab, we have Mr Sloan Wilson's Man in the Grey Flannel Suit, the 'regular guy' who lives across the way. Instead of attempting to emulate Nietzsche, the college student writes a thesis on him. Instead of fashioning his own life, the modern American consults his psychiatrist to discover precisely what he is capable of. His belief in 'the factors that control our lives' may be tempered by anxiety; but he finds it indispensable as an excuse for doing nothing.

I regard my own temperament as peculiarly adapted to existential criticism in that I have always been insufficiently emotional, too abstract and intellectual. The world is only meaningful when interpreted by emotion; intellect finds it baffling. The result is the basic existential experience: the vision of the world's absurdity that Sartre calls 'nausea' in his book of that title. 'Nausea' is the root of existential philosophy. Observed by the intellect alone, physical reality is meaningless. Intellect has no purpose; it is an instrument of analysis. Purpose is a *feeling*.

Nevertheless, it should be understood that 'feeling' in this context does not mean physical sensation, or the emotions it evokes. In *La Nausée*, Sartre's hero speaks of a café proprietor, and comments: 'When his café empties, his head empties too.' Such a man is the opposite of what the 'existentialist' sets out to be. He has no inner reality; his mental life is a series of sensations and ideas aroused by his immediate experience.

Here, then, is the *a priori* of existentialism. Its 'value judgement' is concerned with 'inner-reality.' The opposite of the café proprietor, with his life of sensation that is sustained entirely from the outside world, is the ultimately 'free' man who lives an inner-reality, independent of the present, sustained from within. The café proprietor, (if such a monster could really exist) would be incapable of an act of faith, for faith is essentially faith in that which is not immediately present to the senses.

It will be seen that I have evoked a version of Plato's world of forms or ideas. Plato believed that these 'forms' were the reality, and not their counterparts in the physical world. Later philosophers have criticised Plato on many counts – chiefly on the absurdity of believing that all 'real' tables, for example, are mere physical replicas of some 'ideal' table that exists beyond space and time. But we can see in Plato, nevertheless, the denial of the two-dimensional world of the café proprietor, the assertion of a superior order of reality. An existentialist would say that Plato was mistaken in assuming that his 'world of ideas' was somehow objective, a ghostly duplicate of the 'real world.' From the existential viewpoint, the physical world is undoubtedly a secondary order of reality; but the primary reality is man's vitality, his freedom.

The starting point of existentialism is the alienness of the world. (It will be remembered that Roquentin, in Sartre's *La Nausée*, looks at a tree root and is horrified by its twisting, snaky *inscrutability*.) The purpose of existentialism is to analyse the world's alien-ness in the hope that it is actually only an appearance. The 'abstract philosophers' had only disguised the alien-ness with their metaphysical 'explanations.' For Kierkegaard or Sartre, the constructions of Kant or Hegel are a subtle form of self-deception. (Sartre calls it 'bad faith'.)

But the starting point of poetry is the feeling of man's oneness with the world. Generations of poets and artists have described even the most dehumanised pieces of nature and somehow made them a part of man's 'home' (Emily Brontë, for example). Where a Roquentin looks at the world and finds it meaningless, alien, inscrutable, finally *other*, the poet, working through some intuition that lies below his conscious personality, expresses an acceptance and affirmation, a sense of the world as a home. A minor poet like Rupert Brooke or Julian Grenfell expresses his love of England when in a foreign country. The major poet expresses a love of the world, the physical universe, for his experiences as a poet have taken him beyond space and time, into the world of final un-knowledge, complete chaos. He moves from doubt and despair into affirmation of the world, love of its reality.

This is also the aim of existentialism. Beginning with 'the nausea,' it moves towards mystical acceptance of everything. This is also where I find myself in disagreement with the ideas of Heidegger, Sartre and Camus. Sartre in particular has moved steadily further from the main problems of existentialism into the shallower waters of political squabbles (some of which have brought him into sharp disfavour with the de Gaulle administration in France). And Camus, who once complained that mere political quarrels distracted him from his ultimate 'quarrel with God,' seems to have allowed himself to be influenced by his politically minded contemporaries until his thought has become an unadventurous atheism in the Voltaire tradition. Although he continues to be influenced by Dostoevsky (and has recently adapted *The Devils* for the stage), his scepticism lacks the intensity of Dostoevsky's craving to 'accept' the world.

The first stage in this revolution which I hope to see accomplished in literature is a 'new existentialism'. The roots of existentialism lie in German romanticism; they can be discovered in Goethe's *Faust*, in Nietzsche, in Novalis and Jean Paul Richter. Richter, in particular, has an extraordinary episode in his novel *Flower, Fruit and Thorn Pieces*, entitled 'The Dead Christ Proclaims there is no God,' which might be taken as a model of mystical existentialism (although the overblown, romantic language is likely to make modern readers wince). Richter begins by commenting that men who profess to be atheists are usually as shallow in their conviction as men who profess to believe in God. He goes on to describe a dream that will remind many readers of James Thompson's masterpiece *The City of Dreadful Night*. He finds himself in a churchyard in some strange, apocalyptic landscape, and sees Christ descending on to the altar. When the dead ask 'Is there no God,' he answers: 'None.' 'And when I looked at the boundless universe for the divine eye, it looked at me out of a socket, empty and bottomless.' Richter then describes a vision of the end of the world, the emptiness and the horror of a universe without God. Undoubtedly, this is the vision that led Dostoevsky to plan an immense novel called *Atheism*. Finally, the dreamer wakes up, finds himself on a hillside on a summer evening, and feels gratitude to be able to accept the world as a home. The development curve of the story is identical with that of the chapter, called 'The Breath of Corruption' in *The Brothers Karamazov*. An even more startlingly close comparison can be drawn with that story in *The Diary of a Writer* called 'Dream of an Absurd Man' where a man is on the point of suicide because his life seems unbelievably boring and pointless, and dreams of his own death and a strange world of uncorrupted human beings in some distant solar system. As in Richter's story, the dreamer wakes up with a deepened sense of purpose, a knowledge of what has to be done.

At a first glance, it might seem that existential criticism is useful only in the case of existential literature. In a narrow sense, this is certainly true. Aldous Huxley or Arthur Koestler are admirable subjects for existential criticism because they are sufficiently interested in these problems of human purpose to fall easily within its categories. Their failings and inadequacies are also clearly definable as a lack of consistency within their existential premises. Like Camus, Huxley has allowed himself to be drawn increasingly into worrying about political problems, and the result is an obsessive pessimism that pervades such works as *Ape and Essence*, *The Genius and the Goddess*, and *Brave New World Revisited*. The existentialist's objection to this pessimism is not that it is unjustified by the facts Huxley presents, but that Huxley's facts are far too narrowly selected. The same objection applies to

Camus. It is true that Huxley might retort: 'What facts ought I have presented?' and that it would be difficult to answer in a few words. But those words 'the facts' conceal a million ambiguities. In fact, there is no such thing as 'a fact'; there is only the human perception of each fact. If 'fact' is taken to mean 'That which one can verify by experiment' then it is impossible to escape complete materialism. The optimism of a Blake or Nietzsche is not due to a blindness to facts that any Marxist would be aware of; it is the introduction of the poet's sense of order into the universe of 'facts.'

The Marxist would object that the poet's craving for order is neither here nor there; he is concerned with objective reality. The existentialist would reply that the Marxist is mistaken in supposing that man's subjective vision of order is somehow outside the universe, not 'a fact.' The sense of order and meaning is the direct stimulus of the will, and even mere perception springs from a will to perceive. Huxley, Koestler and Camus might persist in asserting that these are the facts of the modern world, and that on such a showing, they can find no ground for optimism. But such a plea is only possible when no one is quite sure what they mean by existentialism. As soon as certain existential premises have been clearly stated, it becomes apparent that 'the facts' are whatever a man chooses to make himself aware of. If he is sitting in an armchair in a room, then 'the facts' are the physical data he can perceive. If he takes up the telephone, calls his bookmaker, and lays ten to one on the favourite, he has moved away from 'the facts' of the room, and is exercising a faculty of foresight that might be called faith or speculation. If he happens to have his dog sitting at his feet, the 'facts' as perceived by himself and the dog are roughly the same. But the dog would be incapable of phoning the bookmaker, even if (like the famous shaggy dog) he had the gift of speech, for his power of projection beyond the immediate facts is negligible compared to the man's. The power of projection beyond the immediate facts constitutes man's power over his environment, and is the basis of his relation to the world. If Huxley or Camus chooses to project himself as far as the 'international facts,' that is his affair. But if they try to insist that these are somehow the only facts, then they are misrepresenting the situation.

The views of thinkers such as Camus and Huxley depend upon their own peculiar way of assessing the interaction between man's 'spirit' and his world. In fact, their finest works – Huxley's *Grey Eminence*, Camus' *L'Homme Revolté* – have been careful studies of the interaction of 'the human spirit' with the 'political facts.' On the one hand, they consider man's craving for order, his need for revolt, and on the other, the 'realities' of wars and rebellions. But while it is arguable that their interpretation of history is unassailable, their view of 'the human spirit' has weaker foundations. Its foundations, in fact, are the personal characters of Huxley and Camus. A reader of the poetry of Wordsworth or Saint John of the Cross feels himself justified if he turns to a biography and tries to learn about the moments of vision or insight that led to the writing of the poetry. Yet a reader of Camus or

Huxley would feel that he was being somehow unfair if he turned to their novels and commented: 'If this is the experience that underlies your conclusions about man and the world, I'm afraid your vision seems limited.'

Yet such a procedure would be perfectly consistent with existential criticism. The serious writer is attempting, after all, to alter his reader's opinions about man and the world. If he is an expert on mathematics or economics, he has a perfect right to assume that his knowledge is wider than that of his reader. But if he is a creative writer or a philosopher, whose superiority over his reader is mainly one of skill in self-expression, then this right becomes more dubious. It is no longer a question of intellectual qualifications, but of the ability to project oneself beyond the immediate facts. And the most inarticulate reader might possess a far broader perception of facts than the writer. It becomes, therefore, necessary to scrutinise the writer's qualifications for imposing his vision on his contemporaries. In literary criticism, of course, there is no question of this. The literary critic will state 'Pope wrote better verse than Francis Thompson.' But ask him to carry his examination deeper, into the 'states of mind' behind the poetry, and he will either declare that this is not his business, or will state his own temperamental prejudices without apology. And, in fact, it is possibly just as well that literary criticism should lead an independent existence from existential criticism; only a superhuman perception could unite the two, and in the meantime, it is just as well that certain critics should be concerned with comparing the merits of the poems of Burns, Lodge and Drummond of Hawthornden.

Existential criticism, then, is only a criticism based upon a quite definite philosophical position. In the remainder of this essay, I shall try to outline this more fully. First, the issues might be clarified by some examples of existential criticism 'in action.'

The plays and novels of Samuel Beckett have revealed the complete helplessness of the English literary and dramatic critics. Kenneth Tynan, for example, when writing about *Endgame* in *The Observer*, devoted his article to parody of the Beckett manner. This was, in itself, extremely amusing, but it disappointed those readers who hoped to be told how they ought to react to Beckett: and unkind readers might suspect that the parody was only a screen for Mr Tynan's embarrassment and inability to make up his mind as to the standpoint from which the play ought to be judged. Other 'highbrow' critics showed the same indecision. Beckett's novels have been the source of even greater bewilderment. Some critics tried to concentrate on the 'manner,' and praised Beckett's Irish wit or commented on his sense of Irish character. Others confined themselves to outlines of his plays, allowing a tone of reproachful protest to creep in. A minority decided to take the plunge and praise Beckett's profundity and deep humanity.

In fact, the principles of existential criticism make an assessment of Beckett a fairly simple matter. Nothing can be more obvious than Beckett's total despair. (*Endgame* was made so uncompromisingly gloomy because he objected to the way in which *Waiting for Godot* was played as a comedy.) But the critics are not certain whether this despair is based on some profound vision beyond their experience, and whether it is, in fact, an absolute despair. Many have concluded that Beckett feels like Faulkner about the wonderful endurance of human beings. Problems of ultimate despair or ultimate hope are outside the range of literary criticism.

But the sloth and stagnant misery of Beckett's characters is the basic experience of existentialism. Sartre's Roquentin says 'There's no adventure.' Camus' Meursault, in *L'Etranger*, behaves exactly like a Beckett character. (The hero of Beckett's play *Krapp's Last Tape* recollects a past that seems very like Meursault's.) The hero of Dostoevsky's *Dream of an Absurd Man* loses no time in expressing a state of mind identical with that of Molloy, or Malone (in *Malone Dies*): '...what had I to think about? In those days I ceased to think altogether; it made no difference to me... I began to feel that *nothing mattered*.' He goes on to admit that, although he has intended to commit suicide for a long time, he feels too indifferent to everything even for this. The main difference between Dostoevsky's absurd man at this stage, and a Beckett character, is that the Beckett character never even tries to think. (Beckett would seem to have no capacity whatever for ideas.)

Many such parallels could be drawn. One might even evoke Strindberg's *Dance of Death*, in which an anonymous husband and wife get on one another's nerves throughout the length of an extremely long play. Modern critics have no inhibitions about Strindberg; his dramas of futility can be dismissed in a few words about Strindberg's paranoia. But Beckett has not yet been made the subject of a psychoanalytical biography. Even the romantic boredom of Byron's heroes, Lermontov's Pechorin, the narrator of *Wuthering Heights*, or Goethe's Werther, is by no means irrelevant. Having placed Beckett's pessimism in its proper context, the existential critic has no hesitation in dismissing it as a case of arrested metaphysical growth. While the heroes of Richter, Dostoevsky, Sartre, progress beyond the 'nausea' stage, Beckett's heroes remain stuck in it. The critic who suspects Beckett's pessimism of being the despair of deep vision, the despair of a man who has comprehended the universe in one profound insight and found it negative, plainly lacks the qualifications for assessing the simplest statements of existential problems. All the same, it is surprising that literary critics should have found so much difficulty in judging the work of a man who has spent twenty years expressing his boredom and implying that he wishes he was dead. A century ago, Beckett would probably have been deluged with offers of the loan of revolvers. Nietzsche once said cheerfully that he wished all 'despisers of the body' would shoot themselves and stop moaning. The lack of any such comment on Beckett's work reveals the extent to which the 'higher criticism' has introduced an element of self-doubt, a fear of sounding like a Philistine, into the trade of reviewing. The use of existential analysis can only make for greater clarity and precision in literary judgments.

The 'case' of Beckett is relatively simple, but there are a great many other writers whose merits are far more difficult to disentangle. D. H. Lawrence might be cited as an example.

It is interesting to consider the change in attitude towards Lawrence over the past twenty years among the serious critics. When Mr Eliot published *After Strange Gods* in the thirties, his feelings were obviously far from an unqualified admiration. Considering Eliot's dictum 'the spirit killeth but the letter giveth life,' it is not surprising that he should feel some antipathy to a writer who cared so much for the spirit and so little for the letter. But in recent years, Eliot's opinions on Lawrence have shown signs of changing; and in a letter to me in 1956, he dismissed my view that Shaw could be considered the most important writer of the twentieth century, and suggested that Lawrence might be a better choice. Eliot's change of attitude towards Lawrence coincides with the steep rise in Lawrence's stock in the English universities. (Professor Leavis has imparted his passionate enthusiasm to a great host of followers.) There is something very like a Lawrence cult, whose adherents seem to feel the same reverence for Lawrence that Matthew Arnold felt for Shakespeare.

It cannot fail to strike anyone who reads Leavis's book on Lawrence (or any of the books by Leavis's followers) that there is somehow a lack of basic principles in his analyses. They give the impression that they are intended only for those who feel exactly as Professor Leavis feels about Lawrence.

Here again, there is the same vagueness that appeared in reviews of Beckett's work. Leavis's followers imply that what matters about Lawrence is the content, not the tone or the form; the spirit, not the letter. And what is this content? It is the message that Leavis and his disciples discern in Lawrence's work. This message is interpreted as a poetic mysticism, a revolt against materialism, a cult of the personal ('Art for my sake'), a glorification of life. If all this could be accepted at its surface value from Leavis' book, Lawrence would undoubtedly deserve to be considered the English Dostoevsky, the great English mystic. Unfortunately, Lawrence's works exist to spoil the impression. And the reader who turns to them discovers a man who frequently suffers from a sort of verbal diarrhoea, who releases a great deal of pettiness and spite in his writing, and who occasionally gives full rein to a manic egoism – and who, above all, can be appallingly long-winded.

The normal method of literary criticism is to admit the faults, and then to continue: 'Nevertheless...'. This attitude makes no attempt to weigh the pros and cons; it merely states them, and leaves it at that.

Here again, existential criticism has the advantage. I have already pointed out that existential criticism is the normal procedure with certain kinds of poetry. The critic feels he is being quite fair to ask: 'What *experience* of the poet led to this statement?' No literary critic, however, would apply the same method to a volume on mysticism by Huxley, although any novelist provides the critic with a unique opportunity of entering his world, judging the precise texture of his experience. In the case of Lawrence, the novels and stories allow us to judge with great accuracy exactly what it felt like to be D. H. Lawrence. To begin with, of course, the reader feels his sensitivity about birds and animals and the countryside of Nottinghamshire. He next becomes aware of the 'ordinary' quality of Lawrence's characters; there is not a single character in the whole range of Lawrence who makes the emotional or intellectual impact of Ivan Karamazov, Captain Ahab, Faust. Edmund Wilson once pointed out that John Steinbeck's characters are mostly sub-normal, and that Steinbeck is most at home writing about animals. Something of the same sort might be said of Lawrence. There is a cult of the ordinary chap. There are none of the appalling dialectical tensions that one finds in Dostoevsky; Lawrence shares with Beckett a complete lack of interest in ideas. Even the characters who appear to be self-portraits (Morel in *Sons and Lovers*, Somers in *Kangaroo*, Lilly in *Aaron's Rod*) are relatively uncomplicated; they share Lawrence's sensitivity and his egoism, but possess no great intellectual depth.

Lawrence's novels reveal with minute accuracy the way in which he saw the world. And they reveal that his vision, on the whole, was commonplace, differing from 'the average' only because of his violent will to self-assertion, and a certain feeling for nature. At least fifty per cent of his characters are drawn 'from the outside,' with a malicious and satirical eye. His feeling for places is not particularly strong; none of his locales are evoked as unforgettably as the Yorkshire moors in *Wuthering Heights*, Egdon Heath in Thomas Hardy, or the Russian landscape in Tolstoy or Aksakoff.

Nevertheless, Lawrence is not to be completely dismissed in the same way as Beckett. His egoism and malice may be due to arrested development, like Beckett's pessimism, but he possessed a certain authentic vision of a more intense life which can be extracted by ploughing through the pages of commonplace realism. Like Huxley, Lawrence is too concerned with people and the dislike they arouse in him; so instead of concentrating on his positive vision, he spends a great deal too much time sneering at them – and too often, when he attempts to evoke the positive vision, it sounds like a literary back-to-nature act. (Consider, for example, the description of the cock and the hens in *The Man Who Died*.) But undoubtedly, Lawrence's experiences of sex had shown him a vision of the world as wholly affirmative as Van Gogh's painting. This was immediate and intuitive, and surpassed in clarity and strength the 'affirmations' in Huxley, Camus or Sartre. (Sartre's Roquentin feels a strange affirmation as he listens to a record of 'Some of These Days'; Camus's Meursault feels it on the evening of his execution, while his 'woman taken in adultery', in the story of that name, has a curiously Lawrencian experience of marriage with the earth; Huxley's Gumbril has a similar moment of acceptance when he takes Emily to bed in *Antic Hay*.) Unfortunately, the reader has to take Lawrence's word for it, for the evocations of sexual ecstacy in his novels are too verbalised to make a great impact. I cannot recall a single one that is really effective. The scene between Birkin and Ursula in *Women in Love*, between Lady Chatterley and Mellors, between Jesus and the priestess in *The Man Who Died*, all fail to convey the intensity of Lawrence's sexual vision. The language becomes a hedge.[12]

The existential verdict on Lawrence, then, is that his mysticism cannot be taken at its face value. There is no point in talking about Lawrence's 'vision' when the total effect of so many of his books is exhausting and depressing. Lawrence's vision is the way he saw the world; as revealed in a book like *Lady Chatterley's Lover*, it is pretty dreary and depressing. The people are boring, the landscape is dull. Although the book is apparently dedicated to an affirmation of life, it is actually far less exhilarating than a scene like the wolf hunt in *War and Peace*, which was written without 'mystical intent.'

The existential critic challenges the author's overall sense of life. No conclusions are accepted separately. The question is not 'What do you see?' but 'How broad do you see?' Literary criticism assumes that an author is saying to the reader: 'I have reached such and such conclusions about life.' The existential critic is inclined to retort: 'you are not writing about 'life'; you are writing about a small section of the world. So before we begin, would you mind telling me exactly what relation you consider that your small section bears to the whole of life?' A writer like Lawrence, Greene, Huxley, Sartre, implies that his 'camera lens' is far broader than the lens of the reader; that consequently, the amount of 'life' the reader will find in his novel is far greater than the amount the reader could hope to see with his own unaided eye.

---

12 Possibly the conclusion to be drawn here is that sex is best conveyed in the language of understatement. It is interesting to compare the effectiveness of Hemingway's brief description in *Up in Michigan* with the mawkishness of the gondola scene in *Across the River and into the Trees*.

The literary critic might be inclined to take this 'world' of the writer at its face value, since his own vision of the world makes no great effort to achieve completeness. But the ideal aim of the existentialist is to finally summarise life, its ultimate affirmations and negations. Against this background, the work of any novelist is bound to cover a very small area indeed. The area covered is the criterion of value, not the 'message' or conclusions of the book. This is why it is irrelevant to speak of Lawrence's mysticism, as if this in itself constituted the value of his work. It may contribute to that value; but the final value depends upon how great is the *area* covered by the writer's work, when compared with the gigantic background of the possible world, against Pascal's 'greatness and misery of man.' Lawrence knows a little of man's greatness, but very little of his misery. Beckett, Huxley and Greene know a little of his misery, but almost nothing of his greatness. Lawrence may come off best from such a comparison; but it must be remembered that, compared to a writer's possible achievement, Lawrence is a figure of total inadequacy. One suspects that the high opinion of Lawrence held by so many academic critics of today is largely a matter of *faute de mieux*. The fact that they can recognise and applaud the vitality in Lawrence speaks well for them. They are probably the last people in the world that Lawrence would have expected to spring to his defence. But their whole-hearted adoration is also a danger signal; it indicates the same defect in creative judgement that made the academics ignore Lawrence during his lifetime.

At this point, one might make some further generalisations about existential criticism. It is an attempt to bypass intellectual values – the values that literary criticism is so skilled in expounding – and to place the work in the context of the writer's life and his relation to humanity. An essay by an academic critic on Aldous Huxley might provide a brilliant summary of his changing views from *Crome Yellow* to *Brave New World Revisited*, while failing to comment on the 'weakness premise' in Huxley's characters. Most academic critics would feel it downright impolite to observe that Huxley combines a penetrating intellect with a curiously adolescent emotional view of the world, and yet this is the most important fact about Huxley's work. I have known readers who find Huxley unreadable, although they have found it impossible to explain why. The reader who begins a Huxley novel quickly finds himself steeped in the Huxley atmosphere, an atmosphere as distinct and unmistakable as the smells we associate with certain houses – the mixture of wood polish, dust and fruit that will always remind us of Aunt Emily, or the smell of cooking and damp newspaper that hangs around the kitchen of some acquaintance. In Huxley, this atmosphere is far too complex to analyse; it is compounded of his reactions to many people and things. These reactions constitute the essential Huxley, not the 'ideas'. In the same way, one might doubt whether any of D. H. Lawrence's farmers or colliers would be able to read ten pages of *The Plumed Serpent*, for Lawrence's writing has a nervousness and tension that belies the Whitmanesque sentiments. And yet the literary critics continue to expound the ideas and analyse the techniques.

As a final example of existential criticism in action, consider the work of T. S. Eliot. Eliot has undoubtedly been one of the major literary influences in our century. Many books on Eliot talk about his mythological method, his metaphysical conceits, his objective correlative, etc. The existential critic finds these of only secondary interest. On taking up a volume of the early poems, the first thing that strikes him is Eliot's distaste for life. His immediate reaction is to ask: 'How far is this a mature reaction to the world, and how far is it – as with Huxley – an ordinary lack of vitality?' The creative texture of *Prufrock* or the *Preludes* bears close resemblances to the world-weariness of Ernest Dowson or Lionel Johnson. Both Dowson and Johnson became Catholics. It would be interesting to determine how far Eliot's Anglicanism is an offshoot of his world-rejection.

I hasten to say that this is not an attempt to dismiss Eliot's religion as a question of nerves or temperament. This would be a complete denial of his intellectual responsibility, the kind of biased analysis practised by Christopher Caudwell[13] in his volumes of 'Marxist criticism.' This is very far from being the intention of existential analysis.

Eliot's early poetry possesses the quality that Schopenhauer claimed was the purpose of all art – to make the world seem a dream. The harsh reality of London or Boston, as recorded by a realistic novelist, has a brutalis-

13 British Marxist writer, thinker and poet (1907-1937) whose work, including *Illusion and Reality* (1937), was all published posthumously [Ed.]

ing and coarsening effect. Eliot manages to give the impression that he is in no way involved with 'the world.' One feels that he locked himself in a room, read a dozen poems of Baudelaire and Verlaine to induce a mood of resignation and melancholy, and then proceeded to write about 'the world outside,' serenely detached from it. In this mood, he can have 'a vision of the streets that the streets hardly understand.' Then he lays down his pen and goes out for supper, and the reality again jangles his nerves and destroys the detachment. Somehow, all his poetry has this quality of withdrawal from the world; it produces the opposite effect from the poetry of Synge or Burns or Herrick that springs out of an immediate love of existence. *The Waste Land* is the culmination of this technique. The present can only be loved with the help of the past, of a gentle melancholy reminiscent of *The Picture of Dorian Gray*:

> Oh City city, I can sometimes hear
> Beside a public bar in Lower Thames Street
> The pleasant whining of a mandoline...

In *The Hollow Men*, the atmosphere is the same; the poetry is weary of the world, but the world is not evoked by the poetry; instead, it is a strange, dream-like Greek landscape with 'voices in the wind singing' and fading stars. This is Eliot's last poem of total despair. In *Ash Wednesday*, he has begun to accept the Anglican vision. The world is still a 'dreamcrossed twilight between birth and dying' (and not the solid, muddy place it actually is); but now there is a hope of another world. Not after death, perhaps; Eliot's vision of the world of the Virgin mother and the three white leopards is poetic rather than dogmatic. Somehow it co-exists with the ordinary world, and the poet definitely prefers it. Nietzsche would undoubtedly have classified Eliot as an 'other-worlder' who lacks the vitality to 'give a meaning to the earth.' And yet Nietzsche, who had loved the work of Schopenhauer, would also have understood the urge to turn away.

Edmund Wilson has already pointed out the similarity of mood in early Eliot and early Yeats. But the important differences occur later in their careers. Yeats made a determined movement of return to the world, and ended his life a Nietzschean visionary, with a touch of the bawdiness of all the great poets of the earth,

> Out and impose our leadership
> On country and on town.
> Throw likely couples into bed
> And knock the others down.

The later Eliot only becomes more rarefied, although he shows a desire to return to earth by writing for the stage. The stage works verify the impression that, for Eliot, the world is 'too much with him.' The choruses from *Murder in the Cathedral*, full of surrealistic images, do not contain a single line of poetry comparable with *Prufrock*. And when the poet attempts to present 'the real world,' in *The Family Reunion*, *The Cocktail Party*, *The Confidential Clerk* and *The Elder Statesman*, it immediately becomes obvious that his ‘world’ is as limited as Huxley’s, and suggests that, if Mr Eliot were a novelist, his work would be closely related to that of Ivy Compton-Burnett. The same narrow range of constipated upper-class people talking the same sort of language as Wilde’s Lady Bracknell or Shaw’s Lady Britomart Undershaft, the same misty profundities that Henry Reed satirised in *Chard Witlow*: this is Eliot showing all his cards, pulling out all the stops, and still managing to sound like Pinero. Worse still, he has begun to parody himself. Occasional lines in the poetry come dangerously close to parody:

> I could see nothing behind that child’s eye

(upon which Edmund Wilson commented ‘I bet he couldn’t’) and:

> No place of grace for those who avoid the face
> No time to rejoice for those who walk among noise and deny
> the voice,

which sounds rather like a commercial TV advertising slogan. But whole speeches in *The Confidential Clerk* and *The Elder Statesman* sound like self-parody.

The plays, in short, reveal the lack of imaginative vitality behind Eliot’s creative writing, and lend colour to the view that his world-rejection is not based upon some metaphysical vision of horror, but upon the Huxleyan inability to get much of a kick out of living. His mysticism is of the negative type, although he shows flashes of a hankering after something more positive: 'Children's voices in the orchard,' 'Lilac and brown hair'. Compare it with the poetry of Synge, Rimbaud or Blake, or with novels like *Ulysses* or Joyce Cary's *The Horse's Mouth*, and the difference between a negative and a positive mysticism becomes at once apparent.

These comments on Beckett, Lawrence, Huxley and Eliot might well give the impression that the function of existential criticism is wholly destructive. So I should hasten to add that my own attitude to these writers is one of qualified admiration, and that the above analyses are not intended to represent my total attitude towards any one of them. Existential criticism is not merely another name for personal attacks, although in the case of writers whose work has been assessed in terms of 'intellectual content,' this may actually be the effect. The function of existential criticism is to determine how far a writer's attitude towards the world is parochial, based upon some temperamental defect of vision.

Edmund Wilson's essay 'A Dissenting Opinion on Kafka' is an excellent example of existential criticism. As a philosophical attitude, it is close to the pragmatism and empiricism that come so naturally to the English and American temper. But its function is not purely destructive. For example, it would be interesting to set some well-known American or English literary critic to write an essay on the decline of Ernest Hemingway. In purely literary terms, it is almost impossible to define what 'leaked away' between *The Sun Also Rises* and *Across the River and into the Trees*. In purely literary terms, it is quite impossible to say why *The Old Man and the Sea* is so immensely inferior to *Big Two Hearted River*. But once the problems underlying Hemingway's works have been defined in existential terms, it becomes a matter of simplicity to see how he has become increasingly shy of attacking these problems, increasingly prone to a formula of tough sentimentality that solves nothing.

The last part of this essay will be concerned with a definition of the basic terms and ideas of existential criticism.

I have said that existential criticism is simply a criticism directed from a specific philosophical attitude. This attitude is, in the simplest sense of the word, a revolt. But it is less simple to define the attitude that it is a revolt *against*. Nietzsche would probably have defined the enemy as 'academic abstraction'; Kierkegaard spoke of 'the System' (meaning intellectual systematizing). Whitehead (who called his existentialism 'the philosophy of organism') spoke of 'the bifurcation of nature.' And Whitehead was (perhaps unconsciously) echoing the view of Goethe, who said that nature cannot be dissected and anatomized like a corpse since it is actually a living organism. David Riesman, taking a simpler sociological standpoint, has defined our malady as the increasing tendency to 'other-direction' in modern society, to the domination of 'public opinion' and modern claptrap about being a 'good member of society.'

These different diagnoses illustrate the complexity of the subject. No matter what field happens to be under survey – literature, philosophy, sociology – signs of the same canker can be detected, manifesting itself as a trend to de-individualisation, a denial of the importance of the individual.

In my book *The Age of Defeat*[14], I have analysed this tendency in literature and entitled it 'the unheroic premise' or 'the fallacy of insignificance.' The hero of the modern play or novel falls into a number of categories: the defeated man, the insignificant man, the 'average man,' the 'crazy mixed up kid,' etc. The simple hero of the Conan Doyle-John Buchan type has degenerated into the comic strip hero ('Superman,' 'the Saint,' etc.), while the serious hero – Goethe's Faust, Melville's Ahab, Dostoevsky's Ivan and Alyosha, Tolstoy's Peter Bezukov or Prince Andrew – has disappeared altogether. There are no 'metaphysical heroes' in modern literature; only the defeated heroes of Arthur Miller, Tenessee Williams, Ernest Hemingway. The metaphysical hero disappeared, 'not with a bang but a whimper,' after Joyce's Stephen Dedalus and Mann's Hans Castorp and Doktor Faustus. The modern hero is brainless, soulless and clueless.

I have protested that we need a revival of the metaphysical hero, and an attempt to solve the problems that Goethe, Melville and Dostoevsky left unsolved. Literature has reached a point where the weakling hero is taken for granted; one infers that the reader has no difficulty in identifying himself with him. A recent play by Tennessee Williams ends with one of the characters asking the audience 'Don't you recognise yourselves in us?' – after three hours of Mr Williams' usual mixture of frustration,

14 London: Victor Gollancz, 1959. Published in the U.S. as *The Stature of Man*. Boston: Houghton Mifflin Co., 1959 [Ed.]

defeat and sadism; this catches clearly the hypothesis that underlies all literature – the demand that the reader should recognize himself in the hero. But while we might agree that a healthy audience would reject a play by Williams or a novel by Huxley with the comment 'What on earth do you take us for?' this in itself is no solution. It is only a footnote to the diagnosis.

The status of the modern hero is too low. The heroes of Tennessee Williams, for example, are allowed to possess only one virtue – integrity. All others – intellect, determination, ambition, strength – are denied them. Above all, they possess no sense of the stature of man, his 'greatness and misery,' the question of his relation to the rest of the universe.

Existentialism is a philosophy that has a number of quite definite concepts about the stature of man and his relation to... Whatever one takes for an absolute – God, life, the universe, an ideal humanity.

Existentialism is concerned with human nature and human psychology. But these words evoke Freud and Adler, when it would be more to the point if they evoked Pascal or St Augustine. The question 'Is man a god or a worm?' would be meaningless to a Freudian; if its meaning could be conveyed, the answer would probably be 'a worm.' He might support his view by pointing to 'the facts' of human existence; man's limitedness, his ignorance, his neuroses and capacity for self-deception. And it is just this procedure of pointing to 'the facts' that would be rejected by an existentialist. He would reply that no human situation is ever defined by 'the facts.' Any attempt to do so is to leave out the most important element – man's will. For example, the modern psychiatrist might analyse a case of suicide in the following manner: 'He was heavily in debt, and was afraid his colleagues might find out; he was sexually impotent, due to a strong fixation on his daughter; he had been passed over twice for promotion in favour of younger colleagues; he had inherited a tendency to melancholia from his mother. Under the circumstances, suicide was almost inevitable.' The dead man's friends and relatives might agree that this analysis concurred closely with their own knowledge of his personality, thus enabling the psychiatrist to state that, for all scientific purposes, his diagnosis is reasonably accurate. But the method ceases to work if the suicide happens to be a man of genius. A Van Gogh, a Kleist, a Beddoes, refuses to be turned into a neat equation of strains and neuroses; when all the personal factors have been accounted for, their work contains an indestructible *supra-personal* vitality, an affirmation of life that cannot be traced in their personal tragedies. The common language expresses this when it speaks of 'the descent of inspiration,' implying that some force comes from *outside* the personality. But existentialism makes a sharp distinction between the personality and the man. It insists that, ultimately and basically, man is free. Being free, he is ultimately indefinable.

A logical philosopher might say: 'Would you mind defining what you mean by free, and exactly how a man can exercise his freedom?' And the resulting explanations might lead him to comment: 'In that case, I agree with you; but the freedom in man is so microscopically small that I see no justification for basing your 'philosophy' on it.'

Here a simile might make things clearer. The average physicist leaves room in his calculations for 'experimental error,' but he does not allow this margin of error to destroy his faith in accuracy. But Heisenberg's principle of indeterminacy (asserting that one can know either the speed or position of an electron, but never both simultaneously) raised the margin of error concept to a basic principle. Indeterminacy ceased to be a regrettable accident, and became a premise. (In the same way, Catholicism regards sin as a fundamental human condition, while humanism regards it as a regrettable accident.) Most philosophical systems regard man's free will as an interesting but unimportant postscript to their calculations. Existentialism regards it as fundamental. It may function in areas beyond the reach of the human eye – like the Heisenberg principle – but its importance cannot be underestimated. Camus, for example, likens the human situation to that of Sisyphus, condemned forever to roll a stone uphill and watch it roll down again; and yet concludes 'We must imagine Sisyphus happy.' Sisyphus is happy because, although his life is apparently *totally determined*, his inner-freedom remains untouched. In fact, all human beings are imprisoned in a necessity as narrow and tyrannical as Sisyphus. Consider human life 'scientifically,' as the psychiatrist might consider a suicide, and one is overwhelmed with horror; one echoes Van Gogh's last words 'Misery will never end.' Then consider Dostoevsky's words that a man condemned to stand forever on a narrow ledge in total blackness would still prefer to live rather than die, and one recognizes the vast extent of human freedom.

In fact, this freedom requires emphasis. The 'unheroic hypothesis' has culminated in nightmares like Orwell's *Nineteen Eighty-Four*, where man has no privacy, in his thoughts or even on the lavatory. The same pessimistic vision was expressed by Rice several decades earlier in *The Adding Machine*[15]. William H. Whyte evokes *Nineteen Eighty-Four* in *The Organization Man*, in the chapter describing how the 'boss' is beginning to dominate the home life of his employees.

To many readers, it will seem that there is a strange paradox in existential philosophy. Its principles state that it wishes to remove the emphasis from human weakness and stupidity and place it on human strength, purpose, free will. And yet any student who takes a preliminary course in existentialism – commencing, let us say, with the novels of Sartre and Camus – discovers that an immense amount of attention is devoted to proving that men are less free than they think they are, and in depicting the world as a depressingly ugly place. There is a great deal of talk about self-deception, unauthentic existence, salauds, etc.

This is due to the fact that existentialism is still in its early stages, concerned more with clearing the ground than with building new concepts. Besides, there is a tech-

15 American Expressionist play, by Elmer L. Rice, noted for its attack on technology. New York: Doubleday, Page & Co, 1923.[Ed.]

nical difficulty involved too. I said earlier in this essay that the basic concepts of existentialism are 'the nausea' and its opposite, man's sense of his interior power, his reality. Elsewhere I have defined existentialism as an assertion of man as spirit. But novels and plays are concerned with events, not with interior states. A novel written in journal-form (like *La Nausée*) can express the negative aspects; a painting like Van Gogh's *Road with Cypresses* can convey its positive aspects. But all other attempts to convey this positive aspect of human existence have been experimental and unsatisfactory – this can be seen in Chesterton's *Man Who Was Thursday*, Cary's *The Horse's Mouth*, Joyce's *Ulysses* and *Finnegans Wake*. The affirmation of existentialism is *absurd*; consequently, the ordinary novel can hardly express it. And yet literature progresses by striving to express what has so far been inexpressible; without this striving, it stagnates. With this in mind, it is hard to avoid the conclusion that existentialism is the one certain road to creative development of literature in the future.

I do not intend, in this essay, to spend a great deal of time defining Sartre's 'bad faith' or Heidegger's 'authentic and inauthentic existence'; I have done so at length elsewhere, and the terms are almost self-explanatory. Such existential formulae as 'existence precedes essence' or 'authentic existence begins with an encounter with nothingness' must also be taken for granted. A glance at any standard textbook on existentialism will elucidate them.

It would be more to the point to consider how a new existentialism might develop from these continental 'roots.' The terminology of Sartre and Heidegger describes negative states: 'inauthentic existence,' 'bad faith,' 'nothingness,' etc. The first necessity is to develop a positive terminology. And, in fact, Whitehead's 'philosophy of organism' can provide some examples of positive terminology. Whitehead is fond of using the term 'prehension,' which might be defined simply as digestion. The fundamental activity of human life is digestion: of food into the body, of air into the bloodstream, of experience into the mind. The 'unheroic premise' of our time is concerned with denying only the third of these. In refusing to place any great faith in a life-purpose, in human strength and free will, it removes all meaning from the process by which men assimilate experience, become more 'mature.' And yet no man can cease from assimilating experience for a moment (except, possibly, in deep sleep). The desire to cease assimilating experience has been treated in many interesting works – Goethe's *Faust*, Goncharov's *Oblomov*, Beckett's *Murphy*. But in many modern writers, it is taken for granted; Faulkner and Hemingway place all the emphasis on human endurance, as if this were an end in itself. It was accepted that the Romantic hero craved for oblivion, turned away from experience, on the grounds that the real world was too unlike his ideal vision of the world. But the 'crazy mixed up kid' heroes of modern fiction reject experience for no reason at all; they are too mixed up to have an ideal world – Brick in *Cat on a Hot Tin Roof* is an example.

The Germans regarded the assimilation of experience as sufficiently interesting to form the subject of great novels, and invented a name, the *Bildungsroman*, for the novel about human development. The Russians have also specialized in this type of novel, and *The Brothers Karamazov* describes all three brothers being educated at once. Such a novel would be out of place in modern England, America or Russia, since the development of the individual has become a matter of so little importance.

Let us admit at once that no philosopher or saint has ever produced a satisfactory explanation that covers every aspect of human purpose. But it is no answer to dismiss the notion of human purpose, for human beings will never be free of the craving for a sense of purpose, a sense that their lives are not totally meaningless and accidental. Neither can the question be dismissed by declaring that man is a social animal, and has no purpose other than his duty to society. This leaves the question: 'What is the purpose of society?'

In fact, men's lives oscillate between a torment of assimilation and a triumph of successful assimilation. (Nietzsche defined happiness as 'the feeling that obstacles have been overcome, that power is increasing.') The world-weary poet who expresses a pessimistic vision of human life is only generalising from his experience of unsuccessful assimilation. A Van Gogh expresses conflicting visions: despair in his life, triumph in his painting. The mystical vision of Blake expresses the sense that *no matter what obstacles might arise*, man has the power to overcome them. This is the only ground for ultimate optimism.

It is, then, the business of existential literature to comment on this problem, this unending act of assimilation. An existential critic would say simply that it is the business of all literature. It might almost be said that, as a cookery book contains instructions on how to cook, so literature should contain instructions on how to live. Its fundamental virtue is therefore to convince the reader *as life*, as reality. But if the author restricts himself to writing a 'realistic' book, he is in the position of a playwright who relies entirely on scenery but gives his characters nothing to do. In order to demonstrate the element of free will in man, it is necessary for a writer to show his hero in the actual process of assimilation. This becomes clear if one refers back to my simile of the psychiatrist analyzing a case of suicide; he is listing all the difficulties that led to suicide, the factors that require assimilation, but he makes no reference to the man's capacity to assimilate, his will to overcome.

The problem of the 'unheroic premise' could be summarized in this way: All literature deals with men over-coming obstacles, from Homer onwards. The hero is the man who overcomes the obstacles peculiar to his own age; the psychological problems of Goethe's Werther would have been irrelevant in the age of Malory. Civilization is actually the refinement of man's power of assimilation. He no longer has to defend his home against wild animals and marauding tribes, but he has to digest all the complexities of the modern working day. Our modern culture has seen a gradual decline in the tacit sense of human purpose, fostered by materialist philosophies and the 'Protestant ethic' of material success. Consequently, the notion of 'prehension,' of the human effort to assimilate and overcome, has begun to disappear from our literature. The tacit sense of human purpose has been tacitly dropped.

The consequence is that one can read, let us say, a critique of the novels of William Faulkner, with no reference to the fact that his characters are completely static; they learn nothing (except, occasionally, endurance), they assimilate nothing. The reader who comes to Faulkner for the first time, and finds himself profoundly depressed by *The Sound and the Fury*, ignores his immediate reaction to the book, looks for deeper meanings, and finishes by writing a thesis about the brilliance of Faulkner's technique. An existential critic would be more ruthless; he would point out that Quentin Compson is the most sensitive character in the book, and may therefore be regarded as its hero; he would then go on to say that Quentin's suicide, springing out of his sister-fixation and sense of his family's decline, is completely insignificant when weighed in the scales with that of Van Gogh, or Dostoevsky's Stavrogin in *The Devils*. The novel has no vital movement of assimilation; it is static, and reveals Faulkner's fundamental bankruptcy. It deals with weaklings and fools, and their weakness and folly are dressed up to look like tragedy.

The admirer of Faulkner will retort that this is to ignore the book's pathos, its sense of a gathering storm, the charm of its portrait of Caddy and Dilsey, the success of its evocation of atmosphere. To this, the existential critic will reply that he is far from ignoring these things, that no one but a fool could fail to admire them – but that when all this has been said, his objections remain accurate.

This is perhaps the most difficult and controversial aspect of existential criticism. Its major criterion is the concept of the stature of man. From this point of view, very few books can be regarded as masterpieces. Its methods must therefore appear to be destructive when applied in particular cases. But these methods can only be justified by the vitality it succeeds in returning to literature. A good literary critic may underline the merits of the author he writes about, and persuade others to turn from the criticism to the works themselves. The bad literary critic (and this covers most of the authors of theses on modern writers) only exhausts the reader and destroys all desire to read the author. But in either case, the process is a closed circuit; the critic can only convey to the reader his author's vision of existence. If the author is great, the vision will be great. The existential critic possesses a standard that is bigger than any individual author he writes about, bigger than himself; if his criticism is good, it not merely sends the reader to the books in question, but conveys some far greater standard to him, revealing the ideal aim of all art. He has, therefore, the effect of a creative stimulant as well as a sympathetic interpreter.

To conclude this essay, let me offer a final example of existential criticism in action. The choice of a book that is unfamiliar to most English readers will underline its method of attack by removing the possibility of too many preconceived notions about the work in question. For this reason, Ivan Goncharov's first novel *The Usual Story* makes an excellent subject for dissection.

Goncharov's chief preoccupation is the contrast between the old Russia and the new. Readers of *Oblomov* will remember Oblomov's nostalgic dream of peace and leisure in the country. Contrasted with this dreamy, peaceful Russia of the early nineteenth century is the new commercial Russia with its intellectual ferments, its revolutionary sentiments and talk of abolition of serfdom. The Decembrist rising is still a recent memory (1825); the Russia portrayed by Dostoevsky in *The Devils* is not far in the future.

The Usual Story describes how a young man from the provinces – Alexander Fyodorovitch – leaves his peaceful home in the country and goes to St Petersburg. His head is full of Byron, Pushkin, Lermontov and Schiller. In Petersburg he meets his uncle, Pyotr Ivanitch, a successful business man and a realist. The rest of the novel deals with the amusing clash between the views of nephew and uncle. In places, the satire on romanticism is rather heavy handed. Alexander never tires of gushing about true love, true friendship, etc. Pyotr Ivanitch throws cold water on his effusions, and invariably proves to be right. Alexander falls in love; the girl betrays him, preferring a less idealistic but more experienced Count; the reader is not spared a single one of Alexander's ravings about the unworthiness of women and the sacred role of the poet. Later, Alexander falls in love with a sentimental widow who bears a strong resemblance to Emma Bovary, and together they gush poetry over one another. But this time, it is Alexander who tires first; the woman's capacity for wallowing in romantic abstractions is even greater than his own, and he tears himself away from her with relief. After a number of similar episodes, each one proving his uncle's superior knowledge of the human heart, he returns to the country, and spends several years in a state of boredom and exhaustion. Then the desire for St Petersburg returns. He goes back, accepts a good job, marries a wealthy young lady, and shows every sign of following in his uncle's footsteps.

All the same, Goncharov's moral is not simply that the romantic was wrong and the realist right. The uncle marries a beautiful young girl, and she finds Alexander a more satisfying companion than her husband, whom she regards as a cold fish. At the end of the book, Pyotr Ivanitch decides to abandon his career and take his wife to Italy; the anaemic emotional life she is leading as the wife of a tycoon is wrecking her health; and she tells Alexander, when he announces his intention of marrying an heiress, that she preferred him in the days of his 'romantic folly,' when he was a more sensitive and intelligent human being. But the most significant speech in the novel occurs towards the end, when Alexander tells his uncle of his intention of returning to the country. He goes on to reproach Pyotr Ivanitch for throwing cold water on his idealism, saying that it might have been better to allow him to find out for himself. Pyotr Ivanitch gives him a long lecture, telling him that it is folly to plunge into despair because his romantic ideas have proved unreliable. 'It is ridiculous to fancy yourself a special great being when you were not born to be one.'

Here again, the unheroic premise appears. Goncharov has obviously identified himself with Pyotr Ivanitch at this point. The book is a *Bildungsroman* about the education of

Alexander. And the book's ending – with Alexander dropping his idealistic notions and marrying for money – is 'the usual story.' But in fact, what right has Pyotr Ivanitch or his creator to assume that some men were not 'born to be great'? The book is a story about facing facts. But the existential critic is again inclined to ask: 'Which facts?'

Goncharov's book affords an excellent demonstration of the function of existential criticism. From the literary point of view, one might compare it with *Candide* or Pushkin's *Eugene Onegin* or Lermontov's *Hero of Our Time*. Such comparisons throw a certain amount of light on the theme, but afford no criterion for judging it. A politically biased critic might point out that the anti-romanticism of Pyotr Ivanitch has much in common with the views of modern Soviet leaders, and is therefore to be regarded with suspicion, but his judgment is not necessarily sounder for being biased. Alexander and Pyotr Ivanitch pose one of the basic problems of existentialism: the question of bad faith, self-deception. The uncle's objection to 'sincere effusions' and all the rest is that they are a species of *mauvais-foi*. When Alexander says: 'I feel like a man who has been deceived in everything,' his uncle comments: 'Say, rather, a man who has deceived himself and wants to deceive others too.' But how far is Pyotr Ivanitch's realism also self-deception?

To clarify this issue, one might compare Goncharov's anti-romanticism with Bernard Shaw's. In Shaw's work, the issues are treated against a wider moral background – with a profounder sense of what is at stake. *Arms and the Man* is an early work on the same level as *The Usual*

Story, with the realist Bluntschli used as a foil against the romantic idealist Sergius. Like Goncharov, Shaw draws no final conclusions, except to indicate his preference for Bluntschli.

In *Man and Superman*, written ten years later, everything is clearer. In the third act (the 'Don Juan in Hell' scene) the devil is the romantic idealist; like Goncharov's Alexander, he believes in 'sincere effusions,' and talks about the nobility of love and friendship. Don Juan is the realist who pours cold water on the devil's idealistic sentiments. But unlike Pyotr Ivanitch, Don Juan is not a mere 'negative' realist. As an evolutionist, he believes it is man's business to help the 'life force' in its struggle upward. In fact, it is Don Juan who is the true idealist; the devil's idealism is the outcome of sentimentality and spiritual laziness.

From the existential point of view, Shaw is superior to Goncharov because he recognizes that there is no credit in deflating romantic idealism unless it can be replaced by a more discriminating idealism. From the purely literary viewpoint, Goncharov's book is valuable because he was a superlative observer, a humourist and a gifted writer. (In fact, there is no reason why Goncharov's book should not be superior to Shaw's play from a literary standpoint and inferior from the existential standpoint. It is not, of course: but the observation is worth making.) However, the existential judgement on Goncharov's book is concerned with its value *as existential philosophy*. The reader who feels inclined to comment 'But Goncharov didn't intend it to be existential philosophy', has completely missed the point. Any book that sets out to make a comment on human life or society, that is concerned in some way with the problem of illusion and reality, is a work of existential philosophy, and may be judged from that viewpoint. Any book possessing a certain basic integrity may be judged existentially; the method is as applicable to *From Here to Eternity* or *What Makes Sammy Run?* as to *Madame Bovary* or *The Brothers Karamazov*.

It should be emphasised that existential criticism is not intended as a substitute for literary criticism; the two should be regarded as closely connected and complementary. In a sense, the role of the literary critic is more exalted than that of the existential critic. The literary critic is like the interpreter of a symphony; his task is to convey a new understanding of the work. The existential critic is like a musical analyst who considers a symphony in the light of its technique, and of all other symphonies ever written.

Certain music lovers have argued that a technical knowledge of the composer's resources might spoil their appreciation of the music. If this argument is granted, then existential criticism must also be dismissed.

The final defence of the existential critic is as follows: No art can be judged by purely aesthetic standards, although a painting or a piece of music may appear to give a purely aesthetic pleasure. Aesthetic enjoyment is an intensification of the vital response, and this response forms the basis of all value judgements. The existentialist contends that all values are connected with the problems of human existence, the stature of man, the purpose of life. These values are inherent in all works of art, in addition to their aesthetic values, and are closely connected with them. The difference between Beethoven's 'Spring Sonata' and his 'Grosse Fugue' is an existential difference, not an aesthetic one; the 'Grosse Fugue' records a broader and deeper response to life than the 'Spring Sonata'. In the case of Beethoven, the task of defining this difference in philosophical language would be immense; but with works of literature, it is easier, and should not be shirked.

It is inevitable that the existential critic should find himself in revolt against many of the values of our time – or rather, against its tacit assumption that values are unimportant. Ultimately, the existential critic wishes to know precisely *what* a book is saying, not whether it is 'true to life' or tells its story well. In order to be capable of pronouncing on this, he requires a certain standard of meaning. This 'meaning' is not moral, religious or political; it is 'meaning' in the broadest and deepest sense. A thing 'means' something because of the relation it bears to our lives; in this context, irrelevance and meaninglessness are the same thing, since we know nothing of meaning beyond life. Existential criticism is an attempt to develop this standard of meaning.

At present, it is true, the method is in its embryonic stages, and may seem to be hardly distinct from literary criticism. It is like a language which has only recently been invented; only continual use will expand it and make it capable of finer shades of meaning. In another sense, existential criticism has existed for a long time; Berdyaev's book on Dostoevsky and Jaspers's book on Nietzsche are classics of the genre. In *After Strange Gods*, Mr Eliot suggested that literary criticism needs to be supplemented by another type of criticism from a definitely moral standpoint. Professor Leavis's criticism has often been attacked because it is 'moral' rather than literary. But the existential criticism of men like Berdyaev, Shestov, Eliot, is based upon the creative temperament of the writer rather than upon a general method. In the same way, we read Johnson's *Lives of the Poets* because we are interested in Johnson rather than because his views throw a new light on the poets. It is the aim of existential criticism to become an instrument that is in no way dependent upon the moral personality of the man who makes use of it. One of its aims, in fact, is to develop the kind of moral perception that distinguishes a Berdyaev or Shestov.

There are, of course, certain dangers inherent in the method. If taken too seriously and applied indiscriminately, it might easily become a dictatorial cult that would obscure every issue. And yet any attempt to impose a scheme of values at least has the virtue of forcing its opponents to scrutinise their own values. At the worst, existential criticism might stimulate an interest in the relation between literature and society. At its best, it could lead to a revitalising of literature in the twentieth century.

1958

Editor's Note:

This essay was first published in: *The Chicago Review*, volume 13, no. 2, Summer 1959 (**C17**). Reprinted here with slight emendations. It was then included as the Introductory essay to Wilson's *Existential Criticism: selected book reviews* (Nottingham: Paupers' Press, 2009 (**A178**).

3

THE EXISTENTIAL TEMPER OF THE MODERN NOVEL

There are two obvious ways of dealing with this subject. One would be to write about a number of 'existentialist novels', from Unamuno's *Marquis of Lumbria* to Dürrenmatt's *The Pledge*, with all the usual references to *Ulysses*, *La Nausée*, and so on. The other is to try to talk about 'essentials' and hope that whoever reads this book is already familiar with his Dürrenmatt, Sartre and Musil. The second method appeals to me most.

First of all, what is the meaning of 'existential', and what does it mean in connection with the novel? I myself have been using the word for years without having any nice, concise dictionary definition at the back of my mind. Let us admit that it is a word that has meaning only within a limited context. But it so happens that it has a great deal of relevance to the culture of the twentieth century. So although it may seem as superfluous to our great-grandchildren as phlogiston is to the modern chemist, we may as well make what use we can of it. It means literally 'connected with existence'. That means nothing whatever, considered on its own. But consider it in relation to the philosophy of Schelling or Bertrand

Russell, in relation to orthodox Christianity or the modern novel from Anderson[16] to Mailer, and it immediately becomes an octopus of a word, a skeleton key to many locks, a spotlight with a hundred purposes.

When speaking about existentialism, it is impossible to avoid reference to Sartre's novel *La Nausée*, for the book is the end product of a process that has been taking place for more than a century. This process can best be described by quoting three lines of W. B. Yeats:

> Shakespearian fish swam the sea, far away from land;
> Romantic fish swam in nets coming to the hand;
> What are all those fish that lie gasping on the strand?

Shakespearian fish – the detached creation of the great writers, Shakespeare, Balzac, Trollope, a creation that takes its premises serenely for granted and creates in the way that a carpenter makes a table. The romantic fish turned to introspection and felt that art could not be 'honest' unless it talked about the struggle of the individual. Zola and the realists declared that the novel should provide what religion was failing to provide – moral guidance, preaching. But finally came the devotees of Art for Art's Sake, beginning with Rilke's novel *The Notebooks of Malte Laurids Brigge*, culminating in *Ulysses* and *La Nausée*. *Ulysses* sacrificed everything to honesty – or almost everything, and its critics declared nervously that the novel was becoming a scientific catalogue. But although *Ulysses* contains details about the exact capacity

16 Presumably Sherwood Anderson (1876-1941) American novelist and short-story writer. [Ed.]

of the Dublin reservoir, it was not this kind of honesty that Joyce was concerned with. Joyce wanted to say, in effect: 'How can we keep on talking about elopements and forged wills and the feminist problem when the texture of reality is so different from anything you will find in novels?' His revolt was not entirely original; in *Crime and Punishment*, Dostoevsky kept the rudiments of the conventional nineteenth-century plot – the wronged sister, the villainous landowner, etc. – but the thing one remembers about the novel is the smell of St Petersburg's hot pavements, the dirty horsehair sofa on which Raskolnikov sleeps, the cracked window-panes, the cobweb on the ceiling, the cup of cold tea, the smell of cooking. Dostoevsky is concerned about the texture of everyday experience in a way that his contemporary Trollope was not: in a way that is familiar to readers of Joyce and Sartre.

But Dostoevsky learned an important lesson. You must choose between texture and plot. You cannot have both. *The Idiot* was an uncomfortable compromise. There are certain chairs and tables and rooms in that book that we remember as clearly as Van Gogh's chair. But somehow, the book is a failure, and it is a failure because the microscopic method cannot support a complicated plot. Dostoevsky realized that complex plots were necessary to say what he had to say. So without a second thought, he abandoned the microscope. *The Devils* and *The Brothers Karamazov* are told in the first person – which, of course, precludes the 'movie-camera' method that is the essence of texture-writing. The narrator has a story to get on with; he cannot linger around a room, creating atmosphere.

I am speaking now of the existential method in the modern novel, the microscope that moves slowly over the surface of a chair or a wall, observes the sheen of colour on the wing of a dead fly in a glass of water. I am assuming that readers are familiar with *La Nausée* and its slimy grey stone and twisted tree roots and the other objects that dominate the book. This method has been carried to a strange limit by three young French novelists, Alain Robbe-Grillet, Michel Butor, and Nathalie Sarraute. Robbe-Grillet derives from Hemingway in ignoring emotions and concentrating on 'the facts'. Like Hemingway, he never tells the reader, 'This character is in mental agony'; he prefers to record casual conversations, the appearance of a chair, and allow the reader to infer the agony. But he is infinitely less successful (artistically) than Hemingway, for the method demands strong, clear emotions that can make their own impact without the writer's help. Robbe-Grillet specializes in long, dull descriptions of physical objects; his attempt to keep the novel detached and scientific has simply emasculated it.

Michel Butor derives from Sartre, but in a different way; he is more concerned with self-analysis, and his *Passing Time* is written, like *La Nausée*, as a journal. Nathalie Sarraute is the most interesting and talented of the younger French writers. She is far closer to Henry James and Proust than to Joyce, and she writes about the over-sensitive mind – close to insanity – agonizingly trapped in the present and in human relations. The main point about these three novelists is that they are all Yeats's fish 'gasping on the strand', completely static, so preoccupied with the 'texture' of the present that they forget that a book is meant to amuse and entertain.

The writer who seems to me to be by far the greatest in Europe at the moment – Friedrich Dürrenmatt – has no such disadvantage. He is refreshingly in control of his material. He has called himself 'this lover of gruesome fables, this pen-pushing Protestant'. His two novels *A Dangerous Game* (*Die Panne*) and *The Pledge* (*Das Versprechen*) are perhaps the most important novels to appear since *La Nausée*. The style is clean and concise. His existentialism is closer to the Sartre of *L'Etre et le Néant*, a preoccupation with the destiny and psychology of man. Unlike Sartre, he seems to have a broad streak of irrepressible optimism. Let me confess that, as far as I am concerned, this is his greatest recommendation.

Dürrenmatt brings this discussion to the next aspect of existential writing: I mean, existential defined *vis-à-vis* religion. In this sense the first great existential drama of European literature was *Faust*. Existentialism here means 'the search for meaning'. It is the ultimate failure of the Joyce school of writing – which includes Robbe-Grillet – that it uses an existential technique while completely ignoring the existential content. Joyce was in conscious revolt against his successful contemporaries, Shaw, Wells, Chesterton, Galsworthy, and others. Out of a school-boyish desire to be 'different', Joyce preferred Ben Jonson to Shakespeare and Aristotle to Plato. But he took this odd position further and declared that logic meant more than ideas. Stephen had to be a formidable logician and intellectual, but Joyce could not allow him to seem a disciple of Yeats and A. E. by discussing ideas; so Stephen is made to advance a complicated and nonsensical theory about Shakespeare, displaying his erudition and logic but steering well clear of general ideas.

Henry James – the other major branch of the gasping-fish business – also eschewed ideas, although this was mainly because fate had given Henry all the artistic sensibility and his brother all the capacity for thought. He was interested neither in religion nor politics – and in sex only in a rather nervous and cautious manner.

So the two major forces on the modern novel defined its method and limits: endless interest in fine shades of psychological analysis and in the detailed description of physical actuality; a certain vague and melancholy interest in the problem of individual destiny (Roderick Hudson, Stephen Dedalus); but a horrified avoidance of religion and politics.

The next problem is the $10,000 question. Can literature survive within these limits? Are the problems of meaning – of religion, sex, and politics – superfluous in the novel? Can the ascetic novelist do without them, as the religious ascetic does without sex and human relations? Or are they like food and drink – a variable but ultimately inescapable necessity? For a great many years no one asked these questions, and the 'existential method' reigned supreme in the novel. For subject matter, the new novelists followed the lead of Flaubert, and wrote about the 'ordinary man'. Observation, observation was all that mattered. Take any character walking down Main Street, write about his misery and futility and about how he is condemned from the beginning. If he is lucky, this ordinary man may reach the stature of tragedy, like Büchner's Woyzeck. But ask no questions about the meaning of his life and of life in general; concentrate on its social significance.

Sartre was one of the first to break away from this particular tyranny. He was, of course, an 'intellectual', even though his favourite writers were Dos Passos and Faulkner. After *La Nausée* came the war, which pitched him whether he liked it or not, into all kinds of convictions and questions about human life. Sartre was a true pessimist, as confirmed in his world-hatred as Graham Greene. But this attitude was of no use to a patriotic Frenchman. So the word 'choice' found its way into the existentialist vocabulary, and the necessity for revolutionary action was emphasized. From the super-subtle Jamesian analyses of *Being and Nothingness*, with its inevitable pessimism, Sartre suddenly found himself committed to telling men they were free and that they ought to do something with their lives. An embarrassing position for the admirer of Faulkner, who suddenly found himself sounding like the H. G. Wells of *Mr Polly*. Sartre did his best to tone down this Wellsian note by repeating that life is basically horrible (down to his latest play, *The Hermits of Altona*), but the note of optimism had been introduced. Worse still was the implication that the novelist can no longer be content to represent his hero's environment and sense of futility with strict realism. Again, Sartre tried to soften the blow by writing novels of unrelieved futility and sordidness, all expressed with an uncompromising experimentalism; still, the impression persisted that perhaps some kind of idealism – social or religious – should be a part of the novelist's equipment.

This brings us to the cross-roads for the modern novel, the latest dilemma. The novel of the eighteenth and nineteenth century – from Richardson to Trollope – had imposed a meaning on its material, and had done so without apology. Trollope breaks off to have discussions with the reader, and in one novel even asks the reader's advice about how he ought to continue the story. The new novelists wanted to do away with all that. 'The novelist is not God', they said. 'The material should be allowed to speak for itself.' Instead of being a storyteller, the novelist was now more like a tourist guide taking his readers round some underground cave, allowing his torch to rest on some interesting crystal structure, then on a stalactite. (Joyce somewhere or other refers to *Ulysses* as 'Joyce's guide to the City of Dublin'.) Opinions are lies; the 'truth' about the world can best be expressed by allowing the world to speak for itself. But the result of this technique is to create a mindless universe of objects and of men who are always 'acted upon'.

This is the problem. On the one hand, the over-simplified moral universe of Richardson and Trollope. On the other, the more honest but ultimately static world of Sartre and Robbe-Grillet, a world as detached and dead as a moon landscape, in which man's life is meaningless.

Immediately an obvious question presents itself. Does

'meaning' involve some simple religious view of the Richardson-Trollope variety? Or are there other possibilities? Very frequently the writers who seem to subscribe to the Joyce-existentialism are actually cheating. Faulkner, under the impressive facade of experimentalism, hides a juvenile romantic-sadism. Even Robbe-Grillet's technique seems to hide a completely romantic attitude, and an embarrassment about asking the fundamental romantic question: What are we doing here ?

I would argue that the distinction between the 'didactic' novel (Wells, Mann, Hesse, etc.) and the existential novel of Joyce, is a false one. All art asks the same question: What is the meaning of human life? and implicitly answers it. Its 'value premises' may be completely hidden and taken for granted, but they are present. The history of the experimental novel in the twentieth century proves that 'technique' in itself defeats its own object: increased maturity. Hemingway and Joyce have nothing in common except their avoidance of 'general ideas' and their technique of detachment. Both, after a magnificent beginning, went somehow to seed. The reason is the same in both cases: the questions asked and the values implied in their best work were never developed.

The problem is plain enough. The questions that lead to a development of values are moral or religious questions. But in view of the state of Christianity in our time, no writer wants to come up with a religious answer. So before he gets to that stage he simply stops asking the questions, and contents himself with his old attitudes: stoicism, detachment, and the rest.

Existentialism means asking the questions. If the answer is unsatisfactory (as, for example, Mr Eliot's answer is unsatisfactory for most of us), then the questions must be repeated, and a finer analysis developed to deal with them. This, for me, is the meaning of the phrase 'the existential temper of the modern novel'. Literature has been lazy for half a century – has preferred to ignore the questions formulated in Goethe, in Melville, in Dostoevsky and Nietzsche. If things are changing, it may mean a new vitality for literature in the second half of this century.

1960

Editor's Note:
This essay was first published in *Christian Faith and the Contemporary Arts* edited by Finlay Eversole. New York: Abingen Press, 1962 (**C40**).

4
PHENOMENOLOGY AND LITERATURE

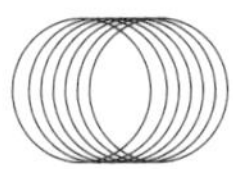

George Crabbe has a poem in which a lover sets out to see his mistress. As he rides towards her all nature seems to express his exaltation. When he arrives he hears that she has left. On his way home he sees the same scenery, but now nature appears to be unbearably dreary.

In writing this poem Crabbe was a phenomenologist. He wanted to show how a man's state of mind can alter a scene so completely that it seems to be a different scene. Phenomenology is concerned with the ways in which the mind grasps the world. When this is fully understood, when phenomenology is recognized as something more than a specialized philosophical discipline, literary criticism as we understand it today – as propounded, for example, by I. A. Richards or Doctor Leavis – will be forgotten.

Most phenomenologists would agree to define their subject as the study of the intentional structure of consciousness. This is accurate enough, but it leaves the non-philosophical reader un-enlightened. Phenomenology amounts to the recognition that we do not *see* the world: we *read* it, just as we read a newspaper.

Philosophy since Berkeley has tended to become tangled in subjectivism – the notion that the mind *creates* whatever it sees. This view, of course, is a dead end; for why should we do anything, make any kind of effort, if the world is somehow a figment of our own minds? Phenomenology has solved this particular philosophical problem by recognizing that the mind does not 'create' the world, but it often creates the *meaning* of the world. Even so, this is not to say that the mind creates meaning. When we read a newspaper, we read a meaning that is already there. Our mind has to grasp and interpret what is there, but if we interpret a paragraph about politics as being about sport, then plainly we are misreading.

But, it might be objected, we have to learn to read and we do not have to learn to see; so how can the two be compared? But we *do* have to learn to see, as any artist will tell you. It is true that we are born with some rudimentary ability to see, but that is only because our distant ancestors have already done much of the work of learning for us. But even so, a baby has to learn to 'read' the world to some extent, learning objects just as it later learns the letters of the alphabet. T. E. Lawrence's Arabs did not recognize pictures of themselves, according to Eric Kennington – did not even recognize the pictures as being of human beings. For them, the portraits were just a series of lines on paper.

Now we come to an important point. It is possible that a newspaper article may be deliberately written so that a knowing reader can 'read between the lines'; that is to say, there is more than one way of reading it. But if we consider for a moment the example from George Crabbe that I have quoted, we see that there are innumerable ways of reading the world.

This is a central insight of such importance that anyone who can grasp its essence has grasped the very essence of philosophy. Let me try to state it clearly.

As I sit in this chair looking at the world around me, I seem to myself merely to be looking, observing. But I am also aware that my attitude towards it is determined by all kinds of factors, for example (to take a random selection) the sun is shining, I have just drunk a cup of tea, and I am expecting an important letter later in the day. Change any one of these factors and it becomes, to a slight degree, a different world. Now what is important is that I somehow take it for granted that the world just 'is'. My attitude towards it is similar to my attitude to reading a newspaper; if my newspaper states that there will be a general election in a month, this fact just 'is'; the editor put it there, and even if I choose to ignore it, the election will take place all the same. Now it is true that the world just 'is' in the same way; but that does not mean that it has only one meaning, like the newspaper paragraph. Neither do I mean merely that I can see the world through any number of moods which will make it appear different. It is not a matter of my feelings any more than the meaning of the newspaper depends upon my feelings; it is a matter of selection and interpretation. I tend to accept the world passively when in fact I might see it crawling with sinister horror, as a paranoiac might, or blazing with inner reality, or in hundreds of other ways. My passivity is a fallacy, and if I could learn to control my perception – my 'phenomenological faculty', to coin a rather clumsy phrase – I should have taken a very important step indeed in human evolution.

Let me try to express what I mean by a different metaphor. Imagine that a man at a fairground has a huge metal frame covered with thousands of coloured lights. A notice outside says: 'There is a familiar object concealed in this machine. Guess what it is and win £100'. A small boy goes in; the man presses a switch, causing various lights to go on, so that the framework appears to be a ship. But when the small boy says 'It's a ship', the man presses another switch, and it now becomes a tree. The man says to the small boy, 'How could you ever have mistaken it for a ship when it is so obviously a tree?' And the boy replies, 'Yes, it *is* obvious now you've pointed it out to me'. No one ever wins the £100 because the man can change the pattern of lights to make almost any object. It will now be seen what I meant when I said that it is not a matter of moods. It was not a mood that caused the small boy to see a ship, but a certain pattern of lights.

The difference between the machine and the actual world is that in the actual world we ourselves choose whether to see it as a ship or a tree. But most of us are not aware of choosing; in fact we are inclined to believe that there is an invisible showman pressing switches. Most of the work of selecting, of course, is done by the unconscious mind; but the conscious mind is not aware of this. In short, when I open my eyes in the morning I am not confronted by a world, but by a million possible worlds.

This, in fact, is the essence of the nature of poetry. To see the world poetically is the reverse of seeing it from the everyday standpoint; it is to see it alive with potentiality, as if the mind of the poet were able to break up the everyday standpoint as a prism breaks up a beam of light. We are inclined to equate this poetic vision with the energy and vitality of youth, for it is strongest when we feel fresh and vanishes when we are exhausted. A moment's thought will show that this is a mistake, for fatigue and dreariness are not necessarily the same thing; a tired person can experience a sense of beauty and potentiality, and sick people very often do: Pascal is an example that comes to mind. But fatigue usually brings with it a sense of the world's sameness; life is drained of potentiality. But it is not my energy that determines the world's 'potentiality', but my vision: that is to say, my phenomenological faculty.

This potentiality of the poet differs in an important sense from the everyday variety. If I wake up in the morning and realize that I have a busy and exciting day ahead of me, the day is full of potentiality for me, but it is imposed from outside: it is potentiality for action. If I come to rely too much upon activity to keep me feeling alive and useful I shall begin to see all objects merely as potential tools. I look at a tree but it has nothing to do with my immediate purpose, so I ignore it. And if a day comes when I have nothing to do, I shall have lost my faculty for looking at the tree with pleasure, and my lack of activity will bore me. The poet, on the other hand, experiences a different kind of potentiality when he opens his eyes in the morning; it is not potentiality *for action* – not in the obvious sense, anyway – but simply for seeing and being. The world is full of a sense of possibilities, of excitement, as on the first morning of a holiday; but this excitement does not arise from the various possibilities of acting, but of feeling. That is, it is no longer simply the world that is 'potential', offering me this or that possibility; I am also aware in myself of different ways of feeling about it, of grasping it. I am aware of the *active* relation of my perceptions to the world. I am aware that my perception usually selects and eliminates according to my own sense of purpose. My perception reaches out hands to grasp the world, and the act of perceiving is actually an act of picking it up. And just as I can pick up a child by the waist or by the hands or under the armpits – or by the feet, for that matter – so my perceptions can pick up the world in many different ways, except that the possibilities are now multiplied many times. The world is a series of meanings; if an artist, a botanist, a geologist, an engineer, and an agronomist were to stand side by side looking at the same landscape, each would see quite a different series of meanings. But all these meanings are actually there in the landscape just as certain meanings are on the front page of my morning newspaper. The mind is not 'adding' them. If I allow myself to sink into boredom and life-devaluation, they will disappear, just as my newspaper will disappear if I close my eyes. If I want to combat my boredom and life-devaluation it is necessary for me deliberately to exercise my phenomenological faculty, to train it as I would train my body for some sporting event. Poetry, or literature, is a by-product of this process.

A further comment on this process: we have all to live in the world as well as see it, and our way of seeing it will obviously affect our living. If the world bores me then I shall not feel like coping with its difficulties; if I suspect that it is hostile, waiting to pounce on me and destroy me, my nervousness will certainly make life unbearable. And if I feel that the world is pointless and futile, I shall probably feel suffocated by its lack of meaning. In this latter case, it will be better for me to see the world as detestable and sinful, for I shall then at least have grounds for feeling something positive about it. Many modern writers seem to have chosen this method of investing the world with meaning:[17] Graham Greene is a particularly obvious example because he describes the sense of futility and meaninglessness in certain essays about his childhood, and it is easy to see how he made the leap from this point of view to the world-rejection of *Brighton Rock*.

As far as I know, the American school of 'transactional psychologists' was the first to point out that the way we see the world is closely tied up with the way we live in it. Our living is obviously a transaction with our environment; but so is our 'seeing'. What we see is tied up with our past experience, so that most of our seeing actually consists of taking a bet on what things are. The transactional school (led by Hadley Cantril and William Ames) specializes in creating visual illusions to illustrate how far our usual perception is a matter of guessing what we are looking at.

17 This is one of the main subjects of my book *The Strength to Dream*.

I think that there is hardly need to emphasize the importance of all this, not merely for literature but for psychology and for human evolution in general. It may well be the answer to the spiritual crises of the twentieth century that we hear so much about. Psychology, for example, is built on the idea of a norm, of sanity. Such a norm does not exist – or rather, it is a freely chosen convention, a general agreement among human beings. The neurotic is usually the man without purpose, and the paranoiac has come to see himself as acted upon by a hostile world rather than as acting purposively. He has simply carried the 'fallacy of passive perception' to an absurd limit. The great question of the modern world is the question of the decline of purpose, of the idea that the universe possesses a God-given meaning. Phenomenology simply points out that man has always been mistaken in seeing himself as a passive creature living in a universe whose purpose is known only to God. The universe may be meaningful and purposive – in fact almost certainly is – but man possesses the secret of perceiving its meaning to any degree he likes. He merely has to learn the secret of the control of the 'phenomenological faculty.' To the objection that this phenomenological faculty is only another name for imagination, it must be pointed out that, on the contrary, imagination is no more than a sub-heading, a special case, of the phenomenological faculty. (And the usual notion of imagination, identifying it with day-dreaming, is a sub-heading of a sub-heading.)

But this essay is concerned with phenomenology and literature. T. S. Eliot and F. R. Leavis have attempted to establish an objective ethical standard against which literature can be judged; but it can now be seen that this is by way of a half-measure, for their ethical standard itself reposes on unquestioned religious foundations. Phenomenology rests on the most unshakable foundation of all: immediate living experience, which can only be undermined by death or loss of consciousness, which negate all standards. But the question of the application of phenomenology to literature is not of great importance. What is far more important is for the phenomenologist – and it is to be hoped that we shall all be phenomenologists one day – to use literature as a useful instrument for turning phenomenology into a living reality. Most of us live in a life-world that is relatively static, and we accept it as a norm. But in a single morning I can browse through life-worlds as unlike as those of Shelley and P. G. Wodehouse, Poe and John Stuart Mill, Tolstoy and Kafka, Bernard Shaw and Samuel Beckett. And will someone then be absurd enough to tell me that these are merely different ways of looking at 'the same world'? (Before answering, 'But surely, yes', think back to the metaphor of the showman and his framework of light bulbs; 'world' as used here is a generic word like 'ship' or 'tree'.)

Phenomenologists are inclined to emphasize that it is a philosophical method, as applicable to science as to philosophy or psychology. This is true; it is for that reason that its founder, Edmund Husserl, is regarded as a more or less 'respectable' philosopher, when Sartre and Heidegger meet with suspicion among academic philosophers. But Husserl himself also wrote that the purpose of phenomenology is to 'unveil the hidden achievements of the transcendental ego', and he spoke about Goethe's mothers in the second part of *Faust*, the 'keepers of the keys of Being'. At the risk of jeopardizing Husserl's reputation with academic philosophers, it must be stated that phenomenology would be nothing if it were merely a method. What matters about it is its aim. Phenomenology regards itself as *the* philosophical method, and the aim of philosophy is, by general agreement, to understand the universe, to grasp the meaning of existence – of pure Being as well as human *Dasein*. Philosophy itself, unfortunately, is a highly unrespectable venture in the academic sense, for 'academic' means nothing if not 'limited'. We lose sight of the basic meaning of phenomenology if we forget that it is, at bottom, a mystical venture – the first mystical venture in human history to insist upon a strictly scientific method. When Blake wrote: 'If the doors of perception were cleansed, everything would appear to man as it is, infinite', he was making a phenomenological statement; that is to say, he was asserting that there is a real world 'out there', and what we perceive is not this real world, or its meaning, but something filtered and distorted by the senses. Husserl would agree with this formulation. The next question is how to uncover the structure of consciousness, or, as Blake would say, how to understand the nature of the distorting glass in the windows. Husserl would not have agreed with the method elaborated by Blake in the prophetic books, for he would object that Blake was exclusively concerned with the noetic aspect of the act of intentionality, ignoring its noematic component. (What this means is unimportant for the moment; I mentioned it only in case anyone should wish to pursue the matter into the phenomenological texts.) But it is very probable that Blake would have ended by agreeing with Husserl if the two had ever had a chance to talk. For if the word 'visionary' means to penetrate through obscurities to the underlying truth, then all science and all literature are visionary in intention.

1965

Editor's Notes:
An important concept to Wilson, phenomenology pervades his work, particularly *Beyond the Outsider* (**A14**). His essay 'Phenomenology as a Mystical Discipline' was published in *Philosophy Now*, Issue 56 (July/August 2006), pp. 15-19 (**C554**).

5

'SIX THOUSAND FEET ABOVE MEN AND TIME'

Remarks on Nietzsche and Kierkegaard

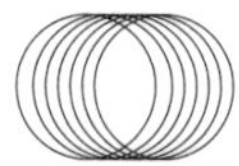

It may seem that so much has been written on these two men that there is hardly anything to add. To some extent this is true; but in the present context – of essays on literature – there is something of great importance that deserves restating.

Whenever I look at the row of Nietzsche's works on my bookshelf, I feel immediately that he *represents* something more important than he ever succeeded in writing down; the same, to a lesser extent, is true of Kierkegaard. He expresses in a particularly pure form the basic human aspiration, the aspiration expressed in all art: to control life by the activity of mind. And his life poses in a particularly pure form the basic question of human life: whether the human mind, whether human effort, can really alter human life, or whether there will always be a fundamental sameness about it. H. G. Wells wrote in his autobiography: 'We intellectual workers are reconditioning human existence', and the question that any 'intellectual worker' asks himself is: '*Are* we?' Man is distinguished from animals by his use of mind to alter his own existence. The child who first discovers the pleasure to be derived from books catches a glimpse of the mind's power to recondition human existence in an immediate and personal way. Yet because of our weakness, the strangely limited quality of human consciousness, we never seem to realize these possibilities that most of us glimpse in childhood.

In Goncharov's early novel *The Usual Old Story,* the two alternative attitudes are shown in the characters of the idealistic young man and his 'realistic' businessman uncle. The young idealist believes that the world could somehow become something like the vision of Schiller or Lermontov; his uncle advises him to concentrate on the problem of security and human relations and forget his dreams. Inevitably, the uncle wins; Goncharov would have had to be a far greater novelist to have shown the nephew winning. But let any reader of this novel ask himself how it could be rewritten so that the idealist wins. Of course, the nephew might become a famous poet, and justify himself in this way; but this is not really the answer. What would it really mean if the nephew were right and the uncle wrong? This is the great question, the most important question a human being can ask. For the novel *could not* be written so that the nephew wins. At least, it would have to become a fictional history of the whole future of the human race, ending in a vision of 'men like gods'.

A few other writers have presented this central issue of human existence – the *Lebensfrage* – with a similar clarity:

Wells, for example, in *The Undying Fire*. But individual works of art are inevitably disappointing because they can so easily be outgrown. In the age of Joyce and Eliot, readers found Wells's style old fashioned, and his later work was forgotten. This can happen at any time to any work of art. This is why Nietzsche is so much more important as a figure than anything he ever wrote. His work is disappointing. Many of us were intoxicated by *Zarathustra* on a first reading, and later found the style an obstacle to life-long admiration. Yet all of the other books are too fragmentary to produce any lasting satisfaction. It is easy to imagine that one has outgrown Nietzsche, until one reflects on what he stood for. And what precisely did he stand for?

In the last act of *Back To Methuselah,* Lilith says of the Ancients: 'Even in the moment of death, their life does not fail them'. But life is always failing the rest of us, like a schoolboy who is bored with a holiday after the second day. Absurd though it sounds, the profoundest of all human problems is that of boredom. If we assess it on the purely historical evidence, human life is a poor and unsatisfying thing, made tolerable only by illusions and our chronic bad memory and laziness. But the activity of the human mind, particularly in the past two centuries, gives the lie to this view. When the idea of Zarathustra came to Nietzsche, he wrote on a slip of paper: 'Six thousand feet above men and time'. Here was a vision that could transform human life. Again, in a letter to his friend Von Gersdorff, he described how he had tried to escape a mood of depression by climbing a nearby hill, and was overtaken by a storm. He took shelter in a herdsman's hut, and there saw a herdsman killing two kids; at the same time the storm broke with thunder and lightning, and he felt an overwhelming sense of well-being. He wrote: 'Pure Will, without the confusions of intellect – how happy, how free.' In these moods he felt an ecstatic certainty that man need not ultimately be defeated. And when one turns to his works, one discovers that he seems to be using his mind with a strange optimism, with a feverish excitement, like a revolutionary planting a bomb or a scientist discovering how to split the atom. When we read Kant or Hegel, we receive a certain intellectual satisfaction; but this phrase would be too feeble to describe the feeling that Nietzsche often produces. What Kant is writing about can never touch the realities of our everyday lives – or the chance seems remote. Nietzsche's work seems more like scientific research. This is not dead philosophy; it is as practical as the discovery of penicillin. Nietzsche never actually uses the phrase 'men like gods', but as one reads his works it somehow becomes far more of a reality than Wells or Morris ever succeed in making it. When the mind is used with this kind of vigour to dissipate illusions and create new values, how is it possible to doubt that the human mind really can recondition our lives? And Zarathustra suggests that health gets the last word – not sickness and defeat, as the other romantics seem to believe.

There is a case cited in Medard Boss's book *Psychoanalysis and Daseinsanalysis* (Basic Books, New York (1963), pp.155), that will help to bring out the implications of this last statement. Reading books on psychoanalysis often produces a feeling that human beings are, after all, miserable and limited creatures, who succeed with difficulty in retaining their normality in the face of the appalling complexities of everyday existence. At first Boss's case gives one this feeling. The patient, Maria, had an immensely fat mother. Until she was fourteen, this did not bother her; then she began to hate her mother and to eat as little as possible. A platonic love affair restored her to normality for a while, then she was almost raped at a dance, and broke with her boyfriend. Intense neurotic symptoms now developed: fits of hysteria and 'possession', heart abnormalities, and finally a compulsion to eat continuously. Her teaching work suffered and she consulted a psychoanalyst. The results of his treatment were entirely successful. Towards the end of the treatment the patient had a dream that showed that her fundamental attitude to existence had become health-oriented and optimistic. She was in an analytic session when a man with an unusually intelligent face entered the room – a professor. She and the professor departed together and went to a party. There they went out on to a balcony and looked at the night sky. She was overwhelmed by a sense of well-being. She knew that she would marry the professor, that they were united in their thoughts and emotions, but that there was no physical urgency. The stars now arranged themselves in the form of a Christmas tree, and she heard celestial music; she awoke in a mood of great happiness. In fact, this dream heralded a new beginning; the patient actually married an unusually gifted professor, and their relationship was satisfactory on every level. She became healthy, creative, and able to cope easily with problems and difficulties.

On a smaller scale, this patient had passed through the same problems as Nietzsche. But the result here was entirely satisfactory. In her early days the patient no doubt felt that she was 'fated' to tragedy – or at least to frustration and illness; the results showed her to be wrong. Unfortunately Nietzsche was not equally lucky. Syphilis contracted as a student undermined his health so that the obstacles he encountered drove him insane. In the light of his final insanity, the optimism of Zarathustra strikes us with a sense of tragic irony. This leaves us confronting the question: Which was the illusion, the vision 'six thousand feet above men and time', or the defeat and death in a mental home? Like the uncle in Goncharov's novel, the latter alternative has 'reality' on its side; but Nietzsche's life and work speak with equal authority of the power of the human mind to overcome any obstacle.

With most art and literature it is possible to take the negative view: that art is the creation of illusions to reconcile man to the harshness of a reality that always has the last word. But the greatest art has an urgency that makes it seem that this is untrue. In that case Nietzsche's life and work somehow contain the stuff of great art. Nietzsche believed that health has the last word, and that sickness and neurosis are a temporary consequence of man's newfound freedom. He possessed enormous moral strength, but not quite enough to demonstrate the truth of his theory.

This seems to be verified by the case of Strindberg, which I have cited elsewhere. Strindberg was also a defeatist from childhood onward, inclined to expect cruel blows from fate and to brood on his various ills and misfortunes. In a successful love affair with a beautiful woman this ingrained pessimism destroyed his happiness – as becomes clear from *A Fool's Confession*. After this, Strindberg became insane, and suffered from various delusions and a conviction that enemies were planning to kill him. The interesting thing is that he did not know he was insane, and so never lost the moral courage that made him go on writing books and plays about his neuroses. Finally he wrote himself out of his insanity, and produced the strange and powerful works of his later years. If, after writing *Inferno* (the most clearly insane volume of his autobiography) someone had convinced him that he was mad, no doubt he also would have died in a mental home, like Nietzsche. Strindberg is clear proof that the will to health can only be destroyed from within by pessimism.

This, in fact, is a view that modern psychological science is coming slowly to endorse. Professor A. H. Maslow, for example, has conducted a series of researches into extremely healthy people that have led him to conclude that health and optimism are far more positive principles in human psychology than Freud would ever have admitted.

Man is a slave to the delusion that he is a passive creature, a creature of circumstance; this is because he makes the mistake of identifying himself with his limited everyday consciousness, and is unaware of the immense forces that lie just beyond the threshold of consciousness. But these forces, although he is unaware of them on a conscious level, are still a far more active influence in his life than any external circumstances. Freudian psychology, for all its achievements, has made a twofold error: it has tried to anatomize the human mind as a pathologist would dissect a corpse, and it has limited its researches to sick human beings. Sick men talk about their illness far more than healthy people talk about their health; in fact, healthy people are usually too absorbed in living to bother with self-revelation. Psychology has consequently been inclined to divide the world into sick people and 'normal' people, regarding occasional super-normality as the exception; Maslow has shown that super-normality is a great deal commoner than would be supposed; in fact as common as sub-normality. Ordinarily healthy people often experience a sense of intense life-affirmation (which Maslow calls 'peak experiences'); and examination of peak experiences has led Maslow to conclude that the evolutionary drive (which is so clear in art and philosophy) is as basic a part of human psychology as the Freudian libido or the Adlerian will to self-assertion.

Maslow is by no means the only one who is working along these lines. For more than fifty years now, a revolt against the reductionism and materialism of nineteenth-century science has been building up, particularly in the field of psychology. When men like Blake and Kierkegaard objected to the scientific tendency to reduce the higher to the lower, science could reasonably object that its principles were pragmatic, not idealistic, and ignore their protest. For the objection of Blake was only that a narrowly materialistic view cannot explain the complexity of human existence; science could reply that it was not concerned with human existence, but with physical laws. In the twentieth century, science itself has come to object to the narrowly materialistic view on the ground that it cannot explain the *scientific* facts. Obviously, from the point of view of the scientist, this is a far more powerful objection. Phenomenologists have been the leaders of this attack against 'reductionism'. For example, Merleau-Ponty's *Phenomenology of Perception* is concerned to demonstrate the inadequacy of the behaviourist school of psychology.

Nietzsche was born half a century too early: one can feel this as one reads his works. At the time he was writing *Beyond Good and Evil,* the citadel of nineteenth-century philosophy and science seemed impregnable. He had a sense of being one man alone against the world. The weapons that Husserl and the *Gestalt* psychologists were to forge were not yet ready to hand. This fact is responsible for his worst faults: his occasional hysteria, his tendency to excess, the disconnected and chaotic nature of his thought. His limitations were essentially those of his position in history. Had he been born in 1900 instead of 1844, he would have found that time had already tumbled many of his enemies from their thrones and was causing the slow disintegration of others. The violence would have been unnecessary. A Nietzsche born in 1900 would never have acquired the same reputation as 'the philosopher with the hammer', the great rebel; but neither would he have become a symbol for anti-rationalism and messianic power-mania. These aspects of Nietzsche are irrelevant historical accidents. The true Nietzsche was a positive and constructive thinker, whose deepest impulse was his sense of evolution, his rejection of pessimism. Nietzsche's present position is paradoxical. He is universally regarded as the philosopher of antirationalism; and yet his work produces its impact because of his obsessive conviction that man can somehow become the master of his life through the use of his mind.

When I wrote a book called *The Outsider* ten years ago, Nietzsche was given a central position in its argument. He symbolized the problem that the book set out to state: whether the use of the mind can really give man control over his life, or whether 'man is a useless passion'. I still have a great affection for *The Outsider;* for, whatever its literary faults, it succeeds in stating the question more clearly than any other work I know. It is the most fundamental question that human beings can ask, and to state it clearly is worth doing. Kierkegaard, on the other hand, was hardly mentioned at all; in spite of his qualifications as an 'outsider', an existential thinker, a rebel, it seemed to me that he had ultimately chosen the wrong alternative in remaining a Christian. Kierkegaard is also a symbolic figure, but what he stands for seems to me less important than what Nietzsche stood for.

Temperamentally, Kierkegaard and Nietzsche had an immense amount in common; both had a background of Christianity; both were small men who suffered from feeble health and who remained lifelong bachelors. Both were devastating critics of the dishonesty and stupidity of their contemporaries. Both recognized that the moral disease of the nineteenth century was nihilism, the collapse of faith due to the rise of science, and that the worst aspect of this nihilism was a complacent limitedness. But here Kierkegaard showed his inferiority to Nietzsche. A man who experiences nothing but impatience and contempt when he looks around him naturally hungers for something of which he can entirely approve, and which he can flourish under the nose of his contemporaries as the ideal to which they ought to aspire. If there is nothing, then he has to go on alone. Now, since the nihilism of the nineteenth century was due to the decay of religious conviction, it follows that religion is in some way desirable. If religion is defined in the words of Julian Huxley as 'the organ by which man grasps his destiny', this is obviously true. But this is a definition of the *spirit* of religion, and the Christianity that was already decaying in the nineteenth century was more body than spirit. It was a Church with certain dogmas and rituals, and its chief dogma was that Christ died on the cross to redeem man from the consequences of original sin. Nietzsche declared, very rightly, that this had nothing whatever to do with the spirit of religion, and that the whole notion of the vicarious atonement was an invention of the guilt-ridden and neurotic St Paul. Therefore, in spite of his respect for the founder of Christianity, Nietzsche would have nothing to do with it as a religion. Nietzsche possessed an honesty that was incorruptible by loneliness or self-pity. Kierkegaard took the alternative course – of justifying Christianity to himself in order to possess a wall to press his back against.

Now this procedure is extremely dangerous, not because there is so little truth in Christianity, but because there is so much. In the same way, a scientific theory that is almost right – like the phlogiston theory of combustion – is more dangerous than one that is obviously and absurdly wrong. Kierkegaard was deeply religious – but then, so was Nietzsche. He was also extremely intelligent. It would have been immensely convenient if a careful examination of Christianity had revealed that it could satisfy his intelligence as well as his religious craving. Kierkegaard performed a subtle piece of casuistry. What he detested about his own time was its lack of conviction, its complacent materialism, its certainty that it was 'without sin'. The centre of the Pauline version of Christianity is its certainty that man is a sinful creature, incapable of saving himself. Kierkegaard worked this into a positive mysticism about man's weakness and sinfulness. Danish protestantism was also inclined to take Christianity for granted as a religion of mercy and cheerfulness; therefore Kierkegaard emphasized that to be a Christian is to invert all one's normal standards about suffering, and to accept that the closer a man gets to God, the more he suffers. In short, Kierkegaard's Christianity is thinly disguised masochism.

All this is not to deny Kierkegaard's deep religious insight, or that his paradoxical and masochistic Christianity was in many respects deeper than the current protestantism of the Church of Denmark. But it does mean that there is something essentially static about Kierkegaard's position, an internal deadlock. If Nietzsche had lived and stayed sane, his thought could have continued to develop indefinitely; his last book, the fragmentary *Will to Power,* does not give a sense of coming to an end; on the contrary, it has a new power and grasp of its problems, and is one of his most rewarding and stimulating books for the twentieth-century reader. Kierkegaard's last works are religious treatises, culminating in the thoroughly negative *Attack on Christendom.* Kierkegaard could not have developed as a philosopher without outgrowing his negative Christianity.

The problems raised by these two great nineteenth-century thinkers are still with us. Neither can be swallowed whole – there is too much about their work that irritates. But neither can be ignored or rejected, except at our own peril. And Nietzsche remains a symbol of all that is best about literature and philosophy: the sense that life is basically meaningful, and that man has no alternative but eventually to become responsible for the whole universe.

1964

Editor's Notes:
Nietzsche is mentioned and/or quoted throughout Wilson's work. Another essay "Dual Value Response'... a new key to Nietzsche?' was published in *The Malahat Review*, no. 24 (Oct. 1972) pp.53-66 (**C119**) and reprinted in *Collected Essays on Philosophers* (Newcastle-upon-Tyne: Cambridge Scholars, 2016 (**A183**)). He included a lengthy chapter on Nietzsche in *The Books in My Life* (Charlottesville, VA: Hampton Roads, 1998, pp. 180-195 (**A152**)).

PART TWO
INDIVIDUAL WRITERS

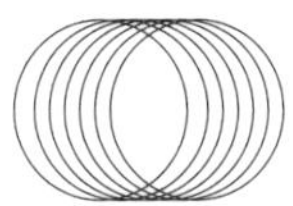

6

THE SWAMP AND THE DESERT

Notes on Powys and Hemingway

The two names at the head of this chapter seem to have nothing whatever in common, and that is the reason that I link them. For me they represent the same problem: What prevented them from being really great writers? I had intended to write an article about the work of the late John Cowper Powys, and for this purpose started systematically to reread his works. But after *Jobber Skald* and *Wolf Solent* I found my energy flagging, and half-way through *A Glastonbury Romance* I had to give up. So I asked myself why I could not read three Powys novels in succession. What was it that had begun to cloy? And it was not until I began to think about a related problem, the decline of Ernest Hemingway, that I began to get flashes of insight.

On 9 October 1962, Professor Wilson Knight organized a broadcast about Powys and his work. It is typical of the extraordinary neglect of this amazing writer – then 90 years old – that the broadcast was confined to the Welsh home service and was not even repeated on the Third Programme. 'Why is Powys so neglected?' asked Wilson Knight, and his bewilderment was echoed by Angus Wilson, H. P. Collins, Malcolm Elwin, and George Steiner.

Well, this is as good a question as any to begin with. No one who has ever read Powys can doubt that he is a tremendous creative force, and one of the great English novelists. He creates characters with a zest that reminds us immediately of Smollett, Dickens, and Trollope. At a first glance, we might think he was another gargantuan throw-back like Harvey Allen, the author of that monstrous best-seller *Anthony Adverse*, which might just as well have been written in 1850 as 1930. But a glance at a dozen pages of *A Glastonbury Romance* will disabuse us. To begin with, there is a feverish eroticism that is definitely of our age. In Chapter one John and Mary meet for the first time as adults; a few pages later they are already making love 'like vicious children' (Powys does not explain what he means, but one can guess). There is quite an amount more of this in the novel. The range of his characters, too, shows a mind that is definitely in touch with the twentieth century; we have a married couple who are communist agitators, a young capitalist with a curious power mania, a sadistic antiquarian, and a half-insane prophet. These are only a few of the more striking characters in the book. Read only ten pages and it is impossible to doubt that Powys has a tremendous and fertile imagination. His brain is like a steamy tropical forest where everything grows at an extraordinary rate; but the price paid for this fertility is a certain morbidity, an unhealthy vapour. Still, this is also true of Proust, Joyce, and (to a lesser extent) Aldous Huxley, and they are regarded as 'modern classics' in every university. How has Powys fallen out?

One reason is that, in spite of his feverish imagination, Powys is in a sense old-fashioned. His books overflow with vitality and sensuality, but one is always a little surprised to hear about motor cars or aeroplanes in them. Nothing really essential would be changed if they were written about 1830 or 1730, with stage coaches and blunderbusses.

The truth is that Powys's vital mind is oddly conservative. He is not an innovator in any sense; and in the twentieth century it is almost *de rigueur* for a highbrow writer to be some kind of an experimentalist, either in ideas or technique. I recently had something of a public debate with Mr Priestley about the question of why certain novelists – like J. B. Priestley, Powys, and Henry Williamson – remain so much less fashionable than Proust and Kafka. Mr Priestley said that he thought that all the fashionable writers were introverts, whereas he is an extrovert. But I'm not at all sure he is right. Powys and Williamson are certainly every bit as introverted as Proust. And would one call an odd bird like Robbe-Grillet an introvert? No, I think the real distinction is that between conservatives and innovators. Read any of the 'fashionable' highbrow writers of the twentieth century and they all have their own tart, distinct flavour, like some curious oriental fruit. It may be an emotional flavour, as in Kafka, or an intellectual flavour, as in Eliot's essays, but it immediately strikes the reader as sharp and new. Hemingway also has it.

Now if you begin your acquaintance with Powys – as I did by reading some of his literary essays, like *The Pleasures of Literature*, or his philosophical volumes, like *The Art of Growing Old*, you are immediately struck by a quality of Powys's mind that an admirer would call directness or enthusiasm, and that a detractor would call amateurishness or old-maidishness. I read them when I was sixteen, and filled pages of my diary with denunciations of the insipidity of Powys's mind. Many years later, when I first met Malcolm Elwin, I infuriated that kindly man by dismissing Powys as a sentimental third-rater. But I had not read any of the novels at that time. A mere chapter of *A Glastonbury Romance* quickly changed my views. So there is no point in trying to hide it: as a thinker and critic Powys has a naïvety, a wordiness and a fulsomeness that are embarrassing. He gives a dreadful impression of 'two-foot-shelf culture', of having carefully read the two dozen best books and admired all the things he ought to admire. It is a relief to turn to the astringency of Eliot's *Sacred Wood* with its machine-gun judgments. Powys gives the impression of having a third-rate mind.

And yet he most emphatically is not a third-rate mind, if we mean by 'mind' the whole of a man's mental make-up. His vision of the universe is completely original, and a great deal more vital than that of Eliot, Joyce, or Kafka. However, he has absolutely no capacity for abstract thought, and is at his worst in the critical books. I hasten to add that if his critical books are read after the novels, one is willing to forgive him almost anything.

Powys was a very late starter. He was born in 1872, but he published nothing of importance until the great novels of the 1930s, beginning with *Wolf Solent*. He had been a lecturer in the United States for many years before that. Perhaps retailing culture to backwoods audiences developed the worst elements in Powys – the naïve, Dale Carnegie approach to literature and life. Talking down to people always produces a deterioration of character.

But Powys was also a nature mystic with a Wordsworthian vision. These expressions are clichés; nevertheless, they describe the essential Powys accurately. Unfortunately, like most romantic poets, he always had a strong tendency to turn away from the present: and the relative neglect of all his best books – and a lot of his worst – made him turn his back on the present and on 'social reality'. The early thirties were a fantastically productive time. *Wolf Solent*, a 600-page monster, was published in 1929. *A Glastonbury Romance* came in 1933 (1,200 pages), and *Jobber Skald* (600 pages) two years later. *Maiden Castle*, the last of the 'great novels', came in 1937. Besides these major works, Powys published several important books of philosophy and literary criticism. The best of them, *In Defence of Sensuality* came in 1930, and was followed by *A Philosophy of Solitude*, *The Art of Happiness*, and *The Pleasures of Literature* (1938). If Powys had died in 1938, at the age of sixty-six, he would still rate as one of the greatest writers of this century. Like any other man of genius he must have known this. Yet although all his books got good reviews, not one of them succeeded in setting the Thames on fire. No one saw that *A Glastonbury Romance* was the great novel of the thirties as surely as *Ulysses* had been the great novel of the twenties. And all the reviews that one finds quoted on Powys dust-jackets somehow make him sound a dull and deserving writer; one would not classify him with Joyce and Kafka, but with Rose Macaulay, Rosamund Lehmann, and Phyllis Bottome. (I intend no disrespect to these excellent female novelists.) Nothing revolutionary.

This is partly Powys's own fault. He is actually as revolutionary as D. H. Lawrence; but reading his work, the first comparison that comes to mind is another conservative genius, George Meredith. Powys has Meredith's love of nature, his wordiness, and his frequent use of the plangent cliché. Powys will not hesitate to tell you that a certain character has 'twinkling blue eyes', or to describe two adults seizing the hands of an old lady and holding them for a quarter of an hour to demonstrate affection. If one casually opened the book at such a passage, one would say instantly: 'sentimental platitudes', and close it again. In fact, as Powys uses them, such phrases or incidents are not in the least platitudinous. He has the courage not to strive for the striking word or incident when an older coinage will serve as well. He realizes that, as with the human body, a certain amount of fat is a good thing, and not all fat is 'surplus'. (This is a lesson that would have turned Hemingway and Joyce – and, more recently, Robbe-Grillet – into better writers.) Still, the unfortunate effect is there for the casual eye. Another – more serious – charge is that Powys, like Meredith, is fond of playing God-Almighty with the reader, and telling him all kinds of things that only the author could know. Unlike the author of *Goodbye to Berlin*, Powys is most emphatically not a camera. Henry James would have shuddered at his novels. He never tells a story from a single standpoint; he is all over the place, inside the brains of every one of his characters. And while this enables him to open wide the sluice gates of his imagination, it also gives a regrettable impression of inconstancy and garrulity.

So the Powys of 1938 was an embittered man, a genius who had poured out his greatest works and seen them neglected – or, infinitely worse, assessed at about a tenth of their real value. No Powys cults grew up; no young writers tried to write like Powys.

Powys's reaction was to produce the panorama of Welsh history called *Owen Glendower*, one of his most difficult if most rewarding books. And from then on he wrote very little of the modern world. The major books of the next twenty years are all well out of touch with what we would call 'reality' – meaning everyday life. The finest of them is the other great Welsh romance *Porius* (1951), the only novel of real size since *Owen Glendower*. *The Brazen Head* is a version of the story of Friar Bacon and Friar Bungay; *Homer and the Ether* is a kind of retelling of the *Iliad* from a 'universal' point of view (the ether). *Up and Out* (1957) and *All or Nothing* are cosmic fairy stories which I would not attempt to describe, but which, like the early novels, are distinguished by the mystical feeling for living nature.

It was indeed a tragedy that Powys got so tired of the modern world and turned to these regions of mist. It has taken many 'big' writers a great deal more than seven years to make an impact. A pertinent example is William Faulkner, another twentieth-century romantic, who was officially canonized as a 'great writer' only after the war although he had been publishing just as long as Powys. Thomas Wolfe – who again resembles Powys in his giganticism, his torrential (and cliché-packed) language, and his mysticism – published his first book in 1929, but became well known only after *Of Time and the River* appeared in 1935. If Powys had kept hammering at 'the modern world' for another five years, I have no doubt at all that he would now be as universally known and respected as Faulkner. Another *Glastonbury Romance* after the war – when all the critics were complaining that English literature was at an end – would surely have focused the attention of every critic in England and America on Powys's work. Instead, he only had *Porius* to offer, which could be ignored as a historical romance; so the critical attention went to another conservative and amateurish writer, Angus Wilson. (In calling Mr Wilson amateurish I intend no insult; he himself has pointed out that his prose has the true amateur ring – lack of sophistication – and has repeatedly spoken of his desire to revive the 'big novel' of the nineteenth century.)

In short, it is partly Powys's own fault if he is less known than he deserves to be.

But what exactly does he deserve, apart from historical accidents? The four great novels (*Wolf Solent*, *A Glastonbury Romance*, *Jobber Skald*, *Maiden Castle*) are certainly a unique achievement, towering like battlements above the rest of the literature of the thirties. They might almost be, like Proust, all part of the same big novel, for there is a curious similarity of scene, character, and event in them. Nevertheless, their imaginative range is so great that this is no limitation.

Their fault – common to all of them – explains why they have received so little critical attention. I indicated it when I spoke of Powys's mind as being like a tropical forest incredibly rich and overgrown. The books are sheer creative explosions, and they have as little inner logic as an explosion. Powys creates simply for the fun of it, and he creates as majestically as that other imbecilic genius, Shakespeare. No one could produce a thesis on the recurrence of Powys's basic themes and symbols, the subtle inter-relations between different characters and events, because none are intended – they may well be there; but they certainly were not put there consciously. *A Glastonbury Romance* is, in this respect, the complete opposite of *Ulysses* or *Remembrance of Things Past*; there is no incredibly complex intention that requires the theses of university professors.

Take, for example, the book that Professor Wilson Knight considers one of the finest, *Jobber Skald*. What, briefly, is the book about ? That is impossible to say, for it is not about any one thing. The sea is the great force behind the book and its major 'symbol' (if it has one.) The main strand of the plot concerns the love affair of a seaman, Jobber Skald, and Perdita Wayne, a lady's companion, and the Jobber's hatred for a local business man, Dog Cattistock. He carries a stone in his pocket with which he intends to kill Cattistock, but at the end of the book throws it away. Another major character is Magnus Muir, a mild teacher of Latin, in love with Curly Wix who is constantly unfaithful with another young capitalist, Sippy Ballard. But all this tells the reader nothing about the book, nor explains its remarkable quality. Like all the author's books, it is saturated with intense sexuality and intense love of nature – a sensuous, passionate craving for nature.

But the weakness of *Jobber Skald* is that the author obviously has no idea of where it is going. When the reader has finished its 600 pages he has no feeling of having been taken anywhere. Although the narrative seems to have a compulsive onward flow, its only real motive force is Powys's delight in his own creative power.

But – this must be repeated – it is centrally about sex, about people being powerfully attracted to one another (to say 'falling in love' would not convey it at all) and having various kinds of relations. Powys is deeply, though not morbidly, interested in sex, and the reader goes on from chapter to chapter solely to see how soon the various affairs will reach their consummation. Sometimes the love is not physical, or at least reaches no physical consummation, as in the affair between Sylvanus, the religious fanatic and mystic, and the Punch and Judy girl. Sometimes Powys plays a game with the reader by hinting at some affair that never develops, as in the episode between the Jobber and Sue Gadget in the chapter called 'Sea Serpent'. The reader is drawn on, wondering where he is being taken, and finally he realizes with a certain disappointment that he is being taken nowhere. If he reads *Jobber Skald* after *War and Peace* or *The Brothers Karamazov* he will feel even more cheated. For when Tolstoy first introduces Natasha, Pierre, and Prince Andrew, the reader can be certain that Tolstoy knows in advance that Andrew will fall in love with her and Pierre will finally marry her. And Dostoevsky, for all his apparently slap-dash style of writing, which sometimes gives the impression that the author is playing blind man's buff, knows exactly what will be happening 600 pages hence. Powys does not. He weaves the destinies of his characters just as cunningly as did Tolstoy, but he can never see more than a chapter ahead. In the first chapter of *A Glastonbury Romance* John and Mary are drawn to one another; in Chapter two they make love. Then John walks all the way to Glastonbury to be close to Mary. And then nothing happens; Powys loses interest in them and goes on to other characters, in whom, in turn, he also loses interest.

To summarize: the reasons for Powys's neglect are historical that is to say, they must be explained in terms of literary fashions. In view of twentieth-century literary trends, the matter for surprise is not that Powys is neglected, but that he ever managed to get published, in England at least. (If Thomas Wolfe had been an Englishman, he would still be unknown.) What publisher of today would accept a book beginning:

> At the striking of noon on a certain fifth of March, there occurred within a causal radius of Brandon railway station and yet beyond the deepest pools of emptiness between the uttermost

> stellar systems, one of those infinitesimal ripples in the creative silence of the First Cause which always occur when an exceptional stir of heightened consciousness agitates any living organism in this astronomical universe. (*A Glastonbury Romance*).

We can understand what Powys is trying to do; that he is tired of the narrowness of contemporary kitchen-sink novels, and wants to express deeper mystical intuitions; but this is not the way to do it. What is needed is a genuine union of the concrete and the universal – the kind of thing that Joyce comes close to achieving in the last few chapters of *Ulysses*, and that he completely failed to achieve in *Finnegans Wake*. Powys went the wrong way; instead of trying to become more concrete, he abandoned the everyday and turned to the universal. The result – as in the writing of another novelist mystic of our time, L. H. Myers – is a sickly escapism. The later books have much to recommend them; but for me the very quality they lack is universality; they are too near to fairy tales.

In certain respects Powys's development is the reverse of W. B. Yeats's. Yeats began as a lover of the vague, the mystical, the general, and gradually turned into a classicist, with a precise eye for detail and a love of the concrete. Powys seems to be ending where Yeats began, in the realm of the vague and the universal.

While my thoughts were occupied with Powys and his work, I picked up the new Penguin *Portrait of Hemingway* by Lilian Ross, a reprint of a New Yorker profile. This turned my thoughts to one of my favourite problems: What went wrong with Hemingway? and it came to me that the development of these two totally different writers throws light on the development of twentieth-century literature.

Lilian Ross's short book describes a week-end with Hemingway and his wife in the early fifties. Hemingway emerges from it as a curiously inauthentic sort of person; or, to use the word that some Americans preferred, a phoney. Stephen Spender once described a meeting with Hemingway during the Spanish civil war, and said then that he was baffled by the contrast between the Hemingway of *A Farewell to Arms* and this bearded actor with the tough-guy mannerisms. All this emerges with extraordinary clarity in Lilian Ross's book. It is obvious from the beginning that Hemingway's judgment has somehow gone completely awry. On the plane he allowed his seat-companion (a stranger) to read the unfinished manuscript of *Across the River and Into the Trees*. The little man made no comment, and Hemingway assumed that the book had been too much for him. Hemingway explained that this book was undoubtedly his best, far better than *A Farewell to Arms*. A subsequent biographer has revealed that Hemingway was shattered when the critics finally told him the truth about the book: that it is very bad indeed.

And one can see why the book is bad from Lilian Ross's portrait of Hemingway. It is not exactly that he is a boaster, as that his whole personality is phoney. He wants to put on an act of being the deep, serious writer who is ten times as big as any of his sissy contemporaries. He knows all the ten-dollar words, he tells Miss Ross, but prefers not to use them. (All this emerges clearly in the controversy with Aldous Huxley which I have described in an appendix of my *The Strength to Dream*.) In between talking about all the cities in the world that he loves, and prize fighters and baseball players, he makes statements like this: 'I started out very quiet and I beat Mr Turgenev. Then I trained hard and I beat Mr de Maupassant. I've fought two draws with Mr Stendhal, and I think I had an edge in the last one. But nobody's going to get me in the ring with Mr Tolstoy unless I'm crazy or I keep getting better.' Hemingway wants to emphasize that he is no lousy intellectual, so when he has to talk about other writers he calls them 'Mr', just to show that for him they are people, not names to be dropped to demonstrate culture. Later in the book he mentions that he learned how to write by looking at the canvasses of Mr Cézanne.

Of the atrocious *Across the River...* he says: 'When I am writing it, I'm as proud as a goddam lion'. He likes to make a bit of a mystique of writing, and to think of himself as a kind of high priest; every book is written with his heart's blood etc. He is worried because he writes so slowly, but tries to convince himself that this is because the quality of the stuff is so high that you can't expect it in quantity. In fact, as he suspected and feared, the quality of the constipated strainings of his last thirty years is pathetic.

Having read Miss Ross's book, I again posed the question that has bothered me for years: How was it that Hemingway could start as a unique, original writer, as fresh as a spring breeze, and turn into the nihilistic ham of *For Whom the Bell Tolls* and *The Old Man and the Sea*? Hermann Wouk has suggested that all major American writers begin to parody themselves in mid-career because they get so nervous of the critics, and lose their talent in anxious self-criticism. There may be something in this. It is unfortunately true that the critics tend to ruin the lives of the modern writers. Success – and the conceit that follows – can also be blamed. But in order to explain Hemingway's decline, explanations have to go deeper; they have to look at the whole pattern of literature since the nineteenth century. And this is where Powys comes in.

The novels of the nineteenth century were 'Powys novels' – big, sprawling, full of vitality, but often careless, undisciplined, and sentimental. The writer was all the time getting between the reader and the 'object'. When Meredith describes the woods in flowery language he expects the reader to sympathize with him. And so, for the most part, the reader does. But the nineteenth century ended with a spate of sentimentality and overblown language. Women were mostly responsible for it: Madame Blavatsky and Ouida, Mary Baker Eddy and Marie Corelli and others. But the twentieth-century mentality distrusts sentiment and verbosity. When Hemingway said that he learned to write from Cézanne's canvasses, we can see exactly what he means. For what is it about Cézanne that gives pleasure? It is his cool objectivity, which he likes to emphasize by painting angular rocks or oddly shaped trees. He is far less successful when he tries painting soft or plastic substances with his technique of objectivity. There is something of the scientific dream in Cézanne and a touch of mysticism too, for he is not only seeing objects objectively, but by tearing away the usual veils of emotions and misconceptions he is also seeing them in a new and intenser way. (One can see why he disliked Van Gogh so much.) Much the same spirit is apparent in the young James Joyce, with his passion for Aristotle and Aquinas in preference to Plato and Plotinus. Parts of *Ulysses* are devoted to devastating parodies of the old, personal, and sentimental school of writing. As Edmund Wilson remarked, he seems to be saying: 'Look at how the old writers distorted reality, then compare it with how clearly I am expressing it'.

Hemingway felt just the same. Gertrude Stein mentions that the young Hemingway used to speak of his mission to revolutionize writing. Hemingway was right. He was saying, in effect: 'The older writers – Anderson, Dreiser, and the rest – always write about the same dreary theme: stupid little people and their silly emotions. I am going to show you a new way of seeing the world, where people count for very little. But you'll be amazed how much beauty you'll find in my universe.' And so he does. He tries to write as flatly as Cézanne painted. People are not important; they are treated as objectively as trees or rivers, just as Cézanne used the same technique for an apple, a stove, or the portrait of a friend. But his favourite subject is the indifference of nature, and it is best illustrated in war. *A Farewell to Arms* is a moving book because it catches the contrast between human emotions and the indifference of 'the world' – a contrast that everyone who has been in the army can remember: the hidden pathos of leaving warmth and comfort behind and getting into a train that is taking you back to a colder world.

I have pointed out elsewhere that Hemingway's vision, in these early books, might be called religious; he is rejecting the warmth and comfort of 'the human dream' as treacherous – and, by implication, creating the condition for the religious search. But if Hemingway was looking for something 'more than human' in the early novels he never found it, for the simple reason that he abandoned the search and settled down to playing the Hemingway character. The urgency disappears from his work.

The interesting thing, however, is to watch how he tries to conceal this bankruptcy. He tries to substitute technique for spiritual urgency, for having something to say. He tries harder than ever to play the objective, Cézanne-like artist. In *For Whom the Bell Tolls*, for example, he tries to create the effect of detachment and strangeness by the device of conversation that is supposed to be literally translated from Spanish. As far as I am concerned, Hemingway has never sounded so inauthentic as in this type of dialogue: 'I, obscenity in the milk of thy obscenity' etc.

When we come to *Across the River*... the total collapse is obvious. What made the earlier books so fine was the atmosphere of spiritual and emotional tension. Here there is only self-conceit and concealed self-praise. The hero of the book is a battered old colonel, tough but badly bruised, who spends a final holiday in Venice with a beautiful sixteen-year-old countess who is in love with him. The basic elements are the same as in *A Farewell to Arms* or *The Sun Also Rises* – human warmth contrasted with a recognition that the world is a hard and cold place, with no room for sentimentality. So in order to try to convince the reader that he is no sentimentalist, Hemingway uses a phrase like 'he kissed her true'. This is strong, silent Hemingway, brushing away the tear with the back of his hand and staring bravely into the distance. He is the simple man, the essential man (I am using essence in Gurdjieff's sense), complex and delicate, and yet as simple as a peasant. One is reminded of Belloc's affectation of being a French peasant, at which Shaw pokes fun in a delightful article; I would guess that Belloc's prose was a great influence on Hemingway.

It never struck Hemingway that detachment is not enough to make good writing. Without detachment, the creative stream will flow muddy; but no amount of detachment will make the stream flow if there is no water. Hemingway, like Powys and Joyce, is at an immense disadvantage in that he is not a thinker. Inability to think analytically, lack of interest in ideas, make no difference to a young and vital artist; but they make an artist short-winded, unable to go the whole distance. Shaw and Yeats were long-distance runners because their unbounded intellectual curiosity never flagged, and provided a driving energy even when their sensations had been enfeebled with age. The basis of good writing is sensation; but it is also movement, vitality. The best writing unites intensity of thought with intensity of feeling; but when the feeling gets tired, thought can often provide an excellent fuel. This is why there is so little falling off in quality between Shaw's *Man and Superman* and his *Good King Charles*, written forty years later.

This notion that technique is enough is the great heresy of modern writing, and the reason that the modern experimental novel is finding the going so hard. The modern writer, like the modern philosopher, has tried hard to get away from the 'pathetic fallacy' of the nineteenth century, and from allowing his own emotions and preconceptions to distort his vision. This is as it should be – the inevitable next step in the cultural revolution. But the result is that the modern writer has come to distrust his own vision; he strains his eyes looking for signs on the horizon and forgets all about his inner world. The simplest example of the destructive effect of this fallacy is Joyce. He abhorred general ideas, and declared that the artist must stick to the concrete. This was the equivalent of nailing one of his feet to the floor; he was forced to go round in circles. Because all that counts with an artist is his response to the world. He has to keep absorbing, filtering, selecting, trying to learn from his experience. And the intellect, although often clumsy, is one of the most reliable means of feeding oneself with new experience, new syntheses. It is not enough to *feel* about the world; one has to think about it too. And where feeling sometimes only succeeds in scraping the surface, the thinking manages to go deeper and strike oil. It is hard to imagine a Yeats who had no interest in theosophy, magic, religion, and philosophy; and quite impossible to imagine Yeats developing into the author of *Last Poems* without that insatiable intellectual curiosity. It might even be asserted dogmatically that, in the twentieth century, the writer who is not a thinker has no chance of distilling the essence of the age.

We might say, then, that the unique literary revolution of our century has been this desire to get beyond human emotions to the reality behind. Its greatest error – which is as obvious in modern *avant-garde* writing as in Joyce or Hemingway – is its belief that merely looking is enough to reveal reality.

In a way, Hemingway was faithful to his basic vision. He said, in effect: 'If you look at the world honestly, unblinded by human prejudice, you realize that it is at the same time far more beautiful *and* far more brutal and powerful than you ever realized'. This is essentially a limited and pessimistic vision, and no man could continue to accept it over a long period without having a nervous breakdown. He would have to learn to go beyond it, as, for example, Mr Eliot did. Hemingway seems to have enjoyed success too much to remain true to his original perception; without its sap, the tree withered.

Now it can be seen that Hemingway and Powys are so completely opposites that they illuminate each other. They seem to have only one thing in common – a kind of nature mysticism, a vision of the goodness of nature and of its indifference. Apart from that, nothing. Arrived at the same crossroads, they chose opposite directions; Powys preferred to stick to his inspiration, and turned inward; Hemingway preferred success, and turned outward. Even in personal life this opposition appears. Powys apparently makes an instant expression of total sincerity and modesty, no 'great man' airs; many visitors have described the gentle, almost saintly, impression of his character, his extreme concern for the feelings of others. Hemingway apparently heard no one's voice but his own, and could only be called sincere in that he deceived himself more than he deceived anybody else.

But the lesson that both of them reveal should be taken to heart by every young writer. One compromised too much with the modern world and was dehydrated by it; his work became drier, until it lost all content. The other compromised too little, and threw away the few advantages of our mechanical civilization: the discipline it imposes, the tension. Consequently his work is a swamp of romanticism. At one end of the highway stands the desert; at the other, the swamp. The writer who wishes to develop has to resist the temptation to be pulled in either direction. Powys has too little of that sense of his own age which is the essential of a great writer. But before a writer can be of any value to his own age, he has to be capable of absorbing it (of prehending it, as Whitehead would say), and for this he must stand outside, not be too involved. In a perceptive phrase John Wain once said that the writer's task is to 'humanize the environment' – or, to express it less humanistically, to impose spiritual values on the glass and concrete. For this he must not only remain richly human; he must also be in constant contact with the environment. No romantic turning-away, no gestures of disgust.

The tragedy of our age is that there is no single writer – except, perhaps, Shaw – who has survived the tension between swamp and desert. Some, like Sartre, Beckett, Eliot, have ended in the desert – in literary sterility. Others, like Lawrence, Wolfe, Hesse, end in the swamp, that is, they fail to develop. In both cases, the early work is the best – a sad epitaph, a confession of failure. It remains to be seen whether our age will produce anyone strong enough to learn from their failure.

1964

Editor's Note:
First published in two parts in *The Aylesford Review*, vol. 6 (Spring, 1964): 85-93 and vol 6 (Summer/Autumn, 1964): 129-135. (**C56** & **C58**). Wilson also deals with Hemingway and Powys in his *The Craft of the Novel* (London: Victor Gollancz, 1975 (**A45**) and dedicates a chapter to the former in *The Books in My Life*: 'Escape from personality: the puzzle of Ernest Hemingway', pp. 141-154 (**A152**).
His views on Powys's sexuality did not meet with the approval of the Powys Society when he spoke at their Conference at Churchill College, Cambridge in 1972. Angus Wilson recalled, in his Introduction to *Colin Wilson, A Celebration* (London: Cecil Woolf, 1988 (**HA8**)): 'His speech was, as always, with believers an enormous shock to the fervent JCP disciples, but a very good shock.' (p. 9). It would be thirty years before he was asked to speak again at the Conference. His review of a book about Powys: 'Cowper Powys's Private World' was printed in *Books & Bookmen* 23 (Feb. 1979, pp. 44-45 (**E165**)) and reprinted in *Existential Criticism: Selected Book Reviews* (**A178**). Powys's sadism is also discussed in Wilson's *Origins of the Sexual Impulse* (**A9**) and *The Misfits: A Study Of Sexual Outsiders* (London: Grafton Books (**A92**)).

In the early 1980s Wilson wrote an outline for an opera of *A Glastonbury Romance*. The music was to be written by Richard Arnell (1917-2009), with the libretto by Wilson and Gavin Ewart (1916-1995). The project was not realised but Wilson's outline can be consulted in his archive at the University of Nottingham.

7

DAVID LINDSAY

A Voyage to Arcturus

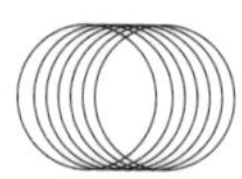

David Lindsay's *A Voyage to Arcturus* is one of the strangest, and most certainly one of the greatest, books of the twentieth century. Yet its greatness is of such a curious order that it is still almost unknown today, nearly half a century after it was first published. When Methuen's issued it in 1920, it sold only 596 copies, and the other 834 were remaindered. It gained a few converts, who gave the book an underground reputation, so that it was republished in 1946 (by Gollancz) and again in 1963. Its author was a musician, and E. H. Visiak, who writes an introduction to the Gollancz edition, offers no biographical details about him except that he also published a novel called *The Haunted Woman.*[18] *A Voyage to Arcturus* was his first novel, and was apparently discovered for Methuen's by Robert Lynd, the essayist.

The book is difficult to characterize. It is an allegory, a kind of *Pilgrim's Progress*, and yet it reads more like a novel of science fiction. It makes a powerful visual impact – one would suppose that the author was a painter, colours and shapes are conveyed so vividly.

18 I have since discovered from Mr Visiak that Lindsay died of gangrene in 1945.

But the most important thing to be said about *Arcturus* is that it is an attempt by a most remarkable man – a visionary – to present his own ideas of the inner nature of the world and of human life. In this sense it is close to the *Prophetic Books* of Blake; that is, Lindsay is deliberately inventing a mythology to explain his ideas of the world's inner nature. Blake's prophecies are an attempt to get beyond appearances; the same is true of *Arcturus*.

Perhaps this kind of prophetic allegory is the profoundest kind of art. The characteristic of human beings that gives them most in common with the animals is their tendency to take life for granted, to accept it in a vague, instinctive way, without asking questions. Now what distinguishes good art from bad art is the depth of the questions it succeeds in raising. All art must begin from common assumptions – the world we accept and live in; but bad art is all common assumptions, unquestioned. One can walk into any bookshop and see dozens of paperbacks that are little more than a libel on human existence. One might read them to pass away an hour, but too much of them produces a sense of spiritual indigestion. As one reads, the horizon seems to narrow; the world ceases to be a place of unfathomed potentialities. Its values are seen in terms of a few pointless and boring emotions, 'human, all too human'.

Blake's *Prophetic Books* are as far from this attitude as it is possible to be. He wants to question so many things, to present such an altered vision of human life, that he relies to the absolute minimum on the common world of everyday experience. He is trying to get beyond the natural standpoint, beyond everyday emotions, beyond appearances. So his books plunge straight into symbolic situations, with immense figures who represent the human intellect or creative faculty or sexual impulse. But no one would regard Blake's later prophetic books – *Jerusalem* and *Milton* – as successful attempts at communication; even the earlier sketch *Vala* is interesting mainly because it presents a series of tremendous images and situations; it has no apparent continuity.

This is not true of *Arcturus*. It is a remarkable work that employs a dream-like technique, and yet its story seems logical so that one reads on to find out what will happen; there is no sense – as with Kafka – that almost anything can happen, and that consequently there is no point in reading it 'for the story'.

I may as well state here, at the beginning, that I am inclined to reject Lindsay's 'message', which is a kind of Schopenhauer-Buddhism, a religion of world-rejection. But it is presented with such creative vitality that the book will bear repeated readings, just as great music will bear repeated hearings. Undoubtedly this is the kind of creative feat of which most writers only dream; Lindsay's imagination is tremendous and enviable.

A Voyage to Arcturus starts badly. For several chapters it is impossible to believe that one is in the hands of an artist who knows exactly what he is doing: the writing makes an impression of amateurishness. This is something of an error. When one re-reads the beginning after completing the book, it no longer seems amateurish, and one realizes that the impression arose because at first *Arcturus* brings to mind the R. L. Stevenson/M. P. Shiel type of fantasy, and one reads it wearing Stevensonian glasses, so to speak.

The hero of the book is an enormous bearded man called Maskull. When he first appears he is accompanied by another character named Nightspore. One discovers at the end of the book that Nightspore is actually one aspect of Maskull – his creative, visionary self. Nightspore seems thoroughly bored by everything – but for the same reason that the poet finds the everyday world boring.

Maskull and his 'other self' arrive at a spiritualistic seance, in the course of which a medium conjures up a beautiful and mysterious looking youth. The door bursts open and a powerful, vulgar-looking man called Krag comes in and twists the neck of the youth; immediately the expression of mystery vanishes, to be replaced by 'a vulgar, sordid, bestial grin, which casts a cold shadow of moral nastiness into every heart'.

This episode must be explained, for something like it recurs throughout the book. Lindsay's purpose, like Nietzsche's, is a 'transvaluation of all values'. Like a true Scottish Presbyterian, he believes that this world belongs to the devil – that is, to pleasure. Krag is actually the devil's adversary, fighting for the ultimately true values, for something beyond pleasure and all our paltry 'human' values. But because our world is so entangled in the snares of pleasure, Krag appears as a jeerer, a vulgarian, a brute. It is his business to unmask 'the devil' (who is usually called Crystalman), who masquerades in various forms that human beings have come to accept as manifestations of the most high – beauty, nobility, mystery, love. So when Krag wrings the neck of the beautiful supernatural youth, the mask vanishes and the true inner nature of this creation of Crystalman appears – the vulgar Crystalman death-grin.[19]

Krag has come to the party to invite Maskull to the planet Tormance, a satellite of the double star Arcturus. He tells him that 'Surtur' has already gone on ahead, and they are to follow him. Now Surtur, we learn at the end of the book, is Krag's alter ego, just as Nightspore is Maskull's. He is a symbol of pain, by choosing which men can release themselves from the sweet and sticky nets of Crystalman.

Maskull and Nightspore go to an observatory in Scotland, from which they are to set out to Arcturus. They visit a chasm overlooking the sea called the Gap of Sorgie (Care?), and there Maskull hears mysterious drum-beats, which he will continue to hear throughout the book. They finally turn out to be the beating of his own heart. It is Surtur beating this mysterious drum, we are told. After this episode Maskull goes into a tower, from the top of which they are to embark for Arcturus; but as soon as he has gone up a few steps, the gravity becomes so enormous that he cannot go farther – his body becomes too heavy. However, he hears a voice warning him against Nightspore, and telling him that he will die on Arcturus. Nightspore later confirms that Maskull will die there, but

19 Looking recently at a huge German *Atlas der Greichlichen Medizin* full of pictures of battered corpses, I was struck by the sense that such pictures seem to be a flat contradiction of all human endeavour and idealism – like pricked balloons, that have become so devoid of the festive spirit. Possibly some such experience led to Lindsay's use of the 'Crystalman grin'.

Maskull does not seem perturbed. Finally Krag appears, slashes Maskull's arm and spits on it to prepare him for the gravity of Arcturus. Then they climb the tower – Maskull no longer feels himself too heavy – and set off in a crystal spaceship, driven by some curious form of light. When Maskull awakens he is on Arcturus, lying alone in the desert.

Maskull arrives on Arcturus at the beginning of the sixth chapter of the book (page 44 in the Gollancz edition). From this point onward, it is impossible to doubt that one is in the hands of a storyteller of genius and astonishing imaginative power. But the chief reason for the book's neglect is certainly the length of these opening chapters and their somewhat undistinguished nature. Lindsay is not at his best when his scene is set on earth. I would therefore advise readers coming to it for the first time to race through these early chapters, and start reading in earnest from the arrival on Arcturus.

Now Lindsay's central intention begins to emerge into the daylight. It is his constant aim to show that everything on Arcturus is a disguised creation of the devil, and this must be grasped if the book is to be understood. Without understanding this, the book is somewhat bewildering; for the first person Maskull meets on Arcturus is a delightful girl called Joiwind, who seems to be overflowing with love. Realizing that Maskull is faint because his blood is heavy and impure, she cuts her arm and his own, places the mouths of the wounds together, and allows her own blood to flow into him, so that he feels renewed while she is exhausted and depressed. She tells him that she and her husband live on water – they will not even eat vegetables because these are living creatures; but the water has an extraordinary electric quality, and, she says, 'As one can really live on anything, water does very well'. This chapter has an air of joy and freshness that is reminiscent of Blake's early poem, *The Book of Thel*. Reading it for the first time, one naturally assumes that Lindsay is creating a picture of a creature and a way of life of which he entirely approves. But it is not so. Joiwind tells Maskull that Krag is the author of evil and misery, whom earth-people call the devil, revealing that she does not know the fundamental truth of Crystalman's world. She loves this world, and feels that love is the highest thing in the universe. Lindsay does not agree with her. Joiwind takes Maskull to meet her husband. He is a poet and a mystic. When they climb a mountain he is so overwhelmed by its beauty that he goes into strange convulsions, and a crystal egg falls out of his mouth. Maskull remarks that on earth this is what happens to poets. Joiwind's husband says that the egg is of no value, and throws it away. He tells interesting stories of his youth, and it is obvious that, like his wife, he is a lover of the universe, completely unselfish. Yet he describes a conversation with a wise man on the top of a precipice; the wise man tells him that behind Crystalman's world there is yet another world whose great principle is not love. He ends by saying, 'You will never rise above mysticism', and jumps into the depths, revealing his own freedom from Crystalman's snares. Joiwind's husband is unable to understand this – and so, at this early point, is Maskull. Lindsay is rejecting both love and mysticism as the 'answer' to the mystery of being; both are snares. The remark that seems to have caused the wise man to leap to his death was, 'Wisdom is mystery'. It will be remembered that Krag had strangled the 'mysterious' young man in the first chapter, and revealed that 'mystery' is only another of Crystalman's masks. Lindsay also reveals Joiwind's fundamental mistakenness when he makes her declare that Surtur is the same as Crystalman, and both are identical with 'Shaping', the architect who made the world and loves all his creation. Throughout *Arcturus*, Shaping is used as a synonym for Crystalman. In other words, Lindsay declares that this world was not created by 'God', but by a demon whose aspects are love and pleasure. This will become clearer later in the book.

It seems, then, that Joiwind and her husband Panawe (the name is obviously symbolic) represent the first illusions that almost ensnare Maskull. But he goes on from them, and has a vision in which he sees Surtur, who tells him that he has been called to this planet to serve him. Surtur offers to answer any questions, but at this stage Maskull does not know the right questions to ask. Surtur vanishes into the sky. It is not clear whether Lindsay intended Surtur to be genuine, or whether he is a counterfeit of Crystalman, demanding from Maskull the universal love and service that God demands of men in the Christian religion. Probably he is intended to be genuine, calling on Maskull to help him in the fight against Shaping and his world. In other words, it will be Maskull's task to encounter all the various delusions of Shaping, and to cast them off one by one. This certainly seems to describe roughly the plan of the book.[20]

Maskull almost immediately meets a woman called Oceaxe, who is quite unlike Joiwind – a savage, sensual creature, something of a vampire. While with Joiwind, Maskull had developed various organs that enabled him to feel universal love and sympathy. At the suggestion of Oceaxe, he destroys these by burning them, and his organ of sympathy changes to a kind of eye called a 'sorb', and becomes now an instrument of will. It causes him to see 'everything as an object of importance or non-importance according to his own needs' – in other words, he has become more of a typical human being. Oceaxe persuades him to eat fish, which she kills by concentrating her will on them through her 'sorb'. She mentions to Maskull that she has often 'absorbed' men (presumably this is what the word 'sorb' is derived from). By this, we presume that she means she has used them solely to give herself a sense of satisfied will-power and vanity – like so many 'vampire women'.

There now follow some of the most fascinating episodes in the book, which somehow produce a tremendous effect of momentousness, even though their meaning is not clear. One gathers that Oceaxe belongs to a world of violence and extreme passions – a completely primitive world. When he asks why the scenery has so few curves, she explains that huge tracts of land are always rising or subsiding; nature here is abrupt and powerful. In this land, will-power counts for everything. They walk up a river against the current, and he is exalted by

20 Mr Visiak points out to me that Surtur is intended to be a fake in this scene.

the pressure against him. Oceaxe calls up some monstrous reptilian birds, and as they fly towards the two human beings, Maskull feels himself nailed to the rock by their will-power. They are coming, Oceaxe explains, to suck their blood and eat them. But as the great reptiles come nearer, Oceaxe concentrates her will and strikes two of them dead; the third lands on the rock tamely, and carries them off through the air, obedient to her stronger will. As they fly, huge tracts of country rise suddenly beneath them, or fall into tremendous depths with a crash. Oceaxe mentions that they are going to see her lover, and that Maskull will have to kill him or be killed by him. Maskull says he has no intention of accepting either alternative, but she tells him he will be unable to help himself. Finally they arrive on a mountaintop and see two figures. One is a boy, slight and slim, the other a powerful muscular creature who is standing above the boy. One assumes that the muscular creature is Oceaxe's lover, but this is another of Lindsay's surprises. The boy is forcing the man to stand there, using his will-power to turn him into a tree. The next day, he says, the man's feet will turn into roots and his arms into branches. Maskull is horrified, and believes the boy is joking, but soon the boy – Oceaxe's lover – turns the will-power of his sorb on Maskull, and a battle of wills commences. Maskull wins, and twists the boy's head round, breaking his neck. Immediately, the boy's face takes on the idiot Crystalman grin.

In these chapters Lindsay seems to be writing with pure inspiration; the power of the writing is extraordinary; it is science fiction increased to the nth power.

Anyone who doubts that *Arcturus* is a masterpiece should begin by reading these chapters (eight and nine). It seems possible that in Oceaxe and her lover Lindsay is symbolizing the upper classes, who turn men into beasts of burden without a second thought; but this is irrelevant; the writing gains nothing by this kind of conscious interpretation.

Another woman now appears, Tydomin, who was also a mistress of the dead Crimtyphon. She quickly kills Oceaxe by directing her to walk over a cliff, and somehow making Oceaxe believe that the cliff is a road off the mountain-top. Maskull looks on in amazement. Then Tydomin asks him to come with her and help her to bury her dead lover; so they go off, Maskull carrying Crimtyphon's corpse. Soon they meet Joiwind's brother, and have a conversation. But when Joiwind's brother refuses to declare that he will keep silent about the murder that Maskull has committed, Maskull seizes him in his arms and 'absorbs' him. 'A feeling of wild, sweet delight immediately passed through him. Then, for the first time, he comprehended the triumphant joys of 'absorbing'. It satisfied the hunger of the will, exactly as food satisfies the hunger of the body.'

Tydomin now persuades Maskull to give up his body to her, and allow her to live in it; Maskull himself will become a disembodied spirit. Surprisingly, Maskull agrees. We presume that Tydomin is using on him the same strange arts of hypnotic persuasion by which she made Oceaxe walk over the cliff. They go into a cave, and Maskull lies down and goes into a trance. Now a strange thing happens. He finds himself on earth again, in the seance that has already been described in Chapter One. But now Maskull himself is the mysterious youth who was conjured up by the medium. Krag enters, and kills 'Maskull' by twisting his neck. Maskull awakes in the cave with Tydomin, and tells her that he is now properly awake, and that she must die. He has seen through the illusion of self-sacrifice that she was using to get him to give up his body to her; his encounter with Krag has brought him to his senses. This kind of noble self-sacrifice is another illusion of Crystalman. They walk on to a volcanic lake, where Tydomin throws the body of her dead lover; but as she prepares to die at Maskull's hands, Maskull sees a vision of Joiwind and changes his mind. They walk on together.

In the next episode Lindsay finally lays his cards on the table. They meet an impressive and powerful stranger called Spadevil, who is a kind of Old Testament prophet. Spadevil persuades Maskull to allow him to transform his sorb – the organ of his will – into twin 'probes', which will give him a vision of the moral law of the world. This moral law amounts to duty.

Spadevil explains that he comes from a country called Sant, where the men have seen through the illusions of Crystalman's world, and prefer pain to pleasure. No women are allowed there. The religion of Sant (presumably meaning 'health') seems to be pure Calvinism, or perhaps Buddhism; the men of Sant have realized that the pleasures of the world are torments in disguise, and have renounced them. But Spadevil has seen deeper still, he claims. In denouncing pleasure, the men of Sant are still giving themselves up to the pleasure of pride. Therefore a new moral order is necessary; the men of Sant must cease actively to condemn pleasure; they must keep their eyes fixed solely on duty, in order to avoid pride.

Both Tydomin and Maskull feel that Spadevil is right. Spadevil tells them to follow him to Sant. Tydomin can now be admitted, for under the new law of duty the old hatred of women will vanish. Finally they arrive in Sant, and immediately meet Catice, one of its wise men. Spadevil tells him about his new moral law of duty. Catice is puzzled. He himself has only one probe on his forehead. He proposes to Maskull that he should destroy one of Maskull's two probes; then Maskull will be in a position to say which is correct – the new law or the old one. Maskull submits, and Catice destroys his probe with a stone. Immediately, Maskull rejects Spadevil. 'At this moment, the world with its sweetness seems to me a sort of charnel house'. He suddenly feels that all that matters is to fight his own pleasure-loving nature, and Spadevil seems to be a weak and confused intellect, not a prophet. Spadevil accepts Catice's decision that he shall be stoned to death (for neither of them cares for life). Maskull is chosen to be the instrument. He kills Spadevil – rather against his will – with a huge stone, crushing his face (so that Lindsay manages to avoid stating whether Spadevil's dead face turns into the Crystalman grin). He then kills the self-sacrificing Tydomin, and cradles her head until she dies. Her face turns into the Crystalman grin, leaving no doubt whatever that noble self-sacrifice is only another of Crystalman's illusions.

This episode at last reveals Lindsay's central contention: that all pleasure is evil, that it only entangles men deeper in illusion, and takes them further from ultimate reality. And yet as an ironical footnote to this episode, Catice adds that he must go away and think about Spadevil's ideas, for probably he was right about pride being another mask of Crystalman. Maskull is horrified, but Catice tells him to regret nothing, but to go on.

The next morning Maskull meets a man called Dreamsinter in a forest, and when he says that Surtur brought him from earth, Dreamsinter contradicts him: 'Not you, but Nightspore' (Maskull's visionary *alter ego* – although Lindsay has not yet revealed this to the reader). Maskull asks why he has been brought to Arcturus, and Dreamsinter answers: 'To steal Muspel-fire, to give a deeper life to men'. (Earlier in the book, Panawe had told Maskull that he was some sort of reincarnation of Prometheus.)

At last Lindsay is beginning to state his meanings unequivocally, and the confusions of the earlier part of the book are vanishing. Muspel is Lindsay's name for the ultimate reality, the 'other world' which is completely different from Shaping's world of pleasure. Maskull is perhaps a kind of Everyman, perhaps a symbol of the poet. *But he does not know his own identity*, does not realize that he is really Nightspore, the visionary and seeker, and does not know that he is on earth solely to destroy the illusions of pleasure, and bring 'Muspel-fire' to men. But, slowly, he is learning.

After the meeting with Dreamsinter, Maskull has a vision in which he sees himself, Nightspore, and Krag marching through the forest to the sound of Surtur's drum-beats. (This vision is induced by a bitter and unpleasant fruit offered him by Dreamsinter – perhaps self-knowledge.) In his vision he sees himself being stabbed in the back by Krag. Nightspore marches on alone, unmoved. Now Lindsay's imagery becomes clearer. Maskull is so called because he is man's outer self – his mask, his body; the inner self is a creature of darkness, of rejection of the daylight world and its values, a spore of night. Maskull must die, and must be indifferent to his own death, for it is not true death; his real self marches on, unaffected.

In the next chapter Maskull arrives on the shore of a strange sea and meets a fisherman, Polecrab, and his wife Gleamiel. The fisherman gives him a meal, and also gives him a little of his wisdom. He confirms that this world is created by Shaping, but that men strive to get beyond to the other world of Muspel. But they are enmeshed in delusions and go in the wrong direction, finding themselves back in the very world they want to escape. Maskull reflects on the fundamental paradox of which every poet is aware: that this world looks real, in fact *is* obviously real – and yet, in a deeper sense, is false. And in a single sentence Lindsay states the essence of phenomenology: 'We are each of us living in a false private world of our own, a world of dreams and appetites and distorted perceptions'. Polecrab's wife is yet another of Lindsay's symbols of female self-delusion and entanglement in Crystalman's illusions. Across the sea is Swaylone's Island, from which emanates beautiful, soul-convulsing music which is said to be fatal to anyone who hears it at close quarters. Gleamiel is determined to cross to Swaylone's Island with Maskull and hear this music, even if it destroys her. Her husband tries to dissuade her, but to no purpose. Finally Maskull and Gleamiel set out for the island.

Here follows another of Lindsay's curious symbolic episodes that baffles the questioning intelligence and yet seems full of imaginative significance. On the island they find a small lake of great clarity; when Maskull tries to walk on it, he receives a powerful electric shock that hurls him back on to the land. At the side of this lake they find Earthrid, the present 'musician', fast asleep. The lake itself is his musical instrument. Earthrid wakes up and explains to them something of his principle of aesthetics. He is obviously another symbol of the artist. His face is weak and pale, and he has an unpleasant smell; when he wakes up, he proceeds to eat earth. And yet he professes to understand the underlying principles of beauty and pain. He explains how this lake once gave off only sweet and beautiful tones, until Krag interfered and made the first musician, Swaylone, play ugly discords. This broke the instrument, so that now it will only play a strange music, a compound of pain and beauty.

Earthrid begs them to go away, for he must now play his instrument. They refuse, and Earthrid plays. Maskull feels tremendous pain, which soon passes, but Gleamiel is killed immediately. Maskull then drags Earthrid away from the lake, and proposes to play himself. Earthrid is terrified, and tells him he will smash the instrument. Nevertheless, Maskull plays. He imitates Earthrid's posture, placing one foot on the lake and one hand on the ground (the artist with one foot in the world of spirit, but one hand on the earth), and then allows his subconscious ideas to flow into the lake, which somehow endows his unconscious mind with its electric vitality. Tremendous exhilaration possesses him; he plays wildly and powerfully, causes the hills to rip apart, tearing Earthrid into two, and finally causing the lake itself to drain away into a chasm that opens up underneath it. Then Maskull leaves Swaylone's Island, and the body of Gleamiel – with the vulgar Crystalman grin on her features. It was somehow inevitable that Maskull should have destroyed Earthrid's 'harp'; the power that inspires him is more powerful than any aesthetic impulse.

One is now two-thirds of the way through the book, and the power of Lindsay's imagination shows no sign of flagging; on the contrary, it seems to increase. The reader begins to wonder how Lindsay can continue at this level of invention. The answer becomes apparent only on looking back on the book. This is not the simple inventiveness often displayed in science fiction; it is a function of Lindsay's intense *conviction*, his certainty of what he has to say.

Maskull finds a tree that is floating past in the sea, and rides on it. (This sea, by the way, has a strange quality: it possesses different densities in different parts, so that Maskull cannot swim in it.) His 'boat' finally brings him to a land called Matterplay (the home of Joiwind's brother, whom he murdered). It is here that Lindsay begins to expose his philosophy nakedly; in fact from now until the end of the book the note of conviction grows stronger.

Maskull walks up a stream which seethes with life: the ground is covered with thousands of different life-forms. Matterplay seems a country where, as Blake says, 'life delights in life'. As in a tropical forest, all kinds of trees and creepers fight for possession of the shore, so that Maskull is obliged to stay in the stream. The reader soon begins to suspect that this stream is supposed to symbolize the Life-Force itself. 'A delightful, spring-like sense of rising sap, of quickening pulses – of love, adventure, mystery, beauty, femininity – took possession of his being'. A draught of the strange, bubbling water gives him 'inner vision', so that he can see into all these creatures. This chapter of the book seems almost pure Blake. Maskull picks up a fruit, and sees that inside it there is a fully formed young tree; he throws it up the current; by the time it comes back to him, it has sprouted six rudimentary legs and is swimming. But where Blake would have felt nothing but delight, 'Maskull felt deeply cynical and depressed'. He is even more astonished as he notices that these strange plant-animals seem to be appearing abruptly out of empty space – spontaneous creation. Then his forehead sprouts several new eyes, and he sees the reason for this. The brook is giving off green sparks as it flows along – life itself. The sky is filled with masses of cloud, and the clouds try to capture the green sparks, which seek to escape upward. If the clouds succeed in catching a spark, they imprison it, and a 'plant-animal' suddenly materializes in space. Maskull is awestruck, and reflects: 'That was like the birth of a thought, but who was the thinker? Some great Living Mind is at work on this spot... It would be ridiculous to go on to other riddles until I have solved these.' But Lindsay is playing his usual double game, and Maskull is once again the dupe of his enthusiasm. This world of seething life is only another of Crystalman's playthings. Maskull discovers this when he meets a strange, ancient creature called a phaen, neither male nor female, for whom Lindsay coins the pronoun 'ae' (instead of he or she – he does not explain why 'it' will not suffice). The phaen explains that it is the last of an ancient race, and that it has spent all its long life trying to get to the source of this stream, the home of 'Faceny', which is yet another name for God the creator – Crystalman, Shaping. The phaen also explains about the stream – how the number of life-forms diminishes as they get closer to its source because matter is not powerful enough to hold the sparks when they are at full strength. In fact, some enormous creature forms in front of Maskull's eyes and explodes immediately, the life escaping. Lindsay's meaning is clear. Man is a vital spark imprisoned in matter, and it is only the weakness of his spark that prevents him from escaping. This idea is closely related to the Platonic doctrine that the philosopher spends his life trying to escape the flesh that imprisons him, and that therefore death is a consummation. Lindsay does not bother to explain about death, but one presumes that the spark simply decays until it vanishes. The phaen also explains why the sea has different densities and keeps rising into water spouts; it is a continuation of this river of life, and the water there does not even possess the rudimentary power to organize itself into shapes; it can only seethe with frustration.

The phaen asks Maskull to use his 'luck' to enable it to find a way into the nether-world which is the source of the stream, where Faceny dwells. Maskull asks why it wants to find Faceny; the phaen replies that it does not know; it feels only the longing of the lover for the beloved. Men, being separated from the female, identify this longing for women with love. Phaens have achieved what men strive for (again, echoes of Plato – this time of the speech of Aristophanes in the *Symposium*), and are simultaneously male and female; they know that their longing does not end there, but still goes on; it is a longing for the source of all life.

Maskull agrees to help the phaen. Sure enough, his luck holds, and they stumble on an entrance into the side of the mountain from which the stream issues. They find themselves in a kind of lunar landscape lit by cold light; the atmosphere is solemn, religious, and tranquil, the air of a cathedral. The phaen dies almost immediately, and vanishes. A man called Corpang now appears, and tells Maskull that he cannot understand why phaens all want to come there to die. 'They regard themselves as the favoured children of Faceny', he remarks cynically. Corpang seems to symbolize the saint and ascetic. (The phaen was perhaps a symbol of the god-intoxicated saint of the Ramakrishna type.) Corpang's face is noble yet with a touch of coarseness, of pride in his own sanctity. That he is intended to represent Christian saints is soon apparent, as he speaks of a Three in One and One in Three. There are three worlds, he explains: of existence, of love, and of feeling (religious or sacred feeling seems to be meant); these are, so to speak, the length, breadth, and depth of the spirit world. Corpang hopes to draw near to the God of the third world, whom he calls Thire. (Faceny – the phaen's God – is merely the God of existence, the first world.)

Now comes one of the most impressive and powerful episodes in the book. They come to three great colossi; they kneel, and soon the first one glows with a kind of rosy dawn-light, and seems to become a beautiful youth. This is Faceny, the God of existence, and Maskull feels overwhelmed with the poetry and mystery of life. The statue fades into darkness, and the second one emerges; this time the light is so bright that Maskull can distinguish nothing, but he feels purified, freed of his selfhood, and a 'passionate and nearly savage mental state of pity and distress. He felt a tormenting desire to *serve*'. This is the God of the Christian mystics, and of George Herbert and Simone Weil. This fades away too, and a voice speaks to Maskull out of the darkness telling him he is to die. The voice adds: 'You have despised life. Do you really imagine that this mighty world has no meaning, and that life is a joke?' Maskull faints, so he does not see the third statue until it is fading.

But now Lindsay produces a typical masterstroke. While Maskull is still overwhelmed with the truth and depth of his vision, a strange light begins to shine – Muspel-fire, that Maskull has come to Arcturus to seek. As soon as it shines on the three colossi, their faces change into the grinning Crystalman mask. Corpang is horrified as he realizes that he has been duped all his life. Maskull states the moral of this transformation, which is the central theme of the book: 'It must mean that life is wrong, and the creator of life too, whether he is one person or three'. Christianity, with its belief that God looked at the world and found it good, is decisively rejected. 'Surtur's world, or Muspel is the original of which this world is a distorted copy. Crystalman is life, but Surtur is other than life.' So much for Joiwind's belief that Surtur and Crystalman are one.

The last stage of the journey is now approaching. Maskull knows he has not much longer to live. Their final objective is the mountain Adage in the country of Lichstorm. Soon a man called Haunte, a hunter, floats through the air in a sort of aerial boat, and Maskull and Corpang climb in for the trip to Lichstorm. Haunte is a disagreeable looking man, a kind of satyr. He explains that in Lichstorm male and female are always in bitter conflict – not as on earth, where man always contains a little of woman and vice versa. He explains that this is the secret of his boat, for gravity is the urge of male objects to return to the female earth, and he possesses two 'male stones' who completely reject the female, and keep the boat in the air. These male stones are Haunte's protection against the sex-mad atmosphere of Lichstorm. When they arrive in his cave, half-way up a mountain, he gives them coarse food and drink – a powerful spirit which releases Maskull's animal lust. Haunte tells him, grinning, that he will now be tormented unbearably by the sexual atmosphere. But in a scuffle between Corpang and Haunte (when Corpang – a typical Christian teetotaller – pours away all Haunte's alcohol) Maskull throws the 'male stones' out of the cave, and they sink into the chasm below. (Lindsay forgets that he had explained they were invulnerable to gravity.) Haunte will now have to share the torments to which he has light-heartedly condemned Maskull. The consequence is that Haunte's 'jeering malevolence… vanished completely. He looked a sick man, yet somehow his face had become nobler.'

They now go out together to search for Sullenbode, a strange woman who is the female principle that causes so much lust and torment in Lichstorm. On the way, Maskull experiences awful torments and imagines he is about to die; suddenly the torments vanish and he experiences 'a… heart-breaking joy he had never experienced before in all his life'. He is able to tell Haunte that he has passed through torture to love, and that this should be the true end of the torments of lust. 'You men of Lichstorm don't go far enough. You stop at the pangs, without realizing that they are birth pangs.'

They find Sullenbode under a tree. She is intensely feminine, yet her face seems only half-formed and 'scarcely human'. Yet when Haunte kisses her, her features suddenly emerge. But the second time Haunte kisses her, he falls backwards as if he has touched an electric cable, his head split open. Now Maskull decides he must kiss her, even if he meets the same fate as Haunte. But although the shock of it makes him lose his senses, he is not killed, and when he opens his eyes again Sullenbode has been permanently transformed; Maskull's maleness has called her from her partial existence into full consciousness. To Corpang's great disgust, she tells Maskull that she will go with him wherever he goes, and that when he ceases to love her she will die. All the women in Lindsay's book seem to have the same characteristics – passion, self-sacrifice, softness; yet all are victims of the delusions of Crystalman.

The going becomes extremely difficult as they climb upwards through mud. (Is it significant that they now clamber through mud, as soon as Maskull has let his emotions become involved with a woman?) Finally, Corpang leaves them alone – perhaps being tactful. Ahead of them are the cliffs of Barey, Maskull's goal. And now Maskull suddenly hears Surtur's drum-beats with deafening volume, and sees the Muspel-light again; he stands there, transfixed, while Sullenbode tries to attract his attention by kissing him passionately. When she fails, she turns and walks away. He emerges from his trance and follows her, but she collapses and dies. The emotional life that Maskull had given her has been destroyed by his vision of his real purpose. Inevitably her face becomes a Crystalman mask after death, but there is so much mud on her that Maskull cannot see it, and 'she had never appeared so beautiful to him as at that moment'. Lindsay's purpose has wavered for a moment; the philosopher with a hammer relents, perhaps out of a desire not to spoil the artistic effect.

The last stage of the journey has arrived, and once again Maskull meets Krag. The reader is still unaware that Krag is another name for Surtur – this is only revealed in the last sentences of the book – or that Nightspore and Maskull are one, so there is a certain effect of tension, as in a detective story. One wonders how soon Krag is going to betray Maskull and murder him. Krag is at his most malicious and cynical, and seems to think that Maskull's long pilgrimage is a joke. He says, 'Perhaps Crystalman will make one more attempt on you', and in fact this is what happens. They meet a man called Gangnet, another poet and dreamer, and for a moment it seems that he is the man who has been waiting for Maskull all the time. He tells Maskull that he reveals his own nobility in mourning for a noble woman, and that Crystalman is not the devil, but love and beauty. 'If Sullenbode can exist, the world cannot be a bad place.' Krag seems to become more and more obviously a malicious liar; he 'seemed to grow sallower and more repulsive every minute'. Maskull loses his temper with him and pushes him at one point; Gangnet advises him to ignore Krag because this is the only way to force him to loose his hold. They now embark on a lake for the last stage of the journey. At this point there is a rather curious passage between Krag and Gangnet. Krag reveals that they have met before somewhere, when Gangnet paid him a visit, and adds that Gangnet is a common thief. It may be that Lindsay means to identify Maskull with Adam, Gangnet with Eve (he is described as looking oddly feminine, and Maskull has a strong sensation of having known him before), and Krag with the wise serpent. If so, why should Krag accuse Gangnet of being a thief, since he tempted her to steal the apple?

Gangnet is certainly Maskull's last temptation. 'His dark hair curled down to his neck, his brow was wide, lofty and noble, and there was an air of serious sweetness about the whole man which was strangely appealing to the feelings.' Precisely – to the feelings – the realm of Crystalman. A moment later Lindsay actually identifies Gangnet with Crystalman himself. As the second sun rises (Arcturus is, of course, a double star) Maskull has a kind of revelation, a feeling that he is nothing. 'I have lost my will... I feel as if some foul tumour had been scraped away, leaving me clean and free.' But this is only another illusion, which is proved when Gangnet agrees enthusiastically, 'Yes, you are nothing'. This is the saint's delusion – that his will is evil, that he must completely abandon himself. But almost immediately this sun is extinguished by Muspel-fire, which causes Gangnet – now seen to be Crystalman – to writhe in pain until he vanishes; his face changes into the slobbering, grinning mask. Maskull sees that the drum-beats of Surtur are actually Krag beating on a blood-red spot with a huge hammer, and Krag tells him that the blood-red spot is his own heart. Maskull knows now that he is dying. As he does so he asks, 'Where is Nightspore?' and Krag tells him, 'You are Nightspore.' Maskull dies, and Nightspore immediately appears in his place. Nightspore asks, 'Why was all this necessary?' Krag answers, 'Ask Crystalman. His world is no joke. He has a strong clutch, but I have a stronger. Maskull was his, but Nightspore is mine.'

They now come to an entrance in a huge, dark cliff, and Maskull-Nightspore knows that he is to be reborn, even though he shudders at the idea. He asks, 'Shall I remember?' and Krag answers, 'Yes, you'll remember' – even when born into the world in a new body'. Nightspore goes through the door and finds himself in a tower. This seems to be some kind of repetition of the tower he tried to climb in Scotland before his first 'birth' on to Arcturus. His body grows heavier as he tries to climb. He is in Muspel itself, and will see a vision of Crystalman's world as it really is. At the first two windows in his ascent he sees nothing, but hears a great driving rhythm like a machine, which is also a kind of mocking laughter. This is the throb of life itself. At subsequent windows he becomes more aware of the meaning of what he is seeing, and the whole plan of the book becomes clear. A light streams from Muspel, but it encounters the vast shadow-form of Crystalman (which is also light – since Crystalman is Lucifer). The green Muspel-light is split by Crystalman's shadow into two different kinds of energy. One is the green sparks of life – now shattered and fragmented – and the other stream is a kind of degraded life, 'fouled and softened by the horrible sweetness of the host'; this stream breaks into small whirls which are individuals, whirls of living will. The green sparks are caught up by these whirls as they try to fight their way back to Muspel. The living wills circulate in a kind of waltz rhythm:

> Sometimes the green sparks were strong enough for a moment to move a little way in the direction of Muspel; the whirls would then accept the movement, not only without demur, but with pride and pleasure, *as if it were their own handiwork* [my italics], but they never saw beyond the Shadow, they thought they were travelling towards it. The instant the direct movement wearied them, as contrary to their whirling nature, they fell again to killing, dancing and loving.

And finally:

> The truth forced itself on him in all its cold brutal reality. Muspel was no all-powerful Universe, tolerating from pure indifference the existence side by side with it of another false world, which had no right to be. Muspel was fighting for its life, against all that is most shameful and frightful – against sin masquerading as eternal beauty, against baseness masquerading as nature, against the Devil masquerading as God.

Nightspore knows that it is his destiny to help Krag in the great fight against Crystalman. When he descends again he says, 'The struggle is hopeless'. But Krag reassures him, 'I am the stronger and the mightier'. And Krag reveals that he is also Surtur, and that his name on earth is Pain. Here the book ends.

The reader lays down the book feeling dizzy and overwhelmed. It is impossible to doubt that Lindsay is a man of astonishing genius. Whether his vision is finally correct or not, he has seen very deep, deeper in some respects than Blake or Milton. The book is a gigantic 'transvaluation of values'. The above account of it will have conveyed some of its tremendous sweep, but given no idea of the imaginative vitality of the writing in which everything is as clear cut and distinct as in a painting.

How, then, has a masterpiece of this kind managed to remain unknown for so long? This is impossible to say. Blake's works were almost unknown in his own time, and have become fashionable only in the last century – Swinburne was among the first to recognize their genius. *Arcturus* makes a bad first impression, with the clumsy writing of its early chapters and its uncouth nomenclature. As D. H. Lawrence said of Melville, you feel as if he is trying to put something over on you. Names like Joiwind, Panawe, Oceaxe, Spadevil, are somehow oddly irritating on first acquaintance; they seem to aim at strangeness and not quite succeed; there is a clumsy, amateurish ring about them, as if the author is an enthusiast without any real sense of the English language. Still, as with *Moby Dick*, the irritating characteristics are only superficial; they are soon forgotten as one becomes absorbed in the story.

What of the book's deeper message? This is a different matter. Lindsay's genius is undeniable, but he is eventually a kind of Manichee, dividing the world neatly into good and evil. When one considers his 'explanation' in the final chapter of the novel, it is seen to explain nothing in a final sense. Who is Crystalman? How did he come to exist in Muspel's universe?

It seems that Lindsay was a man of powerful intuitions, a visionary who tried always to penetrate beneath appearances. *Arcturus* makes the nature of his intuitions very clear. I have several times mentioned Nietzsche's name in this chapter, and this huge task of 'transvaluing values' certainly has no modern counterpart outside Nietzsche's work. Like Nietzsche, Lindsay is obviously obsessed by the 'human, all too human' nature of human beings. The most obvious thing about human beings is that they have many instinctive values that turn out to be false on examination. A hungry man feels that food is the highest good; but if he overeats he feels sick and wonders how he could ever have had such an absurd notion. But all these shifting values of human beings can be summarized in one phrase: what I have called 'the St Neot margin', the indifference threshold.[21] Men are always being stimulated by pain and inconvenience into apparent certainty about what is good and what is bad; but much happiness quickly produces boredom and sometimes a paradoxical desire for pain, or even for self-destruction. They seem to know what they do not want far more deeply than they ever know what they do, and this produces the suspicion that men are mere machines, kept going by negative stimuli but incapable of positive purpose. They easily lose all sense of direction, and so may be destroyed by a few difficulties which demoralize them. They are immensely subject to self-pity, and for the most part lack any kind of self-discipline. They are fundamentally creatures of delusions.

But it is too easy to arrive at such a pessimistic estimate of human beings, and this kind of extreme pessimism may be no more than a sign of a weak but sensitive nature

21 See my *Beyond the Outsider*.

which derives a kind of strength from the contemplation of such a vision. It is the same kind of mechanism that produces religious cranks – almost invariably social misfits – who look forward eagerly to the end of the world at a definite date in the near future. It is difficult to see how a nature like Lindsay's could avoid such pitfalls; he was obviously highly intelligent and sensitive, and yet is still so totally unknown that it seems obvious that he made no kind of a mark as an artist or writer. Such neglect is enough to predispose anybody to extremism.

The sign of such natures is usually a tendency to over-simplification and a kind of moral Calvinism. Ayn Rand is obviously another such. Yet another interesting example is the little-known contemporary writer Michael Byrom, the author of *Evolution for Beginners*,[22] whose intelligent evolutionism forms a strange contrast to his total world-rejection. Blake remarks, 'Angels like to think of themselves as the only-wise', and certainly there is a strong element of this in David Lindsay and Ayn Rand – always the sign of the lonely enthusiast.

The obvious objection to David Lindsay's universe, as I have said, is its unexplained dualism of good and evil. The evolutionist views of Shaw or Teilhard de Chardin see evil as one of the unfortunate consequences of 'complexification'. Evil is simply power out of control. For a man who must spend his life travelling long distances a powerful car is obviously a useful asset; but its possibilities for evil are obviously greater than those of a bicycle. This

22 Some of whose characteristics I introduced into the portrait of Jeremy Wolfe in my novel *The World of Violence*. London: Victor Gollancz, 1963. [Reprinted by Valancourt Books, 2013. Ed.]

view sees the universe as basically good, as a struggle between spirit and matter. There is no 'evil spirit'. Lindsay's view complicates the matter needlessly. Crystalman is a kind of evil spirit. What is more, Lindsay's view does not explain matter. One might assume that when the Muspel-rays are broken up by Crystalman they would divide into spirit and matter, the matter attempting to imprison spirit. Instead, Lindsay declares that they divide into 'life-sparks' and some unspecified energy that has been 'fouled and softened'; this energy, Lindsay says, is individual wills. But in the Matterplay chapter it seemed that individual wills were the consequence of life-sparks being trapped in cloud matter. But even in this chapter the cloud matter seems to have a will of its own, and actively to set out to entrap the life-sparks. So where does matter come in, and how does the cloud come to be alive?

But perhaps the chief objection to Lindsay's universe is that he insists that love, beauty, nobility, and the rest all belong to the world of Crystalman, and so are somehow evil in themselves. Lindsay gives the impression of a man who has struggled for a long time against his own nature, like the ancient ascetics, trying to root out pride, lust, and love of pleasure, always being overtaken by self-disgust so that judgments that appear true at one moment become untrue the next. Finally, the simplest solution is to reject *everything* of this world, and posit the other Muspel-world which apparently has nothing whatever in common with this one, a place rather like Plato's world of ideas. This gives a splendid excuse for an attitude of universal superiority, rather like the tendency of

Jehovah's Witnesses to declare that all other religions are the creations of Antichrist. *A Voyage to Arcturus* gives one the impression that Lindsay has studied a great deal on the subject of religion; has swallowed the religion of the aesthetes, then rejected it for mysticism, then swallowed in turn Blake, Ramakrishna, and St John of the Cross. None gives him the satisfaction he craves, so he writes a book that considers them one by one, and rejects them as inventions of Antichrist. In the final analysis, *A Voyage to Arcturus* is a negative work, although its sheer imaginative vitality makes this a less serious charge than would be the case with a lesser work. Where Lindsay succeeds triumphantly is in finding images and symbols that go to the heart of the complex tangle of human existence. The most familiar human experience is of conflict of values; we want several things at the same time, or completely change our ideas of what we want from day to day. This is really Lindsay's central subject. Visiak declares in his introduction that one reader said *Arcturus* plunged him into a state of 'spiritual terror'. This is understandable, (although it is probable that the reader was only half aware of what Lindsay is getting at, which is not so terrifying.) Whether one agrees with its basic philosophy or not, it has the power of destroying our usual attitude to existence – of taking life for granted – and making human life seem an extraordinary spiritual adventure. Inevitably, as the feeling of everyday security vanishes, different readers will experience varying sensations depending on their underlying assumptions about life. The drug mescalin has this same curious effect;[23] conscious defences are removed; one's inner urges and fears gain the same kind of freedom they have in dreams, and the effect can be one of spiritual vertigo, as if one were on some kind of scenic railway at a fairground, swooping from heights to depths without warning. A work of art must possess a certain kind of greatness, although not necessarily of the highest order, to produce such an effect.

In retrospect, one regrets Lindsay's manicheism, which seems to be an offshoot of puritanism. Joiwind and Panawe make an impression of genuine goodness; why, then, should Lindsay regard them as completely in Crystalman's power? If they knew about 'Muspel', would they not reject Crystalman's illusions? In other words, is not their kind of goodness important and desirable? Besides, Lindsay puts his finger on the real problem of human existence in that passage about the human tendency to live enmeshed in personal dreams and delusions. Phenomenology is an attempt to investigate these dreams and delusions scientifically, and no phenomenologist can accept Lindsay's all-or-nothing attitude to the human world.

But these objections, I repeat, are not of great importance. The chapters dealing with Oceaxe, Crimtyphon, and Tydomin leave behind a tremendous impression of Lindsay's insight into human existence. A carping critic might find *A Voyage to Arcturus* no more than an attempt to write *The World as Will and Idea* as a novel; but, as with Schopenhauer's work, *Arcturus* has a power that enables it to survive one's disagreement with its ideas.

23 See Appendix One to my *Beyond the Outsider*.

Lindsay's second novel, *The Haunted Woman*, again shows him preoccupied with his old interests: the two worlds. It is startlingly unlike *Arcturus*, and demonstrates that Lindsay was a genuine imaginative creator, not a 'one-book man'. But its ending is something of a let-down, and one feels none of the compulsion to reread that *Arcturus* produces.

The 'haunted woman' of the title is Isbel Loment, who, at the beginning of the book, is engaged to a young city man. Her aunt is thinking of buying a house, and they go to look at a very old building in Sussex. The owner of this house, a Mr Judge, has had curious experiences in an upper room – has found a flight of steps leading upwards to storeys that have not existed for hundreds of years, but his memory is always a blank when he returns from excursions up these stairs. Isbel also finds a flight of stairs in the hall, which she ascends, and finds herself in a strange part of the house. Like Mr Judge, her memory is a blank when she returns to the hall afterwards. Mr Judge becomes acquainted with Isbel and her aunt and takes them to the house; then both he and Isbel reach the strange upper rooms by different routes and meet there. Both feel curiously transformed in these rooms and, in fact, become younger. After a few of these experiences they realize they are in love, but this presents something of a problem since the amnesia always returns when they descend the stairs.

All this sounds a promising foundation for a most unusual kind of love story; but the development is disappointing. One feels that Lindsay was not quite sure what his 'upper rooms' symbolized, although their effect is to make people younger, to break down their acquired social façade, and to reveal their inner nature to themselves. The development of the plot bears some resemblance to the old musical-comedy formula: 'Boy meets girl, boy loses girl, boy gets girl', except that in this case Isbel ends by losing Judge. A female spiritualist is hauled into the plot; she wants to marry Judge and hopes to compromise Isbel; however, after a visit to the strange rooms, she hears an ancient musician playing a viola and dies of a heart attack. Judge and Isbel also hear this musician; Judge finally sees his face and also dies of a heart attack. Isbel and her fiancé break off their engagement, but at the end of the book seem prepared to renew it. This is not really a happy ending, because Isbel had told Judge – while they were in the upper rooms – that her engagement was a mistake because her fiancé was too shallow.

The most likely explanation of Lindsay's intention in writing *The Haunted Woman* is that he wanted to contrast the world of 'spiritual reality' with the stifling world of social convention. It was published in 1922, when the Victorian world was still a living reality, and before Scott Fitzgerald and Hemingway had shattered the last remnants of the old conventionality. But this subject can make little appeal nowadays; one is simply slightly bewildered at all the talk about 'compromising unmarried ladies' and the necessity for chaperones. It is all too reminiscent of the world of Pinero, where a woman whose reputation had been 'shattered' by a broken engagement or a scandal crept off to Bath or Harrogate and died in retirement.

The best parts of *The Haunted Woman* are successful for the same reasons that *Arcturus* is successful; one feels that Lindsay is trying to find a symbol for something that strikes him very deeply as a reality. The book leaves behind a lingering atmosphere of poetry quite unlike the harsh colours of *Arcturus*. Visiak's comparison of the book with *The Ancient Mariner* is not entirely without justification, although its magic is actually closer to that of *Christabel*. This plot of walking into the past is not an unfamiliar one: Henry James used it in his unfinished last novel. Lindsay's manipulation of it is expert enough, but it is sadly clear that *The Haunted Woman* should have been rethought and rewritten before publication; he has wasted an excellent theme. Clumsinesses and redundancies that are hardly noticeable in *Arcturus* are here more apparent. The book opens, for example, with an account of how Marshall, the fiancé, has just returned from America, where he has been clearing up the estates of Isbel's brother. All this has no significance whatever to the plot and could have been cut. In fact the story really opens on the fourth page, when Marshall asks Isbel's aunt whether she is still interested in buying a house. When it is all over the reader's mind is full of questions: Who was the musician? Why did the sight of his face kill both Judge and the spiritualist woman? What were the 'upper rooms' supposed to signify? Then there are purely practical questions: Why should Mr Judge have asked Marshall to go and 'investigate' his house, and have enjoined him to secrecy about the upper rooms? Why did it never strike Judge that he only had to take a pencil and paper upstairs with him to defeat the loss of memory? (In fact he does this later in the book, but Lindsay makes very little of it – Judge merely destroys the paper.) The final chapter is all confusion. The spiritualist woman dies, but her ghost leads Isbel back to the house. Judge has written her a note saying he must never see Isbel again, but Isbel meets him at the house. He has now recovered his memory about the upper rooms by scrambling through the window back into his own garden, and he somehow succeeds in momentarily restoring Isbel's memory by vanishing into the house; Lindsay does not bother to explain what he does there.

One can only say that *The Haunted Woman* is not a bad book by the usual low standards of ghost stories – in which a certain immaturity of mind appears to be necessary in the writer. It seems to confirm that Lindsay's vision was basically tragic. When Isbel first goes into the upstairs room she sees her reflection in a mirror, and it strikes her that her face is far more alive and passionate than usual, and also *tragic*. Earlier in the book she tells her fiancé: 'My character is tragic, I fancy'. If this is accepted as the key to the book, *The Haunted Woman* begins to take on some appearance of unity of intention. Lindsay is saying that most people have a hidden nature that never has a chance to express itself in our convention-ridden society; it is possible that he means to indicate that the reason goes deeper than social convention – that the *everyday nature* of our lives prevents self-knowledge. In that case the problem is the destruction of the 'natural standpoint'. This is clear enough from Maskull's comment in *Arcturus* that 'this world' is certainly real enough, and yet in another sense it is not real. We use the word 'reality' in these two senses: as the 'stubborn, irreduceable fact' that presents itself to our eyes when we open them in the morning, and as the 'reality' of which we sometimes become aware in flashes of vision or insight. Phenomenological disciplines attempt to break open the natural standpoint in the way that a prism can divide white light into the seven colours of the spectrum; and yet this is not to say that white light is somehow a delusion.

But if this is true, and the problems presented in *Arcturus* and *The Haunted Woman* can be solved by a phenomenological discipline, then what about Isbel's belief that she is predestined to tragedy? What about the symbol of the musician, who, according to Visiak, is a symbol of evil, another version of Crystalman? It begins to seem that here is another familiar case of an inspired artist not grasping his own meaning – in fact, actively distorting it.

But it would certainly not be fair to Lindsay to close at this point. All artists must do their best to interpret their intuitions, and in some cases they may produce contradictory interpretations at different points in their careers – so that a Shelley, who begins as a militant atheist, ends as a religious mystic. *Arcturus* was an early work. Lindsay apparently wrote three other novels, *Sphinx*, *The Devil's Tor*, and *The Witch*, all of which, according to his friend E. H. Visiak,[24] were far below the level of the first two.

24 Mr Visiak has been kind enough to send me some notes that he once broadcast on the subject of Lindsay.

The diction of *The Witch*, which was left unfinished, was – significantly – inspired by Carlyle, for whom Lindsay felt great admiration in his later years. Lindsay and Carlyle have much in common – including a clear religious vision and a tendency to over-simplify. In *Past and Present*, Carlyle turns his back on the complexities of the industrial age and day-dreams of feudalism and monasteries; this wholesale attitude was always typical of him. He hurls down his intuitions like thunderbolts, and is so irritated by the forces he opposes that he feels no need for subtlety or qualification. This absoluteness tends to be a Celtic characteristic.

Visiak also mentions that Lindsay preferred Beethoven to any other composer – and at once one gains an insight into the creative processes of *Arcturus*. Beethoven stood alone all his life; he never married, and it may be that the deep psychological reason for this was a fear that a wife would soften the outlines of his rock-like genius. Visiak writes: 'The extreme preference he betrayed for Beethoven denoted an appreciation of sublimity in distinction from beauty'. When Visiak asked Lindsay whether the delightful intuitions of childhood are also delusions of Crystalman, Lindsay apparently answered: 'Yes', and dropped the subject.

Now all creative genius feels itself drawn onward by purpose, and consequently feels suspicion of pleasure, which seems an ultimate aim to so many people. Because human beings are not yet truly human – because they are all victims of the 'St Neot margin', which means that they know what they *don't* want more powerfully than they ever know what they do want – pleasure will always produce degeneration; while their greatest achievements are usually the result of the 'challenge and response' mechanism. For a man with a deep sense of evolutionary purpose, therefore, pleasure is to be regarded with suspicion; the mystic's vision of the world as entirely good is to be feared because the evolutionist feels a compulsion to improve it.[25] In *Man and Superman* Shaw says that religion provided him with a mere excuse for laziness, since 'it had set up a God who looked at the world and saw that it was good, against the instinct in me that looked through my eyes at the world and saw that it could be improved'. Lindsay's fierce rejection of religion, mysticism, love, is the rejection of an evolutionist who feels there is vital work to be done. Shaw also rejected love, religion, and mysticism *as ends in themselves*, but he did not make the mistake of supposing them therefore to be evil. The kind of happiness that most people seem to want is static, and would be cloying after a short period. Shaw recognized this when he made one of his characters say, 'I don't want to be happy; I want to be alive and active', and when his Don Juan declares that heaven is not the home of the seekers after happiness but of the seekers after reality, typically Dona Ana replies: 'Thank you: I am going to heaven for happiness. I have had quite enough of reality on earth'.

Lindsay's was a curious tragedy. The total lack of interest that greeted *Arcturus* and *The Haunted Woman* must

25 I have gone into this interesting problem at some length in the 'Mescalin appendix' of my *Beyond the Outsider*.

have taken a heavy toll on his optimism. And yet one wonders whether the author of *Arcturus* really hoped for universal acclaim. He wrote in a notebook:

> One must regard the world not merely as the home of illusions, but as being rotten with illusion from top to bottom... The most sacred and holy things ought not to be taken for granted, for if examined attentively, they will be found as hollow and empty as the rest... Behind this sham world lies the real, tremendous and awful Muspel-world, which knows neither will, nor Unity, nor Individuals; that is to say, an inconceivable world.[26]

The man who could write as gloomily as this could surely have had little interest in being recognized. Yet it is the opinion of J. B. Pick that the decline in the quality of Lindsay's novels 'seems to me the inevitable result of Lindsay's feeling that no one was genuinely interested in what he was trying to say'. Is it possible to detect here the contradiction underlying the philosophy of *Arcturus*? Lindsay had worked as a Lloyd's underwriter for fifteen years before he decided to give up his job and become a full-time writer in Cornwall; *Arcturus* was 'discovered' by Robert Lynd; then the rest was anti-climax: dismissive and uncomprehending reviews, total lack of interest. After *The Haunted Woman* Lindsay wrote a novel called *The Violet Apple* which he did not even bother to try to publish. Mr Pick mentions that its theme is similar to that of *The Haunted Woman* – that conventional life does not touch reality; he seems to feel that, as a novel, it com-

26 Quoted by J. B. Pick in an essay on Lindsay in *Studies in Scottish Literature*, January 1964.

pares with *The Haunted Woman*. Another novel, *The Sphinx*, was published in 1923; it deals with a man who has invented a machine for recording dreams, and with a woman composer named Lore. The dream-record theme provides Lindsay with a mechanism – similar to that in the first two novels – for contrasting the world of strange and deep significances with the banality of everyday life. At the end of the book Lore is drowned, and the inventor dies in his sleep and is somehow united with Lore – to whom, in waking life, he was not particularly attracted.

Lindsay wrote two more novels. Only one was finished and published – *The Devil's Tor*, another novel about a man and woman who are united through miraculous intervention; it is apropos of this book that Mr Pick makes the remark about Lindsay's decline through neglect. A final novel, *The Witch*, was begun (but never finished) at the beginning of the last war; of this Mr Pick reports that it 'is probably unpublishable, being written with an obsessive concentration on a series of speeches by an Earth-Mother figure who speaks in a strange, stilted, archaic rhetoric.'

It would seem, then, that we have in Lindsay a novelist who produced a single great work, and several minor books that certainly do not add to his stature. The blame lies partly on our philistine country that detests ideas and has no interest in religious discussion. In France or Germany Lindsay might have flourished and developed; but in the country that allowed William Blake to die unknown and that refused to take Shaw or Wells seriously, he had no chance of being understood. Apart from E. H.

Visiak, he had few literary friends; no one of any influence took the slightest interest in *Arcturus*. This is hardly surprising; a typical review – in the *Times Literary Supplement* – dismissed it as a 'riot of morbid fancy' and described it as uniformly unwholesome.

But to some extent Lindsay himself is also to blame. It is curious that four out of five of his finished books should deal with the same subject: a man and a woman who fail to realize that they are soul-mates in this world of illusion, but who are able to meet in some 'other world', some strange world of dreams or the supernatural. It becomes clear that Lindsay's constant theme was the rejection of 'this world', and his desire for the 'hidden world' of reality. But the reader of *Arcturus* is inclined to wonder how Lindsay can take the slightest interest in female characters since he so resolutely dismisses everything connected with femininity as an illusion of Crystalman. In the first chapter of *The Haunted Woman* one suspects that Lindsay intends Isbel to be everything he dislikes in women; she has a constant nervous habit of plucking at her dress or patting her hair, and sets out firmly to dominate the man she is going to marry. Her declaration, 'My character is tragic, I fancy', makes her sound an egotistic neurotic. And yet as the book progresses it is obvious that Lindsay has suspended the anti-feminism that is so apparent in *Arcturus*. One keeps wondering how the author of *Arcturus* can find the patience to write a book of this kind; it ought to have been written long before *Arcturus*. Yet, on the other hand, it is possible that Lindsay was genuinely trying to widen his scope in the later books, recognizing that he had gone too far in *Arcturus* and that the book was a dead end.

The later novels certainly enable one to understand Lindsay's character better. (*Arcturus* itself gives little foothold for existential criticism.) He was a lonely and shy man of talent who had wasted the better part of his life in a bread-and-butter job. He had the unbending character of the Scots Presbyterian which inevitably finds personal self-expression difficult. He unfortunately belongs with the men of genius who were never able to come to terms with the world, whose personality could never learn to express the inner nature. Most men of talent feel this way when young, for the personality is formed by social and human pressures that have little relation to the slowly unfolding inner nature. (Many of the novels of Aldous Huxley are about this rather painful comedy of adjustment.) The natural tendency of such a writer is to reject the everyday world and create another world of ideals, a Yeatsian 'land of heart's desire'. After this, much depends upon his personal character. If he happens to be fairly cheerful and optimistic, like Shaw, he will gradually get the world to take him at his own estimate, or something like it. If he is naturally shy and reserved, like Poe or H. P. Lovecraft, he may spend his whole life rejecting the everyday world and creating some compensatory reality with less sharp corners. But it is by no means rare for the man of talent to learn gradually to express his inner nature socially, and to achieve a degree of self-fulfilment that seemed impossible during his 'awkward age'.

It is clear from Lindsay's books that his late development meant that he never achieved this kind of spontaneity. But his extremely solitary disposition also meant that he never had enough contact with the world to discover how far genius *can* create its own conditions; he made the mistake of assuming that his own problem of non-communication was universal. For this reason it is a pity that he never achieved enough recognition to throw him into intercourse with some of his intellectual equals – with Shaw and Wells, for example, or with T. E. Lawrence, whose problems Lindsay would have understood. He would quickly have come to recognize that his favourite theme – that 'this world' does not allow people to be their 'true selves' – was not the universal truth he took it for.

What is more, a little intelligent criticism might have led to a real development of the startling powers that can be seen in *Arcturus*. An intelligent critic might have pointed out to him that the later books appear to contradict the all-out rejection of *Arcturus*. In *Arcturus* 'reality' is the Muspel-world, which has nothing whatever in common with the world in which we live; everything we know is illusion. But in other books the symbol for the 'alternative reality' changes; it becomes the world of dreams or some supernatural world of the past. This makes it clear that what we are up against is a world-rejection like that of the young W. B. Yeats; and Yeats's development reveals that such an attitude is by no means the last word. Under criticisms such as these, Lindsay might have undertaken a more deliberate and precise analysis of illusion, and realized that his wholesale rejection of 'this world' is a convenient simplification. It is remotely possible that Lindsay might have ended by reaffirming the stern vision of *Arcturus*; but at least he would have had to recognize that it is completely incompatible with the vision of *The Haunted Woman* and *Sphinx*.

In any case, there can be no doubt that *A Voyage to Arcturus* will one day take its place as a classic of English literature.

A Note on E. H. Visiak[27]

E. H. Visiak was one of Lindsay's few literary friends; he discovered Lindsay through *A Voyage to Arcturus* and wrote him an admiring letter. Lindsay was so excited by this that he travelled from Cornwall to Sussex to meet Visiak – which seems to confirm the notion that Lindsay was bitterly disappointed by his lack of recognition.

Visiak is a powerful and much underrated writer with more than a touch of genius. On a certain level he and Lindsay have much in common; both are poets and visionaries. Unfortunately, Visiak's remarkable qualities were too similar to Lindsay's own to lead to any cross-fertilizing.

Visiak is a writer who has always been fascinated by the sea, from his early *Buccaneer Ballads* to a recent book on Conrad. His major novel, *Medusa*, is a curious and most disturbing work that has some of the haunting quality of *Moby Dick*. The style is early eighteenth century, reminiscent of Defoe, and the narrator tells how he runs away from school after accidentally killing a school-fel-

27 i.e. Edward Harold Physick 1878-1972 [Ed.]

low, and then goes to sea with a Mr Huxtable, who is on his way to ransom his son from pirates. Strange things happen on the ship, and there are signs of a sea-creature, half man and half fish. Finally the ship arrives at a pillar of black rock, and the narrator finds himself in an underground cavern, lying on a ledge; below him is a great octopus-like monster, lying in a pool of black water; one of the sailors, who is caught in a tentacle, wears an expression of 'abounding, extravagant and antic joy'. The narrator manages to escape by means of a rope that is thrown down to him. One gathers that this octopus-like Medusa is a vision of pure evil; the ecstasy on the face of the victim seems to link him with Crystalman.

Medusa is an extraordinary book, and its style has no doubt prevented it from being recognized as a Kafkaesque vision; the Defoe-like clarity forms a strange contrast to the stifling nightmare atmosphere – in fact reviewers were even more dismissive than with *Arcturus*, and the book was not reprinted until 1963.[28] It is far more elusive than *Moby Dick*, yet the intention seems in many ways similar.

The unique quality of Visiak's vision becomes even clearer in a fragment called 'Medusan Madness'[29] much admired by David Lindsay. Here Visiak comes even closer to the limits of the unsayable. A man in a mental home relates how some vision at sea has driven him insane; although this vision is not specifically described by the narrator, it has the effect of driving the narrator insane also.

28 In the same Gollancz series as *The Voyage to Arcturus* and *The Haunted Woman*.

29 Published in *New Tales of Horror*. Hutchinson, 1936. [See also *Editor's Notes* at the end of this essay. Ed.]

The madman explains that he is kept from total mental collapse by being able to talk about his vision to a woman called Diomedia. But he succeeds in conveying an impression of the intense beauty of a dark sky against the light of the sea (apparently Lindsay particularly admired this passage), and goes on somehow to make his hearer share some vision of total beauty – which he seems to identify with Aphrodite, and which has struck him dumb. The 'vision' turns its eyes on the narrator so that he finds it impossible to leave the asylum. The story ends: 'Diomedia help us. She is coming now'.

One is not surprised to learn that, like *Medusa*, this fragment was written in a semi trance-like state, and that only later did Visiak look up 'Diomedes' in a classical dictionary and discover that he was the one man who was enabled to look upon Aphrodite (by the grace of Pallas Athene) without being destroyed by her beauty. It is even more interesting that Visiak had been asked to produce an ordinary horror story by the publisher, and apparently made several attempts to do so without success until a kind of automatic writing produced the Medusan fragment.

Visiak seems to be haunted by a vision of the unsayable. Primarily he is a poet, not a conscious literary artist, although his books on Milton and Conrad reveal a keen critical intelligence. The very nature of *Medusa* means that, unlike *Arcturus*, it can never make its appeal to the general reader; but it will undoubtedly never lack a small audience of enthusiastic readers.

1965

Editor's Notes

This was Colin Wilson's first major essay on Lindsay, a writer he championed throughout his long career. This essay formed the basis of 'Lindsay as Novelist and Mystic', his contribution to the symposium *The Strange Genius of David Lindsay* (London: John Baker, 1970. (**A28A**)) and was further expanded to form the book *The Haunted Man: The Strange Genius of David Lindsay* (San Bernardino CA: Borgo Press, 1979. (**A55**)). Another essay 'David Lindsay and *A Voyage to Arcturus*' was included as Chapter 16 of Wilson's *The Books in My Life* (Charlottesville, VA: Hampton Roads, 1998. (**A152**)). In an article for *The Mail on Sunday* (April 10, 1983, page 29 (**C325**)) he described Arcturus as '...one of the greatest...fantasy masterpieces ever written.'

He wrote Introductions to Lindsay's *The Violet Apple* and *The Witch* (Chicago: Chicago Review Press, 1976. (**D26**)), *Sphinx* (London: Xanadu, 1988. (**D67**)) and an Afterword to a new edition of *A Voyage to Arcturus* (Manchester: Savoy Books, 2002 (**D135**)).

Keen to encourage other enthusiasts he provided a Foreword to Bernard Sellin's *The Life and Work of David Lindsay* (Cambridge: Cambridge University Press. 1981. (**D41**)) and a Preface to David Power's study *David Lindsay's Vision* (Nottingham: Paupers' Press, 1991. (**D88**)).

He became friendly with E. H. Visiak and encouraged his publisher, John Baker, to publish his memoir *Life's Morning Hour* in 1968 (**D7**), writing a generous Introduction. And when *Medusa* was reprinted (Lakefield CO: Centipede Press, 2010 (**D159**)) he also wrote an Introduction. In 2007 Anthony Harrison-Barbet's study *E. H. Visiak: Writer and Mystic* appeared with, once again, an Introduction by Wilson (Nottingham: Paupers' Press. (**D152**)). This book includes the full text of 'Medusan Madness'.

As a Visiting Professor at various US universities, in the 1960s and early 1970s, he lectured and taught courses on *Arcturus*.

In the symposium presented to Colin Wilson on the occasion of his 80th birthday, *Around the Outsider* (Alresford, Hants: 0-Books, 2011. (**HA33**)), Murray Ewing, host of the Lindsay website (www.violetapple.org.uk), wrote an assessment of Wilson's contribution to Lindsay studies.

8

IMRE MÁDACH'S *TRAGEDY OF MAN* AND MARK TWAIN'S *MYSTERIOUS STRANGER*

This chapter is by way of a footnote to the one on David Lindsay. Both the works mentioned above can be classified with *A Voyage to Arcturus* as attempts to make some final statement about human existence.

It is inevitable that man should try to scrutinize human existence for meaning; but there is an obvious problem: existence is too big; it is too many things.

Let us consider this question of the *Lebensfrage* for a moment from a scientific point of view. Man has always looked to the universe for signs and portents; as a prisoner scrutinizes the face of a judge, and we now consider the art of astrologers and soothsayers as so much nonsense. Still, if it is a mistake to personalize the universe, it also seems contrary to experience to assume that it is totally unaware of us. L. H. Myers[30] was not the first to point out that 'the actual experiences of a man's life [seem to be] determined by his ingrained preconceptions'; James

30 Leopold Hamilton Myers, 1881–1944. See Chapter 9 [Ed.].

Joyce also declared that in considering a man's character, one also has to consider whether he is the sort of man who is left fortunes, or on whom slates fall. And everyone has at some time observed how events often seem to fall into 'clusters' ; for example, I hear a new word or idea for the first time, and I can now almost take a bet that I shall keep stumbling upon it for the next few days, sometimes in completely remote contexts. It may simply be that there are laws at work here of which we have no conception at present. We know ourselves only as conscious personalities, but psychology teaches that below the surface of everyday consciousness there lies a whole world which we seldom become aware of. If our psychic 'bulk' is so immense, it may be that we cause a sort of wash as we travel through time, and perhaps exert on events a gravitational pull of which we are completely unaware. But that is pure speculation. For the moment, I only want to argue that it may be quite unscientific to take it for granted that we live in a universe that is in every way indifferent to our existence.

Quite apart, however, from this question of the universe's indifference, it is certain that we have continually to interact with our surroundings, just as two prisoners sharing the same cell have to take continual account of one another's presence. For practical purposes, therefore, we might as well think of the universe as in some way a person, of whose moods and personality we have to take account – even though, in this case, the moods and personality may be purely natural manifestations. And here the problem arises, which is analogous to the problem of human relations. The less mature a person is, the easier he is to 'know'. It is easy to know a child or a pet dog. If the child is highly intelligent, he will become steadily more difficult to know as he gets older. If he one day develops into a great man, his personality may be fundamentally a mystery to those surrounding him, because he has so many levels, so many depths of self-consciousness and self-knowledge, and because he will find that the easiest attitude to adopt towards the world is one of detachment.

But if a human personality can be almost unknowable in its complexity, in its detachment the universe is many times more so. The problem is complicated not only by the sheer size of the universe and our ignorance of most of its laws, but by our human limitations: by the fact that our vision can only grasp a little at a time, and that our moods change from day to day, and our values with them, so that something we seemed to know yesterday appears false or irrelevant today.

In spite of all this, in spite of man's long-standing recognition of his limitations, bold spirits have never been afraid of the attempt to summarize existence. The earliest summaries all tended to be pessimistic – Koheleth, Solomon, Job, Aristotle. But even the Greeks, whose culture was soaked through and through with pessimism, could not help feeling a certain admiration and astonishment at the achievements of the human mind, so that Plato's *Symposium* culminates in a prediction that man will one day become something closer to a god, by following the 'highest' in himself. And when Kepler, Galileo, and Newton showed just what the human mind could do by way of predicting and controlling the activities of nature, the old pessimism began to lose its grip; it suddenly seemed possible that man might, after all, leave his animal self far behind. Admittedly, men like Blake, Hamann, and Kierkegaard showed that this scientific optimism was to a large extent based on a naïve failure to recognize human limitations. Still, properly seen, their criticisms could be regarded as a corrective, not as a new argument for pessimism. All the same, the nineteenth century saw the return of pessimism, as it became steadily more apparent that science was inclined to negate all those aspects of man that poetry and philosophy had regarded as of central importance. The two works mentioned in the title of this chapter express the nineteenth-century pessimism with considerable force and clarity.

The Tragedy of Man, by Imre Mádach, is regarded as the great Hungarian national epic. To some extent, it is an obvious imitation of *Faust*, but it has a force and originality that go a long way towards justifying the claim of Hungarian critics that it ranks with Goethe's masterpiece.

It is the opening scene that most clearly brings *Faust* to mind. A choir of angels praises the Lord, but Lucifer sneers and mocks until God banishes him. He is told that his dominion will be two trees in the Garden of Eden, and he replies: 'A corner's all I need – enough to afford a foothold for negation.' He then goes down to Earth and tempts Eve; the result is that Adam and Eve leave Eden. Later, when Adam questions Lucifer about his future, Lucifer makes him fall asleep and sends him a dream.

This dream, in several episodes, is the substance of the poem. We see Adam reborn in various incarnations, always the idealist, the man who dares to hope that human life is meaningful and purposive; always disillusioned and crushed. In his first incarnation he is an enlightened Egyptian Pharaoh, building a pyramid somehow to cheat time and death; but the sight of a slave's death makes him recognize his folly; he takes the wife of the slave (Eve) as his mate, and frees his other slaves; he kicks a mummy down the steps of his throne, rejecting this method of obtaining 'immortality', and declares that he will set out to establish a democracy. As he goes out Lucifer sneers and predicts his disillusionment.

In each of the following episodes Mádach shows Adam in different incarnations, becoming disillusioned with some other aspect of human life. As a Greek general, he returns from foreign conquest to discover that enemies at home have turned the mob against him, and these enemies are 'demagogues' who claim to speak for the people; so much for democracy! It is Lucifer who wields the executioner's axe. In the next episode Adam is a degenerate Roman sensualist, and Eve a courtesan. They summon a funeral procession into their carousal with the intention of mocking, then discover that the corpse has died of plague. A fiery cross appears in the sky, and hordes of barbarians are seen bearing down on Rome. Adam recognizes that his life has been a failure, but prays for something to 'put health into our tainted blood', and prepares to go out and fight. But the next episode repeats the pattern of the preceding ones: knighthood and Christianity are shown to be as vain as Roman decadence. Adam is now Tancred, returned from the Crusades, only to find Christendom divided by inner squabbles about doctrine, and engaged in burning heretics. Adam meets Eve, but she is pledged to enter a convent; so he loses her. These are the fruits of Christianity – fanaticism and frustration. Adam turns away, tired and disillusioned.

In the next scene he is reincarnated as Kepler, married to a woman who is his social superior and who is unfaithful to him. (This is apparently an autobiographical touch.) Kepler is forced to waste his time helping a feeble-minded emperor in his alchemical experiments, and casting horoscopes for the nobility. In his misery he falls asleep, prophesying future freedom for man, and dreams of the French Revolution. The next scene is a flashback within a flashback, for Kepler dreams that he is Danton. This scene is no more than a repetition of the scene in Athens; once again the fickleness of the mob is shown, and the futility of the dream of democracy. After Danton has been executed, Kepler wakes up, and has a conversation with a scholar in which he advises the youth not to waste his time in the search for knowledge, but to go out and live.

In the eleventh scene Adam and Lucifer once again assume their true identities, and wander through Shakespeare's London. The content of this scene is less clear than the others; it is a play within a play. To some extent the intention seems to be to satirize capitalism; it is also meant to show a world that has only succeeded in degenerating into quackery, credulity, cruelty, and social injustice. There are again echoes of *Faust* as Adam accosts Eve and her mother and is snubbed. With Lucifer's help he succeeds in gaining her interest, but when some of the devil's trinkets turn into snakes, Adam and Lucifer have to beat a hasty retreat.

The twelfth scene is Mádach's own version of Aldous Huxley's *Brave New World* or Zamyatin's *We*. Apparently it is intended to satirize Fourierism. Adam and Lucifer visit a scientific community, and the scientist discourses, with dry nineteenth-century rationalism, on the folly of poetry and art. In this community workmen are strictly regimented. Luther stokes a boiler; Michelangelo carves chair legs. Eve appears with her child, which is now old enough to be taken from her and brought up by the community (in accordance with Fourierist principles). Adam supports her in her plea to retain the child, while the scientist dismisses them as 'a romantic man and a nerve-ridden woman'. Once again, Adam and Lucifer have to disappear hastily.

In the next scene Adam and Lucifer flee through space away from the Earth; but Adam discovers that he cannot abandon the Earth, even though the scientist has told him about the 'heat death of the universe'. So in the final scene of Adam's long dream he is a traveller on the dying earth, and he meets an Eskimo, who offers him a night's hospitality, with his wife – a shrivelled Inuit hag – as companion. Adam recognizes the hag as Eve, and flees with horror.

In the last scene of *The Tragedy of Man* Adam awakes, and is overwhelmed by his vision of the futility of history. He decides to commit suicide. But as he advances towards the edge of the cliff, Eve tells him that she is pregnant. It is too late to 'stop history'. Adam collapses in the dust, and vows that he is nothing before God – in spite of Lucifer's indignant contempt. The heavens open and God appears. Adam asks who will guide him now that God no longer walks with him in the garden; God refuses to make any promises, but tells Adam to 'strive on, and trust' – the last words of the poem.

As recounted above, *The Tragedy of Man* may sound a typical nineteenth century piece of bombast and confusion; actually, in spite of many absurdities, it has a remarkable power of its own. It is quite definitely a poem, not a play – although it is now presented regularly at all Hungarian festivals of the arts. Things happen too jerkily and arbitrarily for a stage play; for example, in the ancient Egyptian scene, Eve is weeping over the body of her husband at one point and calling Adam 'beloved' two lines later. Still, the sweep of the work is impressive, and in one respect it surpasses *Faust*: that is, it is a tremendous attempt to summarize human history and human destiny, and to 'pass judgment'. *Faust* – a far greater work – is more modest in scope.

Mark Twain's *Mysterious Stranger* is one of his last works – it was written in 1916 – and it seems to confirm the view advanced by Van Wyck Brooks in *The Ordeal of Mark Twain*, that Twain the humourist was a mask covering an altogether different personality. The serious American writer of the nineteenth century tended to be a failure: this holds true, from Charles Brockden Brown, whose *Wieland* is the cornerstone of American literature, to Hermann Melville. Even Hawthorne and Whitman could hardly be regarded as successes in any worldly sense. From the beginning, Twain found himself highly popular; he became the symbol of nineteenth-century 'go-getting' America. Everyone loved him; as he walked through the streets, he was saluted with the same affection and admiration that Norwegians of that period showed to Henrik Ibsen. (As Ibsen entered his favourite restaurant, all the diners used to stand up as a mark of respect; Americans are too informal for any such display, but it often came close to it.) In some ways, Twain's natural affinities were with Poe or Melville; but with the example of their failure constantly before his eyes, he never dared to risk alienating his great public. This, at all events, is Mr Brooks's theory, and he makes it sound plausible. When Twain set off on one of his lecture tours, he was preceded by sandwich men carrying boards that read: 'Mark Twain, Ha Ha'. This is enough to sour the sunniest nature.

To some extent *The Mysterious Stranger* seems to us a little too determinedly Swiftian; but its final pages certainly strike a note that would have alarmed even Swift. The story takes place in sixteenth-century Austria. Three boys are playing when they are approached by an angel called Satan – the nephew of the Prince of Darkness, he explains – who proceeds to perform miracles for them like conjuring tricks, creating a castle full of tiny people. He talks to them and they are enthralled – he seems altogether a great and noble being; yet when some of the tiny people fall to quarrelling, he squashes them between his fingers, then when the others begin to wail, crushes dozens of them by hitting them with a plank. But, as Satan points out, he created them, and he can make plenty more; life is cheap; so is death. Then he causes a storm and an earthquake for the boys' amusement, but only so that it affects the castle; and the boys are horrified as tiny men, women, and children are crushed and burnt to death. But Satan does good as indifferently as he does evil, and helps the village priest, who is having trouble with a money-lender and an envious astrologer.

The point of the story begins to emerge when one of the boys mentions the village loafer, who is always beating his dog, and calls him a brute; Satan tells him sternly that this is to libel the animals; they are never gratuitously cruel like human beings. He even objects when the boy says that the loafer's conduct is inhuman. 'No, it is distinctly human', and he explains that men act in this way because they are tainted with a disease called the Moral Sense. By way of driving home his indictment, Twain juggles with time, and makes Satan show the boys a factory in which half-starved women and children work fourteen hours a day.

The boys want Satan to change people's lives for the better; he proves to them that things are best as they are; a boy and girl who are drowned are only saved from lives of misery and sickness. He promises that the old priest shall be made happy for life, and accomplishes this by driving him insane so that he believes himself to be an emperor. 'Sanity and happiness are an impossible combination', Satan explains. In the closing pages Satan comes to take his leave, and reveals the final truth to the narrator: life is an illusion. 'There is no God, no universe, no human race, no earthly life, no heaven, no hell. It is all a dream... Nothing exists but you, and you are but a *thought* – a vagrant thought, a useless thought, a homeless thought, wandering forlorn among the empty eternities.' Satan himself is only a figment of the narrator's brain. The narrator created the universe to avoid the horror of being alone, nothing. But the universe is always revealing that it is an illusion because it is 'so frankly and hysterically insane – like all dreams'. And Mark Twain finishes: 'He vanished, and left me appalled; for I knew, and realized, that all he had said was true.'

Mark Twain's story is altogether shallower than Mádach's. He is repeating much that Shaw said in the third act of *Man and Superman* on the subject of man's stupidity and cruelty and dependence on illusions, but Shaw also took the trouble to answer his own indictment – most of which is placed in the mouth of the devil. The whole tone of the story is Swiftian; having shown that Satan creates and destroys life without giving it a second thought, Twain then shows that human beings themselves can easily outdo Satan. The story is a collection of episodes indicting human folly and cruelty. But one gets the feeling that the author has chosen a sitting duck for his target, and is often scoring rather cheaply. Much of the satire is reminiscent of Shaw at his worst; for example, Mark Twain writes about a woman who is hanged as a witch because 'she was known to have a habit of curing people by devilish arts, such as bathing them, washing them, and nourishing them, instead of bleeding them and purging them in the proper way'. The woman's daughter looks on as she is hanged, and Theodor, the narrator, joins the crowd in flinging a stone at her because he is afraid to appear unlike the rest of the crowd. Afterwards, Satan tells him that sixty-two of the sixty-eight people were as unwilling to throw a stone as Theodor, but stoned the woman for the same reason. He goes on to draw the moral: human beings are sheep and cowards.

There is obviously much truth here, but still, it is all a little too facile. Satirists have a habit of growing complacent and denouncing human folly with a self-satisfied smile on their faces; this is what happens to Shaw at his worst, and it happens to Twain here. The satire misses its mark because it is not accurate enough, not subtle enough; at times, it is little better than abuse. One then feels that Twain has worked himself into such a mood of violent raging nihilism that he carries the story to its life-denying conclusion without really intending to go that far; he is swept away by his own rhetoric.

The final effect of *The Mysterious Stranger* is not quite what the author intended. Clearly, one of his ideas in writing it was to prove that he was not 'merely a humorist'. In this he succeeds; it is certainly the finest of Mark Twain's stories. But it also makes one aware that the humorous works are not what they pretend to be. From this point of view, the story is a mistake – like a man who pretends to be the soul of tolerance and good humour giving way to a public tantrum. Many English readers find the humour of *Huckleberry Finn* rather hard to take, in spite of the exaggerated esteem in which that book is held by most Americans; there seems to be something forced about it; all its funny situations are taken just a little too far, and its satire is heavy handed. But the reader may be inclined to blame himself for his failure to recognize it as the great American masterpiece that Hemingway claims it is; *The Mysterious Stranger* destroys this doubt, for it makes very plain what one had always suspected: that Mark Twain did not find the world as funny as he pretended. True humour should spring out of exuberance; it should be a part of the genuine character of the humorist; otherwise it makes an impression of bad faith. One also feels that Van Wyck Brooks is right; if Twain had had the courage to write *The Mysterious Stranger* at the beginning of his career instead of at the end, he might have become a truly great writer.

To summarize: *The Tragedy of Man* and *The Mysterious Stranger* may ultimately be unsatisfactory works, but at least they throw down a challenge: they suggest what great art could be. Their formulation of the human predicament arouses one to dissension and to analysis; if they have over-simplified, then what is the truth? As works of literature, they rank below *A Voyage to Arcturus* and *The Near and the Far* because they are less complex; their assessment of the human situation lacks subtlety. But at least they make it clear that a work of literature can provide a contribution to existential philosophy.

1965

9

L.H. MYERS

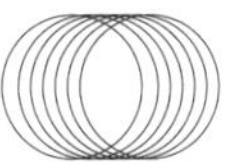

For his admirers L. H. Myers ranks as one of the most interesting and rewarding writers of the twentieth century, yet when pressed to explain they usually experience some difficulty. Myers was the author of four novels – one of them 1,000 pages long – and yet no one could describe him as a good novelist. The contemporary with whom he has most in common is Aldous Huxley, and even more than Huxley he is an intellectual essayist rather than a creative writer. In that case it might seem that his neglect is deserved. Yet there is something about Myers that makes it impossible to dismiss him. There is a clarity about his books that makes them stick in the mind and that induces one to return to them. One might say of him, as Eliot said of Henry James: 'He was one of the most intelligent men of his time'.

One thing is certain: the total neglect into which he has fallen since his death is undeserved. At the time of writing (1964) all his books are out of print, and I have been unable to find his name in any reference work on English literature – although his father, F. W. H. Myers, one of the founders of the Society for Psychical Research, is in most of them. I can think of no comparable example of a writer of merit, who received a fair degree of acclaim in his lifetime, being so totally forgotten after his death.

The facts of Myers's life can be summarized briefly. He was born in 1881, did some travelling, and married a wealthy woman nine years his senior in 1908. His first novel, *The Orissers*, was published in 1922, and attracted favourable attention. For a while Myers was regarded as a member of the 'Bloomsbury group': his second novel, *The Clio*, seems to be a deliberate attempt to rival the Huxley of *Those Barren Leaves*. Then in the thirties Myers turned his back on Bloomsbury and published his major novel, *The Near and the Far*, in four parts. His sympathy with communism increased until he came to regard himself as a communist (although he was never a party member) and broke with most of his old friends. His suicide (from an overdose of veronal) in April 1944 may have been due to a fear that he had cancer; according to his friend L. P. Hartley he was always something of a hypochondriac. A fourth novel, *Strange Glory*, was published in 1936 while he was engaged on *The Near and the Far*.

Myers is a frustrating novelist. In the early chapters of any of his books one has a sense of being in the hands of a true novelist, a writer with an immensely active intelligence who is also capable of creating human beings. The tremendous intelligence is certainly his most exciting quality. But as the novels progress they seem to lose direction, and the characters and their actions become more and more arbitrary; finally they peter out like a stream disappearing into the sand. One of the chapters of William Blake's novel *An Island in the Moon* ends with the words: 'Then Mr Inflammable Gas ran and shoved his head into the fire and set his hair all in a flame, and ran about the room – No, no, he did not; I was only making a fool of you.' One sometimes feels that Myers has the same casual attitude towards his characters, and does not really care what happens to them or what he makes them do. In this sense he is most emphatically not a good novelist. He is like a cook who knows exactly what ingredients should go into a dish but who has no idea of what to do after that, so that when it comes out of the oven it is quite uneatable; and one feels that Myers looks at it with mild surprise, saying, 'I've no idea what could have gone wrong, but it doesn't really matter anyway...' And in a sense it doesn't matter, for what is important about the novels is what went into them. Blake's *Prophetic Books* are also unsuccessful as works of literature, yet they are more exciting than most 'successful' works.

This is what is so frustrating about Myers; in writing about him, the words success and failure take on a different meaning and one is easily lured into apparent contradictions. One can say, for example, that he is a bad novelist, and then add that nevertheless *The Near and the Far* is probably one of the half dozen great novels of the twentieth century. One can say that *The Clio* is probably his most successful novel, and then feel obliged to add that it is his only complete failure. One can only summarize the problem by saying that what Myers stood for, what he was aiming at, is far more important than anything he actually achieved.

But let us try to go to the heart of the matter: the reason that Myers is important is that the 'life-problem' tormented him, and his books are attempts to grapple with it. I have suggested elsewhere that there are two classes of writer: one sails along, contentedly accepting the world as it is, taking its values for granted; the other is inclined to see 'too deep and too much', and his work often has a disturbing feeling of being built over depths. Jane Austen is an example of the first class; Dostoevsky of the second. A writer of the first class may ask questions, may be intensely critical of human beings and human society; may even be deeply disturbed by the problem of human tragedy and death; yet somehow he remains 'of this world'. The second class of writer somehow begins by doubting this world and its values; world-rejection is one of the fundamental constituents of his being, even though he may eventually overcome it and become a life-affirmer. Myers belongs to this latter class, and all his work is a drama of world-rejection and the struggle to affirm. Such writers are exhilarating because one feels that their minds are trying to grip their experience, to prevent it from gliding away like water under a bridge. They are not contented to live; they want to know *why*. They also want to know how they should begin. They are not prepared to be hurled into it blindfolded and rushed along by circumstances until they are carried out of the door of death; they find it incomprehensible that so many human beings seem to take this for granted; they are inclined to wonder whether other people have some secret knowledge which they have been denied.

The Near and the Far

Myers calls his major work *The Near and the Far*. It is the title of the first novel of the tetralogy, and he evidently felt it to be so important that he later transferred it to the whole series. Its meaning is explained on the first page of the novel. Prince Jali (aged twelve) stands on the balcony of a palace and experiences a sense of delight and awe at the sight of the desert and distant mountains. The desert has always fascinated him; evidently it was a symbol for Myers as it was for T. E. Lawrence – a symbol of freedom from the sticky prison of one's own humanity. But, Jali reflected, 'there were two deserts: one that was a glory for the eye, another that it was weariness to trudge. Deep in his heart he cherished the belief that some day the near and the far would meet… one day he would be vigorous enough… to capture the promise of the horizon. Then, instead of crawling like an insect on a little patch of brown sand, swift as a deer he would speed across the filmy leagues…'

Myers has here found a symbol to state the most fundamental problem of human existence. Most human beings have their glimpses of 'the promise of the horizon'; but when they investigate and discover that the reality is hard and dull, they usually assume that the promise was an illusion. It is once again the problem of uncle and nephew in Goncharov's *The Usual Story*.

Now Myers can at least see that there is an alternative. If one were strong enough, healthy enough, it might not be necessary to trudge so painfully through the present. This is the answer that Nietzsche suggested in *Thus Spoke*

Zarathustra – the idea of great health. If human beings could jar themselves out of the self-pity that is so fundamentally a part of the human condition, if they could cease to nurse a certain amount of weakness to furnish them with an excuse for opting out should life prove too difficult, there might be some chance of living in a present that is more like the poet's vision of 'the promise of the horizon'. The main problem so far has been that the poets have been weak and sensitive men – visionary insights often seem to go with sickness, as in the case of Pascal – and have simply lacked the courage to start the work of self-discipline. This unfortunately, was true of both Nietzsche and Myers. When one has read L. P. Hartley's statement, in the introduction to *The Near and the Far*, that Myers was a hypochondriac, one knows in advance that his quest will be a failure. Nevertheless, such is the quality of Myers's intellect that there is a great deal to be learned along the way. Myers was a man of thoroughly independent mind, which is undoubtedly why he so quickly came to reject Bloomsbury. Although a liberal himself, he was inclined to question all the liberal assumptions of his day – another reason, no doubt, for his current neglect. Yet for all his independence he was never able to rid himself of our modern tendency to identify strength with brutality and stupidity, and weakness with sensitivity and intelligence.

The parts of *The Near and the Far* dealing with Prince Jali are by far the most interesting; into Jali's mouth – or mind – Myers puts his most intimate thoughts about the business of living. They tell us a great deal about Myers and about the reason for his ultimate failure as an artist. In the Agra palace, whither Akbar the Great Mogul has summoned many of his subject princes, Jali feels at first pained and bewildered by the stupidity and vulgarity of 'the great world'. And there is the usual theme – common to all existentialist literature from Dostoevsky to Sartre – of the sensitive man's envy of the stupid, his wish to be as simple and undivided as they are. 'A stout heart and a thick skin, a knowing eye and a ready laugh – these, these were what he admired and coveted' (p. 222). 'To live in and for reality was to dwindle and fade, to accept appearances was to wax fat and grow strong… A man should give and take generously in the false coin of appearances.' But then Jali discovers the secret. He gets into conversation with the beautiful (but brainless) slave girl Gunevati, and she initiates him into sex. She encourages him to make his assault on 'the world' – to try to seduce some of the women of the palace. Astoundingly, he succeeds, and 'the women of the palace saw a tongue-tied, self-conscious boy most piquantly transformed into an impudent but charming young rake'. He has learned the great lesson – to rival the world at its own games. That Myers took his own teaching to heart is proved by *The Clio*.

But throughout *The Near and the Far* one is always aware of the narrowness of Myers's sympathies. On the one hand there are the people he likes – intelligent and sensitive people like Rajah Amar and Princess Sita (Jali's father and mother), Prince Hari (Jali's uncle), and Gokal, the Hindu religious teacher, close friend of Amar; on the other hand there is the world – stupid, insensitive or just downright corrupt; and as Myers writes about 'the world' one can almost see his mouth pursing as if he is sucking a lemon. Such a man very obviously lacks the common touch, the cheerful earthiness of Burns, Synge, and Rabelais. But, unlike his contemporary Huxley, he is not fully aware that he lacks it.

The Near and the Far is perhaps the best example among the novels of the statement that Myers is like a cook who has all the right ingredients but no idea of what to do with them. If Myers had possessed the humanity of a Tolstoy as well as his own profound insight and sensitivity, the novel would surely have been one of the world's greatest artistic achievements. The scope is almost epic.

The plot centres around the characters mentioned above. The scene is India in the time of Akbar the Great, a contemporary of Queen Elizabeth I. (His actual dates are 1542 to 1605.) Akbar has summoned various princes to celebrate the foundation of a new capital, so Rajah Amar and his family journey to Agra. Amar is a Buddhist and his wife a Christian, and from the beginning of the novel Amar has decided to renounce the world and become a monk. It is obvious that Myers sympathizes deeply with his attitude of world-rejection. His beautiful wife Sita is all tenderness and love, and she finds the world too beautiful to want to renounce it. Gokal (in whom, apparently, Myers caricatured some of the traits of his friend Hartley) is a Hindu; for him Brahman is the ultimate reality. Yet Gokal, a fat, serene-looking man, is by no means dead to the world, and falls in love with the slave girl Gunevati. Amar's brother Hari is far more a man of action and something of a Don Juan; yet he is also intelligent, and it is obvious that Myers likes him. At the beginning of the novel he is engaged in a love affair with Lalita, the future bride of Prince Daniyal, Akbar's son; half-way through the story he has a love affair with Amar's wife Sita.

Two main threads run through the book: the struggle for succession that takes place between Akbar's two sons, the homosexual Daniyal and the brutal Salim; and Akbar's attempt to establish a new religion, the Din Ilahi, of which he is to be the prophet and the avatar.

L. P. Hartley has pointed out that Myers hated the idea of setting novels in the modern world; he once told Hartley that the thought of one of his characters walking down Piccadilly oppressed and frustrated him. *The Clio* is set on an expensive yacht on the Amazon and *Strange Glory* in the swamps around New Orleans. This helps to explain the extraordinary fascination of the first half of *The Near and the Far*. One is aware that Myers is rejecting all the usual paraphernalia of the modern novel – the realistic details, the sordid adulteries, the stream of consciousness. *The Near and the Far* resembles one of those Hindu or Japanese paintings with an immense blue sky, a golden moon, and with a few trees and mountains painted in with clarity and delicacy. It is as if Myers is saying: 'This is *my* world you are entering now, and I do not propose to indulge any of the usual low tastes. It has depth and excitement, but it is the excitement of adventures of the mind.' An extraordinary calm descends upon the reader as he moves through the opening chapters. This is a book in which religion is going to play a central part; in fact it is the true theme. The characters have been deliberately chosen to represent different religious viewpoints, and the book is in essence a great dialogue, like *The Magic Mountain*. Chapter after chapter begins with words that deliberately set a scene of peace: 'A long, empty corridor, lit by small lamps of perfumed oil, stretched away into the distance' (Chap. 2); 'Huge, dim lanterns stood at the four corners of the terrace, spreading pools of light upon the marble flags' (Chap 4). And Amar's Buddhist longings are symbolized in a natural scene:

> The Rajah went down the steps and along the water's edge as far as the corner of the lake. There he stood pensive, wrapped in an unexpected peace. The place seemed to him to be hallowed; it seemed to be watching itself, communing with itself; it seemed to be happy in the contemplation of an unchanging tranquility. This, thought the Rajah, is a picture of the condition towards which the spirit strives, and with this thought there came over him an intense love of the place. Yes, he loved it with intensity. Some day, it would surely be granted to him to identify himself with this repose, and to exist, selfless, brooding upon the face of these serene waters (p. 46).

It can be seen that Amar is just as much preoccupied as Jali with 'the near and the far'. It can also be seen that Myers is inclined to side-step his earlier recognition that the answer to the problem is great health, and to dream of pure peace. Hence the Rajah's problem is how to escape the world with its endless demands and complications, and whether he has a right to desert his wife and son. But when, in the last novel of the series (*The Pool of Vishnu*), Amar goes blind and joins a band of pilgrims, one has no feeling of a problem finally solved; on the contrary, the Rajah's decision somehow seems to symbolize waste and frustration and futility. One suspects that Myers himself did not feel that it was a satisfactory solution; but by then he was already getting tired of the task he had set himself, and the later novel lacks the haunting quality of the earlier ones.

But in these earlier parts it is all promise and intellectual excitement; it is here that Myers stakes his claim to greatness. There is nothing like them in twentieth-century literature. There are many intellectual novelists – Mann, Hesse, Musil, Huxley; but none achieves this sense of deep-breathing serenity and detachment. For a while Myers seems almost godlike. In *The Orissers* he had already practised this scheme of making various characters stand for certain attitudes towards life, but here he brings it to perfection. It is almost as if the events were simply a parable to clarify and illustrate the argument. For example, on page 3 of the novel Jali sees a cobra crawling along a ledge high up the wall of the palace. There is a small plant in the gutter that moves at every gust of wind. It strikes the cobra, which rears up, then another gust makes the plant thrash down on its head again; the snake coils and strikes at it, but in doing so loses its balance on the ledge and falls on to a roof far below, where it writhes in agony with a broken back. The whole episode only takes a paragraph, and Myers does not pause to draw a moral; but one feels that this is symbolic. Its lesson is control over instinct. This comes immediately after Jali's meditation upon the problem of the near and the far, the promise of the horizon and the pain of the present, and one feels that Myers has neatly added one more line to the equation, with an enviable economy. And when, a few chapters later, we accompany Hari as he goes out to meet Lalita in secret, it is obvious that here again Myers is symbolizing another aspect of human life, this time the power of the erotic instinct. This is made clearer by the continuation of the scene in which Hari finds the beautiful Gunevati sleeping in a forest hut. She is a member of a sect called the Vamachari, worshippers of the goddess of love, whose rites involve sexual orgies in which Gunevati herself represents the goddess. Hari asks her what is to prevent him from raping her. 'Her silence gave him his answer. Compassion again stirred within him. To be so beautiful and to hold oneself so cheap!'

It is in small matters like this that Myers reveals the depth of his insight into human beings. It is yet another ironic twist that Gunevati later tells Jali that Hari did rape her; she finds his abstention a bitter insult.

It should be added that Myers seems to have none of the almost morbid preoccupation with sex that one finds in Aldous Huxley. One feels in Huxley that when a girl yields her virtue or is raped the novelist is participating enthusiastically, even when his attitude seems to be a slightly Swiftian disgust. (This is not intended to be a criticism of Huxley; in many ways he shared the views of D. H. Lawrence on sex.) Myers, on the other hand, seems disturbingly uninterested in sex – disturbingly because this means that he is unaware of it as a liberating force; he tends to rely far too much on the intellect. There are plenty of adulteries in Myers's novels but he can never spare more than a sentence for them, and sometimes they get even less than that. Where sex is concerned, he seems a cold fish; there is not even the detached, Olympian delight that one finds in Anatole France. So it seems quite natural that Hari's affair with Lalita should peter out at an early stage in the novel, out of a lack of interest in both parties. Hari's love affair with Sita, Amar's wife, is probably the most unsatisfactory affair ever described in fiction. One is aware that Myers is positively uninterested in it. Aldous Huxley would have led up to a bedroom scene and then allowed a sense of anticlimax to develop; Myers is not even interested enough to mention whether the love affair reaches the bedroom stage, with the consequence that the anti- climax develops relatively early.

Apart from the various love affairs involved, the novel is mostly concerned with intrigue – the conflict between Akbar's sons. Various prominent characters in the novel, Sheik Mobarek, Narsing, Mabun Das, are merely pawns in this intrigue and play no other part. The intrigue itself is something of a disappointment. Prince Salim is a secret member of the Vamachari sect – the sex-worshippers – and his father has sworn to stamp out all heretical sects. Salim's supporters plot that the other son, Prince Daniyal, shall be accused of being a Vamachari, but it comes to nothing. Again one feels that Myers was not really interested.

It is apparent, however, that he is altogether more interested in Daniyal. Daniyal is a detestable creature; a homosexual, an artistic dilettante, a 'culture vulture', who sets up a camp on the side of a lake full of shallow people with artistic pretensions. Myers is here lashing out at something he loathes. It has been suggested that he was satirizing Bloomsbury, and L. P. Hartley has pointed out that this is hardly fair since the Bloomsbury set went in for plain living and high thinking. But I am inclined to believe that Myers was aiming at something altogether wider, although he may have also been inspired by irritation at Bloomsbury cliqueishness and its certainty about the rightness of its opinions. Any serious writer may be filled with rage at the intellectual scene in most civilized countries today, because the foremost place is inevitably occupied by intellectual middle-men with no creative capacity and with the self-conceit that comes of continually setting intellectual fashions and passing judgment on other people's creations. An impulsive writer like D. H. Lawrence found it impossible to control his fury, and spoiled a great deal of his work in consequence. Myers's attack is all the more deadly for being restrained, and for being aimed at no specific targets. He shows Daniyal as self-indulgent but by no means stupid. But Daniyal's pleasure comes from imagining that he is an advanced thinker, an iconoclast; and, as Myers points out, much of it depends upon his notion that the rest of the world is regarding him with horror and indignation. The camp's battle-cry is the phrase 'avant garde'.

Everyone flatters Daniyal, since he is the prince and may be the future ruler of the empire. (The historical

Daniyal never was; he died of delirium tremens in 1604.) When Daniyal writes an anti-religious play that is cheap, blasphemous, and in shocking taste, everyone professes to find it wickedly funny and brilliantly witty. At the climax of the third part of the novel, Daniyal crushes the head of a white cat under his foot,[31] and Amar is so revolted that he tries – unsuccessfully – to kill Daniyal. Here Myers seems to be implying that the Buddhist has no right to his detachment; that it is man's job to combat the world's evil or to try to add to its good. It may also be that Amar's blindness, when he finally renounces the world, is also meant to be a symbol expressing Myers's disapproval. This interpretation would certainly be consistent with the Guru's advocacy of commitment in the final part.

This, then, is the strength of the novel – its detachment, its ability to treat the complexity of human life in terms of symbols. This detachment is also its weakness, and this criticism applies to all Myers's books. They finally produce a sense of airlessness, so that the reader longs for something real and solid. They stand at the opposite extreme from the novels of Hemingway, in which the reader never loses touch with the earth and its smells. The people and events are simply not real. Myers is splendid when creating a serene atmosphere in which the problems and contradictions of human existence can be clearly seen, an atmosphere that has something in common

31 L. P. Hartley objects that Myers is here inconsistent, since he earlier describes Daniyal as being unable to bear physical pain. This is not necessarily so. Daniyal is represented as a weakling, a self-indulgent drifter, and such a person would probably be inconsistent, and quite capable of killing a cat out of sudden caprice.

with the Socratic dialogues. But when the book ceases to be a Socratic dialogue and describes Salim's uprising, Mabun Das's intrigues, Hari's disgrace and return to favour, it seems to make no concessions at all to realism. One cannot believe that anything has really happened; it is as if someone were to read the *Iliad* aloud in a gentle, toneless whisper; it is simply unconvincing.

Now, plainly, a novel differs from a volume of philosophy or a Socratic dialogue because it deals with characters in action; if it fails in this respect, then it has failed as a novel. The passages I have quoted about Jali show Myers's strength and his weakness. He is telling the reader *about* Jali's thoughts and feelings, philosophizing and using Jali as his example. He is not presenting Jali but reporting him; there is a second-hand flavour about it all. And this is unfortunately true of the whole novel; it is all reported and second-hand. The novelist differs from the historian in that he tells about events as if he were present, while the historian, unless he happens to be a Caesar, only claims to report 'from other sources'. Myers writes novels as if he were a historian.

The Near and the Far is Myers's best novel because it brings us closest to Myers as a human being. The other three novels are comparatively lightweight, even *The Orissers*, which is bulky enough in sheer volume. And it makes clear something that one had come to suspect from the other three volumes: that Myers was a man who spent his life in a search that was a total failure. At various points in Myers's books different theories of human life and how it should be lived are propounded; it is obvious that none of them works. This is undoubtedly why all his novels become more boring towards the end; he has lost contact with the original impulse, or perhaps examined it and found that it was less promising than he imagined. I personally find the last volume of *The Near and the Far* very nearly unreadable. The central character is an old Guru who nurses Hari when he has been wounded. He is undoubtedly an admirable character; he is not only a holy man, he is a social reformer who tries to help the miserable human beings in the filthy Hindu villages. Still, as a character, he is rather a bore. Myers seems to have come a long way to arrive at this extremely simple conclusion: that one should help one's fellow men, that we are members of one another. Possibly the Guru is ultimately unsatisfying because the reader suspects that he does not really satisfy Myers. (The Guru was apparently a portrait of Max Plowman, whom Myers admired.) After all, if it is important to commit oneself to ameliorating social misery, is not the Guru also a failure? He only tries to improve things on a tiny individual scale; with a stronger social conscience he might become a revolutionary. But Myers could never have become an 'activist'; his need for a life of poetry and contemplation was too deep. Yet he never achieved his ideal life of poetry and contemplation; the near always triumphed over the far, and he spent his life trying to work out a compromise, a way round. His attempt to become a communist was a typical compromise. Through the person of Stephen in *Strange Glory* he admits that Russia is very far from being his spiritual home. The one answer that Myers never seriously considered was to be a man of deep conviction, a real spiritual revolutionary of the type of Shaw or Wells. These men may have been unsatisfying in the ultimate sense, but their work brings precisely that sense of vitality and exhilaration that Myers can never catch. Myers clung to his weakness; he remained a quietist, a man who wanted to be left alone. This is the root of his tragedy.

The Orissers

Mr Hartley has stated it as his opinion that *The Orissers* is Myers's best novel.[32] In the traditional sense this is so. But compared to *The Near and the Far* it is a crude and immature work. Myers's chief failing as a novelist is his tendency to melodrama; one could draw up a table of the 'good characters' and 'bad characters' in each of his books, just as in an early Hollywood film. The fact that Myers's idea of good and evil is more sophisticated than that of Hollywood is beside the point. A truly great novelist has no villains; he understands human beings too well to paint them in one colour.

The central impulse of *The Orissers* seems to be the author's desire to symbolize the kind of life he loved. It is set mostly at Eamor, an ancient mansion somewhere in Wales, a place with grey walls and smooth lawns and deep woods. The 'good characters' are the inhabitants of Eamor: Allen, Lilian Orisser, Lilian's stepson Nicholas, and Isabel. The 'bad characters' are John Mayne, an industrialist, Walter Standish, his second-in-command,

32 Letter to the author, September 1964. I wish here also to acknowledge Mr Hartley's kindness in supplying me with biographical details about Myers.

and Madeline, engaged to Walter. The story of the novel (there is not much, considering the book's length – it would have made a good long short-story) is concerned mainly with the struggle for the inheritance of Eamor.

As with all Myers's books, this one begins excellently. In the first pages, we are introduced to Allen and Cosmo Orisser. Cosmo is a kind of rogue elephant, the son of Allen's former friend and employer, Sir Charles Orisser the archaeologist. Allen wants Cosmo to go abroad and leave his stepmother Lilian alone; Cosmo's terms are that Allen should go abroad with him. It is a hard choice, but Allen decides to sacrifice himself for Lilian's peace. However, a few chapters later, Cosmo simply changes his mind about going abroad. This is typical of Myers's tendency to treat his plot with extreme casualness.

There is a long flashback during which we are introduced to Sir Charles Orisser, and told how Allen became his friend and assistant at certain excavations in the Nubian desert. And here, for a few pages, we feel that Myers is thoroughly at home; this is the kind of thing he enjoys writing about: the brilliant savant Orisser, who is nevertheless the perfect English gentleman. 'As time passed, it was borne in upon Allen... that the community of feeling between his companion and the contemporary world was singularly slight. At first he thought that Sir Charles must suffer from this isolation of spirit, but later he perceived that his friend was troubled by no desire for a closer connection with humanity'. This is a typical Myers sentiment; here he expresses his heart of hearts. It is in sentences like this that we find the reason why Myers is a cult for a small number of readers. He expresses fastidiousness, fineness of spirit, intellect, a kind of spiritual aristocracy. And when he writes of Sir Charles's total absorption in his archaeological work, his feeling that the present is only an unimportant moment in the great flow of history, we feel that Myers is writing with approval and enthusiasm.

Sir Charles marries the beautiful Lilian, many years his junior. But he is involved with various crooks in the City, and one day his finances collapse and he commits suicide. Eamor is now Lilian's property, but it is so heavily mortgaged that she seems certain to lose it. At this point an earlier suitor, John Mayne, renews his offer of marriage and she accepts. Mayne is one of Myers's pet aversions – the brutal business man who salves his conscience with 'good works' but whose life is fundamentally a sham. He wants Lilian as a possession, but he cannot understand her fundamental aloofness, her detachment of spirit. On the other hand Lilian finds his brashness and stupidity unbearable, so after a few months of marriage they part. Mayne allows her to stay on at Eamor as a kind of revenge; his condition is that she never leaves the place; it will become her prison. He also sends to stay with her his niece Madeline. Madeline is another of Myers's aversions. She *needs* people, and wants to involve them with her in order to convince herself that she exists; she professes to be religious, because it gives her another stick to beat people with; she is fundamentally empty – another of Myers's studies in inauthenticity that link him with Heidegger and Sartre. Myers's habit of setting up puppets to be knocked down is, however, far more reminiscent of Ayn Rand; *The Orissers* and *Atlas Shrugged* have a great deal in common, although Ayn Rand would certainly have disapproved of Myers's attitude towards industrialists. Mayne's right-hand man Walter represents another type of inauthenticity. There is at least a kind of grandeur about Mayne's ruthlessness and wickedness; Walter is a cold fish, deeply self-approving, as unctuous as Madeline and as empty. Myers has very little trouble in showing how the Orissers are infinitely preferable to Mayne, Walter, and Madeline.

Cosmo Orisser, Sir Charles's other son, introduces a complication into the plot. He is a man whose whole life has been one long act of rebellion, a continuous expression of his dissatisfaction with life. When the book opens, he is half insane and something of a dipsomaniac. But he decides he would like to stay in the village near Eamor, and his presence involves threat, for if Mayne found out he might decide to leave Eamor to Cosmo just to spite Lilian. (He has promised, at all events, to keep it in the Orisser family.) Mayne has discovered that he is dying of a cancer (again, one feels that Myers is loading the balance against the characters he dislikes). Eventually, Allen solves the problem by killing Cosmo. One might expect that there would be an exciting scene here, but as usual Myers disappoints; the 'murder' – it seems to be no more than a blow struck in anger – is committed off-stage. This takes place about half-way through the novel, which falls off from this point onward; there are too many conversations that seem to get nowhere, and too many long passages of rumination and explanation on the part of the author. When he is not at his best Myers can be a most irritating writer. He devotes whole chapters to conversations that take the action no further, and dismisses important action in a couple of lines in his favourite 'reporting' manner. For example, Cosmo's brother Nicholas is a fairly important character, and much space is given to his various problems and perplexities. He is in love with an attractive girl Isabel, another inhabitant of Eamor. Isabel finally becomes his mistress: but this is how this comparatively important event is described: 'It so happened, too, that he was ready to take the lead just when Isabel showed signs of faltering. He was able to catch her up in the flow of his vital spirits, and to sweep her off into a sphere where the enactment of his sensual fantasies was possible.'

That is all. Hardly a very satisfying seduction scene. Myers sounds as if he were summarizing the plot of someone else's novel instead of writing his own. But, worse still, he later subjects the reader to immensely long conversations about the importance of sex.[33]

The rest of *The Orissers* can be briefly told. John Mayne dies; Madeline continues to plot against Lilian, and ends by trying – unsuccessfully – to tamper with the will. This scene is the climax of the novel. After this, Madeline marries Walter and is instrumental in getting him a peerage; and Allen marries Lilian, who was already his mistress. Nicholas, for some reason, does not marry Isabel. We gather that Lilian becomes even more

33 Strangely enough, Myers had a reputation among his friends as something of an amorist. This is yet another of the contradictions of his strange character.

detached and aloof after her marriage, achieving some of the independence of material things which characterizes a Hindu saint. The final scene shows Lilian and her step-son sitting on the lawn in silent communion, while Allen watches them 'with heavy sorrow in his heart'. This is on page 538 of the novel. The reader cannot help feeling a certain irritation. He has been brought a long way to this inconclusive and unsatisfying ending, and has ploughed through a great deal of joyless and abstract writing. The ending seems to be Myers's confession of his own failure. In Chapter 22, which gives an account of an argument between Allen and Nicholas, it becomes clear that Myers knows what is wrong with himself; Allen tells Nicholas that his life is too cerebral; he has become separated from the 'deeper movements of organic life'. This is what D. H. Lawrence also recognized; but Lawrence at least had a kind of solution; his novels are full of the presence of nature and the reality of sex. Myers's take place in a vacuum.

The Clio

In certain ways *The Clio* is Myers's most satisfactory novel. It is light, witty, and manages to keep moving fairly briskly up till the end. It is a light-weight piece of work, and in the early chapters the tone is strongly reminiscent of Saki, or even Oscar Wilde. It emphasizes Myers's connection with the 1890s, the continuity of the tradition.

'The Clio' is the most expensive steam yacht in the world, and it is owned by the still attractive Lady Oswestry. On board are Sir James Annesley, a sixty-year-old baronet whom Lady Oswestry is hoping to seduce into marriage; Lady Oswestry's two sons Hugo and Harry, and a number of pretty girls. The plot is thin; the 'Clio' goes up the Amazon, becomes slightly involved in a revolution for which Harry is partly responsible, and finally sets out to return to London, minus Sir James who has died of fever. Nothing of much importance happens. One of the girls becomes Sir James's mistress – very briefly, before he dies; another, who is already Hugo's mistress, throws him over and he falls in love with yet another young lady. The revolution goes on in the distance but never comes very close. It is obviously a musical-comedy plot, whose major interest is who will end up in bed with whom. For the first few chapters Myers puts himself out to sound gay and cynical: 'Most people, she reflected sadly, did so lack finish. They looked terribly shop-soiled and untidy and misshapen. One had to fall back upon their moral qualities in order not to dislike them'.

He seems quite to approve of the magnificent steam yacht and the beautiful girls in their coloured dresses, and the atmosphere of culture and light-heartedness. In the hands of Aldous Huxley the book would have become a delightful romp. As it is, one becomes aware – as usual – that Myers is not really very deeply interested in it. He does not seem to know quite why he started writing it. Since the whole interest of the plot is more or less romantic interest, the story obviously needs to be told by a novelist with a certain penchant for romantic situations – that is to say, by almost anyone but Myers. There is one somewhat Huxleyan scene where Angela is frightened by some small animal that has got into her cabin, and climbs on to a piece of furniture. Sir James traps the animal in a sewing basket and tries to help Angela down, but her dress catches. Holding her legs, Sir James cannot resist kissing the thigh above the stocking. Then, 'during the next half-hour, after he had locked the door, he found her of an exquisite docility'. This is as far as Myers is willing to go in creating Huxleyan situations; he passes on hastily to other matters...

At the end of the book Harry decides to stay in Brazil to help the revolution forward – in fact he has dreams of being a South American dictator. He explains to his mother that fashionable life in London bores him; but one doubts whether Myers was here speaking from his heart; it is more probably a convenient way of ending the novel. And on closing the book, the reader has the usual feeling of having been cheated. What does it all amount to? Why did Myers write it? There is no answer, except that Myers wanted to show he could do something just as good as *Those Barren Leaves*.

Strange Glory

Unfortunately Myers's last novel, *Strange Glory*, is his least satisfactory. But at any rate its unsatisfactoriness (I am unwilling to say 'badness') gives an insight into the author's creative process. It is possible to see precisely what he set out to do. The novel is set in the forests around New Orleans, and its chief male character is an eccentric old hermit called Wentworth who once spent some time in jail for killing his wife's lover. A pretty young society woman, Paulina, wanders out into the forest and meets the hermit. In subsequent years she often revisits the forest to renew her acquaintance with Wentworth. She inherits a fortune and marries an English lord; later, dissatisfied with her life, she takes lovers and is divorced by her husband. Then she returns to the forest and meets Stephen, Wentworth's son-in-law, a young scientist who is a communist. The second half of the book is devoted to this highly unsatisfactory and inconclusive love affair. At the end of the novel Stephen is rather casually killed off – he dies of typhus in Russia.

It is clear that Myers was fascinated by the idea of a quiet retreat in the forest, and that a hermit who has survived two unsuccessful marriages and lost three fortunes should find peace there. When Paula describes to Wentworth how her marriage has finally broken up, it seems that she is now rather painfully learning the same lesson. Wentworth himself had once been married to a very beautiful half-caste girl who turned out to be a nymphomaniac who cuckolded him even on their honeymoon; later, this girl drank herself to death. Stephen, the young scientist, then married Wentworth's daughter – another exceptionally beautiful but completely empty-headed girl. So when Stephen and Paulina fall in love, it looks as if they have both outgrown their youthful follies and will now lead a useful and fruitful life together. Myers disposes of Stephen's present wife by making Stephen remark, 'She is so beautiful that anyone will marry her'. The girl's father – Wentworth – seems to make no objection. Then Stephen returns to Russia to clear up his affairs there, and he and his wife die of typhus. At the end of the book Paulina prepares to go to Russia to take charge of Stephen's son.

The reason for the unsatisfactoriness of Myers's novels can be clearly seen in this case: he was simply not interested in 'developments'. It is obvious that his heart is in the early chapters of the book, describing how Paulina and the hermit become acquainted, and how the peace of the forest exercises a steadily increasing fascination on Paulina. But what then? Unfortunately a writer cannot publish half a novel. One alternative would be to leave it unfinished and unpublished – but this is unsatisfactory. So the story has to be dragged on for another hundred or so pages, as artificially as the last act of a musical comedy where the boy and girl have to quarrel in order that they can make it up and be reunited in the grand finale. In the meantime, all the life seems to seep out of the novel like a slowly-deflating tyre; the feeling of airlessness and suffocation increases; the reader finally puts it down feeling drained and exhausted. Great novels have the opposite effect: the power to recharge the reader's batteries; so that after the sleigh ride in *War and Peace* the reader's cheeks also are tingling with the cold air. But very few novels of the twentieth century have this power, for one of the chief characteristics of this century is its tendency to life-devaluation. Inevitably, the intelligent and sensitive suffer from this tendency more than the unintelligent, for intelligence has the power to convert experience into unconscious knowledge in the quickest possible time; experience has to be packed down into the subconscious mind so that the conscious mind is left free to grapple with the next problem. But this is tantamount to saying that the intelligent are quicker to acquire habits, and habit is usually associated with boredom. In reading Myers, we are always aware that he has been drawn into the great twentieth-century vortex of life-devaluation, and that the fine qualities of his mind were powerless against it. What he needed was the one quality he did not possess – a little crude vitality, or at least the recognition of its importance.

I said earlier that the writer with whom Myers continually invites comparison is Aldous Huxley. The comparison is by no means to Myers's disadvantage. There is always something a little over-done, a little clever-clever, about Huxley's intelligence. Sometimes his cleverness is impressive; but more often it misfires because one feels that he cares deeply about being thought clever and is performing for applause, like an intellectual acrobat. In comparison Myers seems to be made of stronger stuff; he seems to be driven only by interest in the situation he is presenting. To some extent this makes him a worse entertainer than Huxley, but the reader finds it easier to grant Myers his liking and admiration.

This helps to define why many readers, myself among them, return to Myers's novels a second or third time, even though the first reading left them irritated and dissatisfied. His virtues are so unusual in a twentieth-century novelist – a certain aristocratic intellectualism, a refusal to be associated with any clique or any fashionable opinion. Purely as a literary figure, there are few novelists who make such an excellent impression as Myers. The ultimate criticism of him is that he lacked raw vitality; but his positive qualities place him very high on the list of modern writers. If we compare him with Proust or Joyce or Faulkner he seems refreshingly un-neurotic, and we become aware of the very high quality of his intelligence. In all the novels that came after *The Orissers*, the reader also becomes unmistakably aware of a certain warmth and generosity of spirit. (L. P. Hartley confirms that Myers was an unusually affectionate man with a strong gift for friendship; the generosity is confirmed by his action in buying up a hundred or so copies of Lindsay's *A Voyage to Arcturus* – which had been a complete failure – and giving them away to his friends.) One becomes so used to accepting the neuroses and spites of the twentieth-century novelist as part and parcel of his genius that it is exhilarating to find someone so relatively free of them.

Whatever reservations we may have about Myers's novels, he undoubtedly belongs on the list of major writers of the twentieth century. The reader who stumbles upon *The Near and the Far* is likely to ask: 'But why haven't I heard of him?' It is, indeed, a relevant question. The literature on Joyce is so abundant that Professor Levin spoke of 'the Joyce industry'. In recent years the Lawrence industry has been catching up with it. Mann, Proust, Kafka, Hesse, Wolfe, and Hemingway may not have so many books devoted to them, but they are on the modern literature syllabus of every college. Other members of the Bloomsbury group are well documented – Virginia Woolf, Aldous Huxley, Lytton Strachey, E.

M. Forster – and their works are all in print. So to what accident does Myers owe his neglect? The reason may be purely historical: that he died at the wrong time, in the midst of a world war, and several years after he had published his last novel. Whatever the reason, it is time the neglect was remedied; the twentieth century has not produced so many major writers that we can afford to forget one of them.

1965

10

THE SHAW PROBLEM

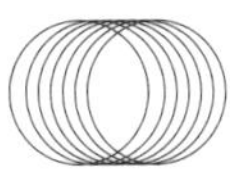

Five years after the death of Bernard Shaw, I wrote an appreciation of him to be published on his centenary.[34] As far as I know, my article was the only one to appear that week that did not assume that Shaw was completely outmoded and would be forgotten within the next twenty years. And even then the editor of the Sunday newspaper in which it appeared took the precaution of printing on the same page another article by an Oxford don, in which Shaw was dismissed as a boring egoist with a flair for publicity.

I doubt whether there has ever been another centenary in the history of literature when critics have been so unwilling to express the usual pieties. For some reason Shaw seemed to bring out the worst in everyone. 'The intensity of my impatience with him occasionally reaches such a pitch, that it would positively be a relief to me to dig him up and throw stones at him', Shaw once wrote of Shakespeare. This seems to summarize the way that every single respectable critic felt about Shaw in 1956.

By the early 1960s the hostility had simmered down a little. But Shaw's stock is still low. It is worth considering why this should be so.

34 See *Editor's Notes* at the end of this essay [Ed.].

Shaw was one of the first writers of the twentieth century to discover that newspaper publicity can produce a wider audience than good reviews. Like most artists, he felt a certain contemptuous hostility towards the critics. ('Don't mind the critics', Sibelius said once, 'No one ever erected a statue to a critic'.) So he took pleasure in thumbing his nose at them and using the gossip columns to advertise his plays. Whenever he arrived off a train or caught a boat he could reckon on the presence of at least one reporter, who would headline his more provoking statements. Being the first to use this method, he was not aware of its consequences. But it is significant that digs at his critics began to appear in his prefaces some time after 1910; in the earlier years of his writing life, he was a critic himself and seems to have harboured no hostility against the tribe. The war with the critics began with *Fanny's First Play*, and reached a kind of culmination in a violent and bad-tempered introduction to *The Intelligent Woman's Guide to Socialism and Capitalism*, called 'First Aid to Critics', which he actually had printed as a pamphlet and glued in the front of the cheap edition. This can be taken as a measure of how far Shaw had been baited by the critics; as a skilled debater, he had always made a point of never losing his temper in public, and never showing resentment.

By the mid 1930s a new type of anti-Shavian had appeared. These were no longer the old-fashioned theatre critics, who regarded themselves in some sense as Shaw's equals. They were the new influences in literature, whose intention was not to criticize Shaw but to finish him for good. Ezra Pound called him a 'ninth-rate coward', and Eliot has some curiously feeble and bad-tempered sneers about him in his early critical essays. Joyce allowed his opinion of Shaw to appear as one very brief and contemptuous reference in *Ulysses*. The generation of Auden and Spender, trained under Eliot, took care never even to mention Shaw's name.

Not surprisingly, Shaw revealed a schoolboy streak of defiance. Unlike Yeats, he made no attempt to understand the new writers; he simply became more jauntily and provokingly Shavian. The Shaw of the last period appears in the books by his friend Stephen Winsten, and they read like a satirical parody of Shaw written by an enemy. Shaw had become the perpetual boaster and epigrammatist, still doing his best to be provocative and shocking. His last preface, written when he was niney-two, must have confirmed his enemies in their belief that he was a senile clown. He announces defiantly that history will find the Second World War a boring triviality, and asks: 'I wonder how many people really prefer bogus war news and police news to smiling comedy with some hope in it! I do not. When they begin, I switch off the wireless'. The smiling and hopeful comedy was the incredibly feeble *Buoyant Billions*. When he died, the general feeling seemed to be that he had overrated himself for fifty years, and it was now time to forget him for a very long time indeed.

And yet it is impossible to look into masterpieces like *Man and Superman*, *John Bull's Other Island*, or *Major Barbara* and not to feel that their author is still very much underrated. As early as 1905 Tolstoy had warned him that he was spoiling his best effects by clowning. One of his favourite forms of clowning consisted in announcing that he was the greatest literary genius of our time. For Shaw, the joke was improved by the fact that it was true. Even the critics might have come to that conclusion if Shaw had kept silent and allowed his plays to speak for themselves. But why did he seem to feel this compulsive need to talk about his genius? The probability is that he was basically a frustrated and disappointed man. He once wrote: 'I have solved every major problem of our time, and people still go on propounding them as if they were unsolved.' This also happens to be literally true. After fifty years of solving major problems he remained a man who was never taken seriously. Goethe had been a State Councillor, Tolstoy had been the most influential thinker in Russia; Shaw was still an irresponsible comedian at eighty. The debater's rule of never showing himself to be ruffled forbade him to lose his temper. But the irritating grin became broader, and the assertions of his genius more persistent.

To understand how all this came about, it is necessary to go back to the closing years of the last century. For Shaw was a true descendant of the Victorians – of men like Carlyle and Dickens, Trollope and Thackeray, Ruskin and Macaulay. What these men had in common was an optimistic attitude towards society and the possibility of progress, and a sense of being social figures as well as writers. By the 1880s the fashion was already changing: Trollope was no longer read, and young followers of Swinburne dared to state publicly that Ruskin and Carlyle were pontifical bores. In the 1890s literature was again regarded as a private business. The image of the poet was no longer of the full-bearded national hero, but of a young man with long hair and a shy manner. Wilde provided this new generation with a gospel – and Wilde, for all his worldliness, was fundamentally an anti-worldling, a seeker after the tragic. This new attitude, it must be admitted, was conducive to better literature than the ostentatious public-spiritedness of the older generation. One has only to read Horne's *New Spirit of the Age* to see that much Victorian literature was bad because it was pretentious, because it did not dare to be deeply subjective. 'The tragic generation' (as Yeats called them) changed all that. The change of attitude was as complete as could be. Instead of Browning's 'God's in his heaven' and Tennyson's faith in 'the parliament of man, the federation of the world', we have the total nihilism of James Thomson's *City of Dreadful Night*, or the determined other-worldliness of Newman and Francis Thompson.

If we follow the progress of European literature from the mid-eighteenth century onward, we can see quite clearly that a new sensibility has developed, and also a new sensitivity. Inevitably, sensitivity means weakness – but no one would therefore assert that stupidity and strength are preferable. When the older generation – the Victorian survivors – accused the *fin-de-siècle* generation of weakness, the younger generation hurled back an accusation of pompousness and inauthenticity. In England there came a brief reaction against the *fin-de-siècle* generation, novelists like Galsworthy and Bennett, and the Georgian poets, but it was soon forgotten and subjectivity – and pessimism – achieved a new force in the work of Eliot, Joyce, Proust, and the rest. The novels of Aldous Huxley state the 'subjectivist' position with clarity. His heroes are all weak and all sensitive. The Huxley hero is the 'chinless-intelligent man', and the Huxley villains are all big-chinned and stupid. I have gone into this matter at length elsewhere, so shall not dwell on it now.[35] But it is clear that Huxley finds something completely incompatible in the ideas of strength and intelligence; he goes further than any of the *fin-de-siècle* poets in identifying weakness with intelligence.

Unfortunately, there were very few notable examples of intelligence and strength in the latter part of the nineteenth century; in fact the only one worth noting was Tolstoy. He somehow managed to combine the physical strength and mental balance of a peasant with a profoundly self-critical intelligence. There was one other – Bernard Shaw. But two swallows do not make a summer. Ever since the 1890s there have been a few solitary protests at the equation of self-criticism with self-hatred, of weakness with intelligence; none was effective. Thomas Mann tried exalting the bourgeois virtues, and succeeded to a remarkable extent in mastering his own Germanic tendency to subjectivity and despair; but his solution had no wide appeal. Stefan George and D. H. Lawrence preached the artist-prophet; but they could be dismissed

35 See my 'Existential Criticism and the Work of Aldous Huxley' included as Appendix One of *The Strength to Dream*.

as hysterics and crypto-fascists. Wells and Shaw preached the least attractive doctrine of all – social commitment and common sense. Both have been unfashionable since the end of the First World War.

But is there any *a priori* reason why a strong man should be destroyed by intelligence and self-criticism? Plainly not. We can understand well enough why increasing sensitivity should lead to a loosening of the grip on life. To begin with, intelligence and sensitivity are acquired by mental discipline and study, and these in themselves can undermine physical health if pursued too single-mindedly. But it is possible for a highly critical intelligence to inhabit a healthy body, as in the case of Tolstoy, without producing mental or physical sickness.

This is what happened in the case of Shaw, and he himself was fully conscious of the situation. It must be recognized that most of the *fin-de-siècle* poets established a reputation early and died young; few of them had time to develop much resistance to the romantic virus. Shaw, like Carlyle, was nearly forty before he began to make himself known. George Sampson has pointed out in the *Concise Cambridge History of English Literature* that Shaw's early novels show a dangerous over-sensitivity and romanticism. One has only to read the last of them, *An Unsocial Socialist*, to realize that this is true.

An Unsocial Socialist produces some other insights into the mind of the young Shaw. In none of the earlier novels had the hero figured as a lady's man; in fact the hero of his first novel, *Immaturity*, does not even get around to falling in love. The lovers in these early novels are usually weaklings, of the type of Octavius in *Man and Superman*. Conolly, the engineer-hero of the second novel, *The Irrational Knot*, has an unsuccessful marriage but makes no fuss about allowing it to break up, and is glad to get back to his major interest – science. Owen Jack, in *Love Among the Artists*, is again too strong a man to bother with falling in love. But Trefusis, the hero of *An Unsocial Socialist*, is the first typical 'Shavian Man', and one has a feeling that Shaw has at last found a persona that suits him. None of the earlier heroes could be lovers because they were not ready for it; they are oddly negative – even Jack, who seems to be based on Beethoven. Trefusis has tried love and found it wanting – or rather, boring; he flees from his beautiful wife and takes refuge in a girls' school. Why in a girls' school? Because it gives Shaw the opportunity to indulge in a long romantic day-dream. Three attractive young schoolgirls find the conduct of the school gardener baffling, and are led to suspect that he is a 'gentleman' in disguise. Then it turns out that the gardener is the rich socialist Trefusis, who has left his lovely wife because he cannot bear a life that is a 'carnival of love'. 'For five weeks I have walked and talked and dallied with the loveliest woman in the world, and the upshot is that I am flying from her, and am for the hermit's cave until I die. Love cannot keep possession of me: all my strongest powers rise up against it and cannot endure it.' But what is obvious is that Trefusis is not a hermit, any more than Shaw was. He does not want to live a totally sexless life; it is only that his heroic romanticism is revolted at the idea of being a slave to woman. Shaw makes it clear that

Trefusis is attractive to women, in fact is almost irresistible when he wants to be. But his idealism is as strong as his sexual romanticism. This is the first clear statement of this theme in Shaw: it will have many reincarnations in the plays.

Ten years later a slightly altered version of Trefusis appears as the hero of *The Philanderer*, perhaps Shaw's worst play. Once again we have the socialist who is an idealist before he is a lover – and who owes his success in love to precisely this. Another ten years pass and Shaw lays the ghost of Trefusis by reincarnating him as Don Juan in *Man and Superman*. Trefusis and the philanderer were only socialists, but Don Juan is in the grip of an even deeper passion: philosophy. We feel of Trefusis that although there can be no doubting his intellectual sincerity, his idealism will burn brighter with an audience of admiring women. Don Juan produces the feeling that he has outgrown this need. This was probably wishful thinking, for a decade later Shaw is allowing himself to indulge a romantic passion for Mrs Patrick Campbell. Not until he is in his sixties do we feel that sexual romanticism has ceased to be a vital driving force behind Shaw's thinking. So Shaw was, in fact, a typical romantic who was lucky enough to have been born with a strong head. Equally important was his shyness – which he has described in several of the autobiographical prefaces – which prevented his exposing himself to possible rebuffs, and so again allowed his genius a long period of incubation. The importance of this can hardly be underestimated. Both Ernest Dowson and James Thomson produced their finest 'poetry of despair' in their twenties; Dowson was dead at thirty-three. At this age Shaw had only just obtained his first journalistic job, as music critic on the *Star*; and these early music criticisms show that he is still immature. He only hits his intellectual stride at the age of forty, when he becomes dramatic critic for the *Saturday Review*.

All this suggests that if Shaw had been a less shy and less patient man he might easily have burned himself out as a romantic in his twenties. Yeats, Chesterton, and others later used the word 'methodical' as a stick to beat Shaw; but a man who can spend twenty years in London as an unknown writer – with no sign of either social or literary success – needs to discipline himself beyond despair; he has to learn to endure, and this requires the cultivation of patience and methodicalness.

It is significant that Tolstoy was also a late developer; he married at thirty-four, and published the first volume of *War and Peace* when he was thirty-seven (the age at which Carlyle also published *The French Revolution*.) These men had learned patience and self-discipline; this is why they were stronger than their contemporaries – not because they were fortunate enough to be born without romantic 'sensitivity'. And the proof of this lies in the development of Yeats, who began as a thoroughgoing romantic and developed into a life-affirmer whose evolutionism in *Under Ben Bulben* is hardly distinguishable from Shaw's. What distinguished Yeats from such contemporaries as Dowson, Johnson, and Wilde was that he was relatively free of self-pity, and consequently had no self-destructive instinct. The romantic is committed to self-destruction because romantic values lead inevitably in that direction. A poet who thinks that youth and love are the most important things in the world is hardly allowing himself much chance of survival. Shelley's Alastor *had* to die when he failed to find his ideal woman; no other end was possible. Yeats occasionally identified his ideal with death, as in *The Land of Heart's Desire*, but by the time he was thirty-five – at the turn of the century – he was already recognizably the tougher Yeats we know from the later poems. Yeats is admired today more than Shaw, perhaps because he never made an indecent parade of his strength; but what we admire about him is his strength, not his weakness.

We find it difficult to sympathize with Shaw because his strength came from a slow, leisurely development while we live in a high-pressure civilization that seems to feel that time is running out. We find it easier to sympathize with such an obviously careless and rhetorical writer as Thomas Wolfe because his voice is urgent; he is driven by a fever we recognize. And yet it becomes steadily more apparent that leisurely development is the answer to the greatest problems of our civilization. Young leaders – like Hitler, Mussolini, and Stalin – created a great deal of chaos in our time; the least we could say for de Gaulle, Adenauer, and Khrushchev was that they apparently learned something from their experience. The few writers of our century who have achieved anything like greatness have been the slow developers – Mann, Hesse, Musil, Powys, Yeats, Joyce, Gide. The writers who have produced characteristic work early – Wolfe, Dylan

Thomas, Hart Crane, Hemingway, Faulkner, Kafka – either died early or very obviously failed to develop.

But Shaw still stands out from the list of slow developers as an exception. Mann, Hesse, Musil, and the rest were all romantics, subjectivists. The only major writer with whom Shaw has much in common is Brecht. How, then, did it come about that Shaw moved so naturally into the 'objective' tradition?

Again his early life provides the clue. Apart from the works of Shelley and Byron, Shaw imbibed very little morbid romanticism in his youth. While James Thomson and Ernest Dowson read Novalis, De Musset, and Hugo, Shaw studied the piano scores of Mozart's *Don Giovanni*, Meyerbeer's *Robert the Devil* and Gounod's *Faust*. In short, he was getting his romanticism from a less tainted source. Shaw's passion for music seems to have saved him from drinking too deeply of contemporary disillusion. His family was musical, not literary. There was always plenty of sheet music around the place, but not a good deal of literature. When Robert Smith, the hero of *Immaturity*, unpacks his books in his London room they consist of Shakespeare, the Bible, Byron, and a few more 'standard works' which he does not name. (Other sources lead us to surmise that they included Scott, Charles Lever, and Dickens.) Shaw's literary culture later became fairly wide, and one biographer even speaks of his 'enormous erudition', but he could never at any time have been described as a voracious reader.

Now musical romanticism is a totally different thing from literary romanticism – at least, it was in the 1870s, when Wagner was relatively unknown in England and Mahler and Debussy had not properly started their careers. Music has a tendency to soften outlines. Merimée's novel *Carmen* is a brilliant and brutal piece of sophisticated realism, Bizet's opera is a very good musical comedy; Hugo's *Le Roi s'amuse* is a bitter attack on royalty and privilege, Verdi's opera (*The Masked Ball*) is just noisy and melodious grand opera; Goethe's *Werther* caused a wave of suicide in Germany, Massenet's *Werther* is only likely to promote a delicious melancholy.

As to Goethe's *Faust*, it is probably just as well that Shaw made its acquaintance through Gounod. Its doubt is even more radical than that of Descartes, for it raises the question of whether man's mind is of any use whatever, whether the idea of evolution through knowledge is a delusion. Gounod has turned all this into a Christmas pantomime, complete with village green and soldiers' chorus.

So while Shaw became a thoroughgoing romantic, it was not the Yeatsian other-world romanticism. Shaw's 'other world' was the world of heroic romanticism – of Scott and Dumas and Charles Lever. He admired the acting of Barry Sullivan, the last of the 'superhuman' school, and recalled how one night Sullivan's sword snapped in the last scene of *Macbeth*, and flew over the audience to bury itself in the front of the dress circle. Yeats never believed in the existence of his 'land of heart's desire'; Shaw did; it was 'out there', in the world outside Dublin.

On the other hand there were influences that pulled him towards realism; he speaks of his father's 'humorous sense of anti-climax, which I inherited from him'. For example,

> ...when I scoffed at the Bible he would instantly and sincerely rebuke me, telling me... that no educated man would make such a display of ignorance; that the Bible was universally recognized as a literary and historical masterpiece... But when he had reached the point of feeling really impressive, a convulsion of internal chuckling would wrinkle up his eyes, and... he would cap his eulogy by assuring me, with an air of perfect fairness, that the worst enemy of religion could say no worse of the Bible than that it was the damnedest parcel of lies ever written.

Shaw also mentions the impression made on him by a curious novel by Charles Lever called *A Day's Ride*. Lever is a fine writer who is undeservedly forgotten today. It is true that some of his novels are little more than a string of anecdotes, and construction was never his strong point; but *Harry Lorrequer*, *Charles O'Malley*, and *Tom Burke of Ours* are among the funniest, and at times the most exciting, novels of the nineteenth century. In *A Day's Ride*, however, he tried something different; it is about a chemist's assistant with a romantic temperament who sets out to look for adventure. As in *Don Quixote*, the humour of the book arises from the contrast between the hero's day-dreams and the reality of his life. It is not as uncompromisingly unromantic as *Don Quixote*; the hero's day-dreams are not always pricked by reality; he holds his own with a crowd of aristocratic young men who mistake him for one of themselves, and at the end of the book gets the girl of his dreams. Still, it was an exercise in a vein that would later have been called Chekhovian; and Dickens, who published the book as a serial in *All the Year Round*, urged Lever to curtail it because it was affecting circulation. Shaw was no doubt so impressed by it because he saw himself in Algernon Sidney Potts, the chemist's assistant full of heroic day-dreams.

When Shaw left school, his heroic day-dreams received a check for which *A Day's Ride* had no doubt prepared him; he was sent to work in a land agent's office as a junior clerk. He worked there for five years, and was surprisingly efficient. He explains his reasons in *Immaturity*:

> ...he hated the duties of his clerkship as barren drudgery, which numbed his faculties and wasted his time. Nevertheless, his unjustifiable contempt for Figgis and Weaver... induced him to do his work conscientiously, lest he should become their debtor for any part of his salary... His employers thought highly of him concluding that he liked his functions because he so scrupulously fulfilled them... When he addressed Figgis as 'sir', despising him in his heart, he loathed his own servility. (Chapter 2).

One of his jobs was collecting money from poor tenants, which he found particularly disagreeable and depressingly unromantic; nevertheless, it laid a foundation for his later development, as will appear in a moment.

At the age of twenty he left Dublin and came to London. By now his father and mother had separated; his father being a drunkard. There was just enough money to support Shaw without working. He lived with his mother and sister; a second sister – his favourite – had died of consumption a few weeks before he arrived in London. Shaw later stated that he allowed his mother to support him. This is not quite true, since he had a small inheritance from a relative; but times were often hard, and he admits that he felt guilty for doing nothing to improve things. These early years in London were, for Shaw, the most difficult time of his life. He was unknown and down at heel in a strange city, determined not to work for a living unless the family came to the actual point of starvation. It was during these early years that Shaw became ripe for socialism. He had been brought up in an atmosphere of slightly decayed gentility; his father's alcoholism made it difficult to keep up appearances. It was an uncomfortable way of life. And in London, he felt just as awkward and out of place – as he tells in the preface to *Immaturity*:

> The truth is that all men are in a false position in society until they have realized their possibilities and imposed them on their neighbours. They are tormented by continual short-coming in themselves; yet they irritate others by a continual overweening.

And this was soon rationalized:

> The born Communist, before he knows what he is, and understands why, is always awkward and unhappy in Plutocratic society... in short, wherever spiritual values are assessed like Income Tax.

A later passage is even more revealing:

> Thus a bee, desperately trying to reach a flower bed through a window pane, concludes that he is the victim of evil spirits or that he is mad, his end being exhaustion, despair and death. Yet, if he only knew, there is nothing wrong with him: all he has to do is go out as he came in, through the open window or door. Your born Communist begins like the bee on the pane. He worries himself and everybody else until he dies of peevishness, or is led by some propagandist pamphlet, or by his own intellectual impulses... to investigate the economic structure of our society.
>
> Immediately everything becomes clear to him. Property is theft; respectability founded on poverty is blasphemy; marriage founded on property is prostitution... . He now knows where he is, and where this society that has so intimidated him is. He is cured of his *mauvaise honte*...

Shaw's background provided him with reasons for social revolt: the years of keeping up appearances, the 'respectability founded on poverty', his parents' unhappy marriage (which was founded on property in that his father believed his mother to be an heiress; however, she was disinherited as a result of her marriage). Socialism provided him with what he needed – a belief that would enable him to feel at home in the world, to condemn it instead of being overawed by it. It provided an explanation of why reality was so unlike his romantic day-dreams. It gave him self-confidence and intellectual stability, a sense of self-justification.

All this is to say that Shaw's socialism was inevitable,

given his romantic disposition and the circumstances of his life. In many ways his circumstances and temperament were like those of James Joyce, twenty-five years his junior. Joyce's father was also a drunkard; Joyce also came from a family in decline. But he had cut adrift from his family by the time he was twenty-one. His mother was dead by then. His religion of art, of 'silence, exile and cunning', was the religion of a lone wolf. Shaw was not a lone wolf; he was living with his mother and sister, so there could be no question of withdrawal into artistic subjectivism.

This long persistence of family ties also explains Shaw's attitude to women, which has puzzled so many commentators. The heroine of his first novel is an attractive Scotswoman, and he records that Smith was 'fascinated by the sweetness of her smile, and awed by the impression of power which he received from her fine strong hands and firm jaw'. No other writer of his time would have been capable of writing this sentence. But it was important for Shaw's mental peace to believe that women could be as strong as men, that they needed no pity or protection. Pity can be a destructive emotion, and Shaw was healthy enough to resist the temptation, recognizing that pity for others is usually accompanied by self-pity. Shaw was determined not to believe that life is fundamentally tragic. To some extent this was a mechanism of self-protection; but there is an abyss of difference between self-protection and self-deception. Shaw created a consistent philosophy out of his rejection of the 'tragic sense of life', and in many ways it is better and profounder than the tragic philosophy of a Kierkegaard or Graham Greene, who mistakes his own weakness for a universal condition.

When we understand the factors that created the 'Shavian personality', we also become aware that Shaw had no choice except to develop this personality. Like Nietzsche he created his philosophy out of his will to live. This will to live was threatened by the tragic – as epitomized, for example, in the death of his sister. Shaw had the choice of believing that her death was the result of a 'tragic destiny', or that it was the outcome of carelessness and stupidity and could have been avoided. Well, Agnes Shaw had caught her consumption from a servant girl; in those days it was not believed to be infectious. Therefore her death was avoidable, and the sense of tragedy could, without intellectual dishonesty, be converted into distrust of the medical profession. So one more typical element of Shaw's personality fell into place.

The unsentimental side of Shaw created more enemies than his socialism or his admiration for women of strong character. But his admirers realize that it is an essential part of his vision, his will to live. 'Heartlessness' is a negative name for it. When Undershaft tells Cusins (in connection with his desire to marry Barbara), 'Like all young men, you greatly exaggerate the difference between one young woman and another', we hear the voice of Shaw's will to be something more important than a slave to romance; this attitude reaches a climax in the scene between Strephon and Chloe in the last part of *Back to Methuselah* when Chloe tells him: 'Really, you must have a very empty head if there is nothing in it but a dance with one girl who is no better than any of the other girls'. And she goes on to explain that she is suddenly possessed by an interest in far greater issues than love and dancing.

But most of the world's great literature is taken up with the subject of tragic love – either that or war. Yeats actually thought that literature could not exist without them: 'What theme had Homer but original sin?' What Shaw is proposing is a break with something that humanity has always regarded as essential. It is hardly surprising if most people reject the idea.

This, then, is the fundamental issue between the Shavians and the non-Shavians. The Shavians, and there are not many whole-hearted ones,[36] argue that Shaw is one of the few specimens of a really grown-up adult that the human race has produced, and that this is the reason for the unpopularity of his work. The anti-Shavians reply that Shaw was never really adult, that he was just a case of lop-sided development who owed his remarkable intellectual powers to a curious deficiency in feeling and intuition. As often as not they add that his intellectual powers were not so very unusual anyway: that his philosophy was half-baked, and would not be taken seriously for a moment by any serious philosopher. I do not propose to argue this latter charge now, since I have never heard it made by anyone who was qualified to judge Shaw's status as a philosopher.

36 I am inclined to believe that most of the people who regard themselves as Shavians are merely admirers of the superficial brilliance of the plays. My own experience of the Shaw Society, to whom I have lectured on a number of occasions, certainly gives me grounds for thinking so. The late Hesketh Pearson was the president of the Shaw Society; his remarks on *Back to Methuselah* in his biography of Shaw reveal that he was better qualified to appreciate Shakespeare.

All this is certainly not to say that Shaw had no failings; only that the attacks on him are usually wide of the mark – in fact sometimes completely irrelevant. Shaw himself once said that the biography of him by Frank Harris told the reader more about Harris than about Shaw. Now I believe that this is true of almost every contemporary account of Shaw. I myself discovered Shaw's works less than ten years before his death, at a time when his doings were very seldom reported in the newspapers, and so came to know Shaw solely through his works. The only available biography in the local public library was Archibald Henderson's *Bernard Shaw, Playboy and Prophet*, which, unlike its later versions, was incredibly feeble, and I never succeeded in reading more than a few pages of it. Consequently when I came to read about Shaw in Frank Harris's book, or in Chesterton's books about him, or in Yeats's autobiography, I found it almost impossible to connect the author of *Man and Superman* with the conceited figure conjured up by his contemporaries. Shaw's protests about being misunderstood, about the 'imaginary monster with my name attached to it that may already have taken possession of your mind through your inevitable contact with the newspaper press', are usually taken to be an inverted method of self-praise, of 'backing into the limelight'. But anyone who has had the experience of discovering Shaw through his plays, and then later of seeing him through the eyes of contemporaries, knows that Shaw had a genuine grievance there. In the same way I suspect that it will be obvious to the generation born in the 1950s that Shaw spoke no more than the truth when he described himself as being a century ahead of his time. In an age that was still in the midst of the *angst* of romanticism, Shaw was in every sense a man of the future. The romantic poets found nothing good to say about modern civilization; its complexity horrified them, and there was a strong 'back to the womb' tendency. It was impossible that a play like *Major Barbara* should be understood in 1905; I doubt whether it will be fully understood even in 2005.

Shaw's faults are connected with his inability to make himself understood. It is very difficult for a man to develop if there is no one alive who can understand what he is saying. Shaw ceased to develop about 1910; nothing he wrote after that goes any deeper into the problems that concerned him. The preface to *Back to Methuselah*, while it contains some of his best writing, shows a man who is not making the best of his powers. He states that he knows most people will never grasp anything so difficult as the difference between Darwinism and Lamarckism, when in fact the distinction is within the grasp of any fifth-form boy. What is more, Shaw had only to take the trouble to talk to Julian Huxley or J. B. S. Haldane to discover exactly why Lamarckism is untenable for a modern biologist. This need not have meant an abandonment of his evolutionist position; on the contrary, it might have been strengthened by Thomas Huxley's views on the 'radical break' between animal material and human material. In the same way, Shaw could have deepened and developed his position if he had been aware of contemporary trends in philosophy and psychology; in fact it is arguable that his position could *only* have been deepened in this way. Shaw was like a man with an intuitive grasp of music but no professional training; if such a man wants to develop into a composer, then he must start at the beginning and learn about the technical side of music. Without such knowledge, development beyond a certain point is impossible. Because Shaw did not posses the tools – the philosophical concepts – there was no way in which he could deepen or widen his philosophy. Why was this? Why did he never take the trouble? It was not out of intellectual laziness. The man who read Karl Marx in French in his twenties, and the whole of *Arabia Deserta* in his seventies was not intellectually lazy. It was simply that he felt there was no point in trying to deepen his philosophy; what he had already said was not yet understood. In Act III of *Man and Superman* Don Juan had declared that the philosopher's brain is the highest creation of the life force so far; yet from *Back to Methuselah* it seems that Shaw's brain was not a philosopher's brain.

But why should this matter? Surely most philosophy is a game played by philosophers? Anyone who glances into a volume of Kant or Hegel is likely to form an immediate conviction that a creative writer like Shaw would do better to avoid this sort of thing. But this is a superficial view. The truth is that we are all entangled in a world of assumptions and prejudices, and in order to gain any kind of knowledge we have to question *everything* we take for granted. We would still believe that the earth is the centre of the universe unless it had occurred to an astronomer to question something that seems so self-evident. But it would have done no good if Copernicus had merely said: 'I think it quite possible that the earth may go round the sun, not vice versa'. To the common man this would only have been to deny the evidence of his senses. Astronomers had to show that the common-sense theory conflicts with the facts that become apparent when the matter is studied more closely. It is necessary to get down to particulars, to facts and figures, to undermine the fallacies of our 'common-sense' standpoint. Now Shaw spent his life asking questions and challenging generally held assumptions, but he did it in the general manner of a reformer, not the particular manner of a scientist. This meant that he never really got to grips with the problem in an organized way – he merely made brief guerilla raids on it. But while it is true that a great deal of philosophy has been nothing but confusion and misunderstanding, there remains a sense in which philosophy is an organized attempt at a science for 'grasping the universe'. To use a rather inadequate simile, it is as if the universe were an engine, and the philosopher a mechanic who tries to create tools capable of taking it to pieces. Shaw simply did not possess the tools for advancing beyond a rudimentary stage. (It is true that Joad wrote a book called *Matter, Life and Value* which is an attempt to express Shaw's philosophy in 'philosophical language'; but Joad was not really the man for the job, being a popularizer rather than a true philosopher.) For all his greatness, all his brilliance, Shaw remained fundamentally entangled in 'the natural standpoint'.

It was all to Shaw's disadvantage that he remained a dramatist and never ventured into philosophy. His achievement was to have outgrown romanticism, to have solved the problem that killed Schiller and Novalis, that drove Kleist and Hölderlin to suicide, and that led Rimbaud to abandon poetry for ivory poaching. He had done this instinctively, intuitively. And he never attempted to analyse what had happened to him – and to the age he lived in. It was therefore easy for anyone who found his temperament unsympathetic to dismiss Shaw as an insensitive freak who was not qualified to understand the subtleties and spiritual agonies of a Proust or Eliot. It was too easy to declare that Shaw's philosophy was simple to understand because there was very little to understand. In fact, Shaw is interesting as a philosopher because, like Bradley and Whitehead, he unites the English empirical tradition with a historical idealism that recalls Hegel. In certain important respects he resembles William James; in others, modern existential thinkers like Heidegger and Jaspers. If he had wanted to, Shaw *could* have produced a 'philosophical testament' like Samuel Alexander's *Space, Time and Deity* or Smut's *Holism and Evolution*. A book like *The Intelligent Woman's Guide to Socialism* shows that he was capable of a flight of sustained thinking in another field. He was never tired of talking about the artist-philosopher; but he left it to Sartre and Camus to produce the kind of work that really entitled them to that description.[37]

Why? There could have been many possible reasons.

37 The excitement created ten years after Shaw's death by Teilhard de Chardin's *The Phenomenon of Man* goes to prove that Shaw's philosophy could have been academically acceptable – it is fundamentally identical with de Chardin's.

Shaw was committed to politics rather than to philosophy. He may also have felt that it was his duty to remain comprehensible to 'the common man' – which is another way of saying that he may have been afraid of being labelled a 'difficult writer' and losing some of his popularity. Another reason, and I mention this purely for the sake of completeness, was that Shaw was oddly neurotic about money, and may not have wanted to write anything that would not immediately reach a large public. The late Esme Percy told me many stories about this curious contradiction in Shaw's character – for he was, in most ways, a generous man – of how, for example, he once arrived late at a rehearsal, cursing because a cab-driver had charged him a shilling from Kings Cross to the Strand (and he had never paid more than ninepence), and was still snorting irritably about the extra threepence three hours later. Shaw's secretary has also told how he was constantly worried, in the last years of his life, in case he lost all his money, although his will later showed that his finances were in an extremely healthy state.

Finally, Shaw regarded himself as a public figure as well as an author. This was true of many of his contemporaries: Belloc was a Member of Parliament, Chesterton edited a newspaper, Bennett wrote the most influential book page in England, Wells was the founder of a movement for world government. All were asked to pronounce on any and every public question several times a week. From the perspective of the sixties, it now seems obvious that Shaw was in every way a more important figure than these contemporaries (although, in my own opinion, Wells comes very close). In the first thirty years of the present century he was simply one of a galaxy of public names. Living in this kind of limelight, with a constant sense of rivalry with Wells, Chesterton, and others, it is not surprising that he did no work of real weight and importance. If Shaw had died in 1902, after *Man and Superman*, his importance in literary history would not have been diminished. We should have lost a few fine plays – *John Bull's Other Island, Major Barbara, Back to Methuselah, The Apple Cart* – but nothing that could be called a masterpiece.

I have said that Shaw died a disappointed man, a man who could write: 'I have solved every major problem of my time, and people still go on propounding them as if they were unsolved'. To some extent this is true; but in another sense Shaw was ultimately a failure because he was not sufficiently at grips with the deepest problems of his time. The really important work in the first twenty-five years of this century was being done by men like Kafka and Wertheimer, the founders of Gestalt psychology, by Husserl and Heidegger and Jaspers and Whitehead and Wittgenstein. Shaw was completely out of touch with all this – he was not even aware that it was going on. Although he was never quite so irritatingly frivolous as Chesterton and Belloc, he nevertheless made no real attempt to deepen his foundations. Tolstoy was right when he rebuked Shaw for taking himself too lightly. If Shaw had really understood the importance of what he was doing, he would never have taken the trouble to oppose Belloc and Chesterton in public debate; he would have recognized that they were intellectual light-weights and that he had more important things to do.

In short, if Shaw died a disappointed man it was largely his own fault. By his own definition, his life deserves to be called tragic because its last forty years were a waste of magnificent opportunities. The remarkable thing is that he can survive even this. For there can be little doubt that, in future centuries, he will be regarded as the greatest writer of his time.

1965

Editor's Notes

Shaw was an enormous influence on the young Wilson particularly (although he remained a staunch supporter of Shaw all his life). In his autobiography *Dreaming to Some Purpose* (London: Century, 2004) Wilson revealed how he first discovered Shaw:

In 1946, when I was fifteen, I switched on the radio one night to the BBC's new Third Programme, and found myself listening to the third act of Shaw's *Man and Superman*. In the previous year I had seen the film of *Caesar and Cleopatra*, and thought it an impressive historical extravaganza, but felt no desire to explore Shaw's other work. But this third act of *Man and Superman* – Don Juan in Hell – left me stunned, and convinced that Shaw was the greatest playwright since Shakespeare...

What impressed me so much was that Shaw is asking: what is the purpose of life? It was the first time that I had heard anyone ask the question that had haunted me since the age of thirteen. Wells had written a little book called *What Are We To Do With Our Lives?*, but it was basically about politics and sociology. Shaw obviously understood the basic problem: meaninglessness.' (p.14)

The early essay, defending Shaw, was 'Shaw: Psychologist and Mystic'. It appeared in *The Sunday Times*, July 22, 1956, p.6 (**C4**).

On July 20, 1956 he appeared on BBC Television in an unscripted discussion about Shaw (**LB1**) and in 1957 he was seen discussing Shaw in the film *Bernard Shaw* (Triangle Films); a copy of which is held at the British Film Archive (cat. No. 5599) (**F1**).

He did indeed lecture to the Shaw Society on April 26, 1957 and April 29, 1960, contributing two essays to their journal *The Shavian*: 'Shaw and Strindberg' (no. 15, June 1959, pp. 24) and 'Shaw's Existentialism' (vol. 2, no. 1, Feb. 1960, pp. 4-6) (**C16** & **C23**). He spoke at the Shaw Festival at Niagara-on-the-Lake, Ontario in 1977. His essay 'The Making of a Playwright', about the writing of *Widowers' Houses*, appeared in that years' *Shaw Festival Programme 1977* (**C279**).

It was inevitable that he should write a book on his hero: *Bernard Shaw: A Reassessment* (London: Hutchinson & Co.) was published in 1969 (**A21**). Although politics never interested him greatly, throughout the 1950s, due to Shaw's influence, Wilson considered himself a Socialist. Ironically it wasn't until he began writing this book on Shaw, that he changed his political allegiance. In a rare essay on the subject, *The Decline and Fall of Leftism* (Nottingham: Paupers' Press, 1989) he wrote:

What Shaw seemed to lack, as a Socialist, was any psychological insight into the problem of human freedom. He understood economics well enough to see the fallacy of Marxism. He understood social history well enough to know that the real sin against the light is not capitalism but poverty. But he failed to see that in that case, the aim of any political system should be the abolition of poverty, not of individual enterprise.

In 1979 he contributed the essay, 'A Personal View', to *The Genius of Shaw*, edited by Michael Holroyd (London: Hodder & Stoughton) (**C285**). When invited to write a book about the books that had influenced him *The Books in My Life* (Charlottesville, VA: Hampton Roads, 1998) naturally included a chapter on Shaw (**A152**).

Invariably, whenever the Editors of *Books and Bookmen* or *The Literary Review* (two journals for whom Wilson regularly wrote reviews) received a new book on Shaw, his expertise was called upon. Several of these reviews were gathered together and included in his *Existential Criticism: selected book reviews* (Nottingham: Paupers' Press, 2009) (**A178**).

11

THE WORK OF AYN RAND

When I was lecturing in America in the autumn of 1961, a great many university students asked me my opinion of Ayn Rand. I had to admit that I had never heard of her. Somebody presented me with paperback copies of her two major novels, *The Fountainhead* and *Atlas Shrugged* – the latter more than 1,000 pages long. I opened *The Fountainhead* – and was immediately put off by the rhetorical tone of its opening page:

> Howard Roark laughed.
>
> He stood naked at the edge of a cliff. The lake lay far below him. A frozen explosion of granite burst in flight to the sky over motionless water. The water seemed immovable, the stone – flowing. The stone had the stillness of one brief moment in battle when thrust meets thrust and the currents are held in a pause more dynamic than motion. The stone glowed, wet with sunrays.

I knew something of the story of the book: an intransigent young architect who wins all his battles through sheer will-power, a sermon on the glory of individualism. I turned to *Atlas Shrugged*. Then I remembered that I had seen some of this book before. A correspondent had sent me its last hundred pages: an immensely long speech, made over the radio by a man called John Galt, again to justify individualism. I had found it too wordy and given it up.

So when, after lectures, students asked my opinion of Ayn Rand I was inclined to be dismissive – a kind of modern Marie Corelli, much given to preaching and grandiose language.

A year later, being confined to bed with influenza, I made another attempt to read *Atlas Shrugged*. This time I persisted beyond the first twenty pages, determined to give it a fair trial. The result was that I read the book from cover to cover in two days, and immediately followed it with *The Fountainhead*. I had to admit that I had done Miss Rand a considerable injustice. It is true that this is partly her own fault. The cover of *Atlas Shrugged* has a rather badly drawn picture of a naked titan, his head thrown back, his arms spread apart, against a fiery red background; the back cover has a picture of Miss Rand, her head also thrown back, her eyes very wide open, the lips slightly parted as if seeing a vision. It was all a bit Wagnerian; and although I love Wagner's music, I am inclined to be impatient of literary Wagnerianism – as in Faulkner or Wolfe, for example. But one thing was immediately obvious from *Atlas Shrugged*. Miss Rand has the ability to tell a story, and she can tell it with a minimum of clichés.

Atlas Shrugged has a great deal in common with Aldous Huxley's *Brave New World* and Orwell's *Nineteen Eighty-*

Four. It is a tirade against collectivism and government interference with individual freedom. But the heroes of Huxley and Orwell are little men, modest souls. Ayn Rand's book has a romantic sweep, an undeniable grandeur, and one is not surprised to learn that one of her favourite writers is Victor Hugo.

Atlas Shrugged has an interesting and original plot. It takes place in an America of the future, a socialistic America where everyone talks of altruism and the individual's duty to society. But something is wrong with this society; it is obviously going rotten and collapsing. Its men of talent keep mysteriously vanishing: artists, philosophers, business-men. Finally the reader becomes aware that a mysterious figure called John Galt is in revolt against the whole idea of collectivism, and is persuading the men of talent to withdraw from society and let it collapse into one big, soggy, altruistic mass of mediocrity. Towards the end of the book Galt makes his speech on the radio (sixty pages long!), and finally the men of talent agree to return to society, on their own terms – complete freedom of the individual from government interference, and the general acceptance of a new morality: 'I swear that I will never live for the sake of another man, nor ask another man to live for me'.

There is no doubt that this book is an astounding feat, and deserved to become a best-seller on the strength of its narrative power alone. Its picture of a collapsing society has a kind of *Götterdämmerung* splendour, like an erupting volcano. One reads it with a kind of destructive delight, as one goes to see films depicting monstrous disasters.

My own response to the book was twofold. I have always detested the 'fallacy of insignificance' in modern literature, the cult of smallness and meanness, the atmosphere of defeat that broods over the twentieth-century novel; I devoted a book to attacking it and announcing the need for a new, positive existentialism.[38] So I was delighted by the sheer health of Ayn Rand's view. Spengler once wrote that he preferred the form of a fast steamer or a precision lathe to all the modern arts and crafts, and that he would give all the Roman statues and temples for one Roman aqueduct. Ayn Rand would obviously agree. There is a Shavian ring about many of her judgments; she is as unsentimental as Shaw. And her heroes are not at all unlike Shaw's; one is reminded particularly of Shaw's Andrew Undershaft in *Major Barbara*.

But at this point I began to have my doubts. I have always loved Shaw because he is one of the few modern writers who is not afraid to create extraordinary men. But one gets the feeling that Shaw's delight in great men is sheer admiration for vitality. It is never tied to any particular ideology. He creates a Caesar, but this is not indicative of a love of the military man, as *Arms and the Man* demonstrates. He creates Andrew Undershaft, but this is not a sign of a romantic attitude to power and wealth, as his portrait of Boss Mangan or Tom Broadbent proves. And to baffle his socialist followers he even creates a king, in *The Apple Cart*, who outwits his socialist cabinet with the author's obvious approval.

Now all Ayn Rand's pleading for individualism is tied

38 *The Age of Defeat* (London: Victor Gollancz, 1959).

to her own ideology – *laissez faire* capitalism. Ayn Rand was born in Russia in 1905, of Jewish parents; she hated the Revolution, and glad to get to America in 1926. The motivating force of her two early novels *We the Living* and *Anthem* is hatred of communism, or of any philosophy that allows the state to tyrannize over the individual. It seemed to her that America of the nineteenth century had the ideal political system, where the talented individual could become a millionaire or the President. In the twentieth century, America, like the rest of the world, is inclined to drift left. Ayn Rand sees the Democratic ideology as one step closer to Stalinism, and loses no opportunity to denounce it in her monthly news-letter, issued by her Nathaniel Branden Institute in New York.

It seems to me that her hatred of communism led her to certain extremes. Communism preaches that all men owe their first duty to the state, including the artists. Understandably enough, she loathed the idea. But communism springs from the nineteenth-century idea of altruism, living for others rather than for oneself, as preached by Comte. This leads Miss Rand to declare that selfishness has always been man's vital principle – not in the sense of meanness or indifference to other people but in the sense of intelligent self-interest. Expressed in this form, there are few intelligent people who would deny that she is right; Blake pointed out that even men and women in love need 'the lineaments of satisfied desire' from one another. Shaw said that our interest in the world is only the overflow of our interest in ourselves; consequently no one can expect the individual to commit moral suicide by trying to take an interest in the world before he is ready to 'overflow'. The greatness of saints springs out of sheer abundance, a magnificent ability to overflow and feel for others, not out of self-negation.

Now this seems sensible enough. How, then, does it lead to her attacks on all forms of state medicine, for example? It would seem that her fundamental idea is: Everyone must be as free as possible. A doctor should work for himself, not for the government. But what about the people who die because they cannot afford the cost of some expensive operation in a privately owned hospital? Miss Rand would reply: Leave capitalism totally free, and the standard of living will rise so steeply that eventually everyone will be able to afford it. But, one might point out, human nature has its blemishes; when businessmen were 'free' in the nineteenth century the result was not a uniform rise in the standard of living, but a few men eating themselves to death on foie gras and caviare and the majority living close to starvation. Still, she would reply, leave everyone free and these temporary inconveniences will be ironed out.

There seems to be a fallacy here that can best be exposed by narrowing the discussion to the question of the artist's relation to the government. When an Englishman reads of the affair of Pasternak's *Dr Zhivago* or the censure passed by the Soviet minister of culture on the music of Shostakovitch and Prokoviev, he naturally feels indignant and says: 'That couldn't happen in a free country'. This is partly true. But he must then recognize that the government in Russia takes a great deal more interest in its musicians and writers than the government in England. It is true that the government expects composers to produce music that can be appreciated by the people; it is also true that you can buy records of almost any modern Soviet composer in Russia for about 5 shillings per 12-inch L.P. In England, 90 per cent of modern composers are not even represented in the catalogues, and even international names like Michael Tippett, Alan Rawsthorne, and Humphrey Searle are very badly represented. One must also take some account of the quality of the music produced. Western music and literature are 'free', but our literature exhales a poisonous atmosphere of defeat – a legacy of the nineteenth century – while our music is inclined to become steadily more abstract and formal. It is significant that Miss Rand's taste in music inclines to romanticism; she likes light musical comedies, and the music of Rachmaninov, and detests the 'neurotic' experimental music of the twentieth century. If she wishes to find modern composers who are producing music that is unneurotic and distinctly romantic in idiom, she will have to buy records of Khatchaturian, Glière, Rakov, Shaporin, Shostakovitch, Maiskovsky. The conclusion seems to be that total artistic freedom in the West has produced 'neurotic' music and literature, while the government's optimistic ideology in Russia has produced a romantic and popular music.

The mistake, of course, lies in going to extremes. One cannot say arbitrarily: 'Total freedom will produce a glorious and unneurotic art'. Men work by a challenge and response mechanism; total freedom may only produce stagnation. Bartók and Schoenberg were neglected in America, and both were seriously inconvenienced by poverty; in Russia, the government might have made a nuisance of itself and demanded a more popular music, but they would have been saved from the poverty. Admittedly Schoenberg is such an extreme case, and would have been so unpopular with the Soviet minister of culture, that citing his name hardly helps the argument; but then in this matter Miss Rand would ally herself with the minister of culture in rejecting Schoenberg's music.

Miss Rand's basic ideology seems to have something in common with Rousseau's romanticism. She also disbelieves in original sin; she also feels that 'man is born free and is everywhere in chains'. Politically, she might be described as a capitalistic anarchist.

It seems to me that Miss Rand is a writer of extraordinary perception – probably of genius. Like Shaw, she instinctively recoils from the decadence and pessimistic romanticism of our age, and declares that the motor of society is individual greatness, not 'the wisdom of the majority'. One cannot help admiring the way in which she has stood alone for more than twenty-five years, preaching her own revolt against nihilism, against weakness and laziness disguised as humility and self-knowledge. But like other lonely fighters, she has allowed herself to become an extremist in all things. She is a writer of extraordinary contradictions. *Atlas Shrugged* reveals that she possesses a considerable intellect; yet it is a narrow and incurious intellect. Having established to her own satisfaction that all that is wrong with the world is lack of faith in reason and its muddled ideas on self-interest and altruism, she seems to take no further interest in the history of ideas. Collectivism has been established as the scapegoat that explains the decadence of our civilization. She has a powerful instinct of health, and the usual desire of the person of strong character to find a simple explanation for the sickness around her. Instead of taking some trouble to analyse the root causes of the 'sickness of mankind in the mid-twentieth century', she finds her scapegoat, rather as Hitler found the Jews, and then begins her crusade.

I have offered, in various books, my own analysis of the 'sickness'. Like Whitehead, I am inclined to look for cultural causes – a bifurcation of nature – rather than political. And it seems to me that Miss Rand has walked into the trap set for her by her own insight and enthusiasm. It is always tempting to resolve situations into simple terms of rights and wrongs, blacks and whites. Let me offer an example. Admirers of the serial composer Webern sometimes cite a story in which Webern was forced to stand at the back of a concert hall (because he was too poor to pay for a seat) and listen to the music of Carl Orff and Richard Strauss – the composers officially approved of by the Nazis. This story is apparently true; Hitler disapproved of Webern's music because Webern's teacher, Schoenberg, was Jewish, and because he thought it neurotic and tuneless.

The simple approach to this situation – and one sometimes taken by Webern's admirers – is roughly as follows. Hitler was evil because he murdered Jews. Therefore anything he admired must also be tainted. Therefore Strauss and Orff must be bad composers because Hitler approved of them, and Webern must be a good composer because Hitler disapproved of him.

It would be comforting if we could accept this simple line of argument. Unfortunately we cannot dismiss the music of Strauss and Orff because it is tuneful. Strauss is undoubtedly a great composer, and Orff is certainly very fine in places. Webern may be a great composer; on the other hand, his music may one day be regarded as largely an unsuccessful experiment. And it *is* possible for a 'free society' like our own to go to absurd extremes to praise that which is rejected or difficult. The truth is that Strauss, Orff, and Webern must be carefully evaluated on their own merits, not on an emotional blanket-judgment. Now Ayn Rand's philosophy is an attempt to pile all the blacks on one side of the fence and all the whites on the other. She produces her simple antitheses: reason and irrationalism (which includes religion), altruism and self-interest, decadent art and healthy art, tuneful music and neurotic music, collectivism and individualism. All the desirable things are piled on her own side of the fence.

Still, before pressing these criticisms, it might be more profitable to try to understand how Miss Rand became the kind of writer she is. Her biographer, Barbara Branden,[39] states that Ayn Rand was born in St Petersburg in 1905, daughter of well-to-do Jewish parents. She was romantic by temperament but not introspective. She disliked the goody-goody children's tales that were pre-

39 In *Who is Ayn Rand?* by Barbara and Nathaniel Branden.

scribed reading for children of the well-to-do, but was delighted when she read a detective story at the age of eight. Later, when she was fourteen, she grew enthusiastic over a magazine serial called *The Mysterious Valley* with an arrogant, dare-devil hero. The only music she enjoyed was light operetta, presumably works like *Mam'selle Nitouche*, *The Merry Widow*, etc. This music had the kind of untroubled gaiety she dreamed about. She wanted a world without weakness, or tragedy. At the time of the Revolution she discovered the novels of Hugo, and was excited by their superhuman heroes. In 1962, introducing Hugo's *Ninety-Three*, she writes typically:

> Is man by nature to be valued as good, or to be despised as evil? Is the universe intelligible to man, or unintelligible and unknowable? Can man find happiness on earth, or is he doomed to frustration and despair? Does man have the power of *choice*, the power to choose his goals and achieve them, the power to direct the course of his life – or is he the helpless plaything of forces beyond his control which determine his fate? Such is the category of questions which are the source and the concern of art, the questions which every art-work answers, whether the artist is consciously aware of it or not... Art is the concretization of metaphysics.

In the same introduction there is an even more revealing passage about the cultural disintegration of our age 'which is bringing man's intellect down to the concrete-bound, range-of-the-moment perspective of a savage'. This last has a Blakeian ring and feeling; and in fact one does not have to read much of Ayn Rand to realize that, fundamentally, she has much in common with Blake and – inevitably – with Shaw. Like Blake, she is a kind of visionary whose ultimate vision is of 'men like gods'. But unlike Blake, she is hardly interested in the question of how man got into his present position of degradation – the question of 'the fall'. Blake invented symbolic personages to try to represent the psychological subtleties he had in mind; for Ayn Rand there is only one cause: Socialism.

It takes a person of quite exceptional character to live in opposition to the whole trend and metaphysic of the age, and not to be broken or embittered. Most of the defeat in modern literature is the defeat of idealists who have found the age too much for them and who are subconsciously working for its destruction by preaching nihilism. Shaw avoided this by leaving Dublin and joining in the socialist movement of the eighties, in which his idealism could find practical expression. Blake did it the more difficult way, by withdrawing from the age and sniping at it in the name of a paradoxical mysticism: the way also chosen by Hamann, Kierkegaard, Kafka.

Now Miss Rand undoubtedly had on her side the fact that she is a woman. Women are less susceptible to the abstract than men. A man can be dragged far from his instinctive certainties by the desire to be fair-minded and look at every side of the problem, and in consequence he becomes weak. A woman remains close to her instincts and treasures them like children.

Ayn Rand was brought up in a decadent Russia, and

she imagined America to be the land of the free. This explains the extraordinary paradox that she has become the prophet of all that Blake would have rejected – big business, money, and materialism. (I am not now suggesting that Blake was entirely right; only trying to empathize my way into Miss Rand's attitudes.) She rejected Russia and the Marxian-materialistic ethic. She held tight to her vision of a free and happy society where, in a kind of continuous sunlight, the businessmen bring material prosperity and an end of poverty, the great artists create their works for the uplift of the human spirit, and man is at last a truly rational creature. (It is amusing to note that this vision is closer to the Soviet ideal than the American.) She saw government interference as a great, sinister octopus lying across this sunlit land, strangling business with black tentacles. She then proceeded to rationalize the whole thing by declaring that romanticism – the literary spirit of which she approves – was the outcome of the political freedom and the scientific faith of the nineteenth century. Now it is undoubtedly true that romanticism was an immediate outcome of the scientific spirit and the feeling that man is the master of things. But one has only to read a book like Van Wyck Brooks's *Ordeal of Mark Twain* to see that, in fact, the political ethic of the nineteenth century produced the opposite effects from the ones she predicts. It produced a series of rebels who rejected it violently: Poe, Thoreau, Hawthorne, Melville. And when Mark Twain, a potentially great novelist, swallowed the 'protestant ethic' of success, it emasculated him as a writer so that his inner conflict produced the blackest pessimism.

Atlas Shrugged sticks very close to Ayn Rand's basic vision. Like C. P. Snow she is fascinated by the 'power men', and she does not regard power in itself as an evil. Like Henley she admires men who can say, 'I am the master of my fate'. But this leads her to take a step in a direction where few readers can follow her. Prosperity is good and freedom is good. Money is a country's life-blood, and it is the businessmen who are the heart of the country, circulating this blood. Therefore, all hail to the glorious businessmen. Let the government keep its thieving paws off them. For when business reigns supreme the great artists will recognize their destiny to lead men on stepping-stones of their dead selves to higher things. (One can imagine the spirits of Melville and Poe grinding their teeth.) It goes without saying that all the businessmen will be proud and courteous, free spirits, like Hank Rearden, Ken Dannager, and Francisco D'Anconia in *Atlas Shrugged*.

It seems to me that Ayn Rand's ideas are such an ingenious mixture of inspired insight and mistaken conclusions that it would be difficult to sort it all out. My own book *The Outsider* was an attempt to trace what happens to the idealists and romantics in a society that 'negates' them. And I pointed out in that book that the increase in 'outsiderism' (which Miss Rand would attribute to creeping socialism) is simply due to the sheer size of our society, and the fact that the individual is bound to feel unimportant when his newspapers and televisions remind him daily that he is one of half a billion just like himself. In smaller societies, the man of genius or ideals has less trouble making his mark: a child prodigy like Mozart soon found himself mixing with kings and queens. The first result of the more difficult conditions of the nineteenth century was a defiant response from the artists, and the huge structures of Beethoven, Wagner, Hugo, Balzac. Melville's Ahab is the typical nineteenth-century hero, recognizing that he is setting himself up in opposition to the metaphysical forces of the universe, and still shaking his fist at the sky and ordering full steam ahead. But Melville ended a disappointed and broken man; so, to some extent, did Beethoven and Wagner. It was inevitable that the challenge should overwhelm the artists of later generations. It was also inevitable that occasional figures like Shaw and Ayn Rand should try to turn the tide of defeat and proclaim again that man is the master of things.

It may be that the tide is ready to turn at last. Miss Rand remarks that romantic literature is concerned with values, and the greatness men are capable of achieving when they fight for their values. The same might be said of the work of Sartre and Camus, of Romain Gary (particularly *The Roots of Heaven*) and Dürrenmatt and Kazantzakis. But Miss Rand has staked out her lines, black on one side, white on the other, so Sartre and Camus would have to be dismissed as communist sympathizers; Dürrenmatt would be found to have a morbid interest in crime; Kazantzakis would be dismissed as a religious mystic as well as a communist sympathizer. Even Romain Gary would have to be condemned, since he began his novel *The Colours of the Day* with the hope that America would drift further to the left and Russia further to the right, and that the two would finally unite to form the greatest civilization the earth has ever known.

This is the upsetting thing about Ayn Rand; she is so sweeping that the result is continual over-simplification. She declares that man has only to adjust himself to 'reality', and that he possesses reason to distinguish reality from illusion. And although one cannot help sympathizing, it still seems that she is using 'reason' and 'reality' here with no idea of the complexities involved. This tendency to over-simplify leads her sometimes into bathos. At the end of *Atlas Shrugged*, as the 'men of talent' prepare to return to society and lead the world, John Galt 'raised his hand, and over the desolate earth he traced in space the sign of the dollar'. One feels like asking: But what about your 'spirit of man'? Will the dollar guarantee new Beethovens and Blakes and Hugos? Obviously not. It will create conditions in which they can flourish – but then all an artist needs in order to flourish is a society that listens sympathetically to what he has to say, and a society concerned with dollars may not be so much better than a society concerned with Marx.

It is the same kind of over-simplification that makes one smile when one reads her condemnation of 'neurotic' music – presumably music such as that of Berg or Stravinsky. What kind of music does she approve of then? And the answer is, light opera, Rachmaninov, Chopin's 'Butterfly Etude' and the slow movement of Saint-Saëns's second piano concerto.[40]

40 These details are given by Barbara Branden on p. 220 of *Who is Ayn Rand?*

It seems to me that this accusation of over-simplification is the basic objection to Ayn Rand's theories of politics and ethics. She is continually throwing out the baby with the bath water. And the fault seems to lie in her lack of any vision of what T. E. Hulme called 'original sin'. I am not now speaking of original sin in the orthodox sense, but in the precise sense of a recognition of man's curious limitations. It seems to me that there are more ultimate questions than the ones Miss Rand poses. Her idea of political free enterprise does not answer the 'existential question', the question of why man is alive and what he ought to do since he finds himself flung into the world. The romantics made an interesting attempt to answer the question; certainly it received its classical statement in *Faust*. The existentialists developed a terminology for getting to grips with the problem – religious existentialists like Berdyaev, Marcel, and to some extent Eliot, as well as purely philosophical thinkers like Heidegger and Sartre. The problem is the problem of man's freedom and his limitedness, of the purpose he seems to carry inside him and his conscious ignorance of it. These are the questions worth answering, and these are the questions that, to read Miss Rand's pamphlets attacking the economics of Galbraith or one of Kennedy's speeches, you would not dream existed. I am not now condemning this kind of engagement; neither would Shaw nor Sartre nor Camus. But it would seem that Miss Rand feels she is able to give it her wholehearted attention because she believes, like the logical positivists, that she has finally solved the metaphysical question. And she solves it in a way that is reminiscent of Wittgenstein's statement, 'The riddle does not exist'. In his long radio speech John Galt mentions the persistence of legends of Eden, Atlantis, etc., and declares that these are a memory that 'somewhere in the starting years of your childhood, before you had learned to submit, to absorb the terror of unreason and to doubt the value of your mind, you had known a radiant state of existence, you had known the independence of a rational consciousness facing an open universe'. One might point out that no child knows the independence of a rational consciousness facing an open universe (although a boy of twelve might do so when he discovers science); the child's world is riddled with fears and doubts. But this passage makes very clear Ayn Rand's basic Rousseauism. Man is born innocent, but society distorts him. All that is necessary to restore the balance is faith in reason and the recognition that self-interest is the highest motive. Miss Rand objects to attributing man's confusions to original sin and prefers to blame society. Since I devoted a whole book – *The Outsider* – to deflating the simple-humanist misconception, I doubt whether it could be done adequately here. But it seems to me that she is once again a victim of her own optimism and urge to over-simplify.

I have tried to make clear exactly where and why I disagree with Ayn Rand. Like her I reject the pessimistic view of human nature and human life, whether expressed by Thomas Hardy or Graham Greene. I also reject the view of dejected romantics that modern civilization is one vast mistake, and that we shall all be better off when fields and rivers once again occupy the land at present covered by London and New York. Civilization was made to express the 'spirit of man', not to stifle it; if it has tended to stifle the 'outsiders' so far, this is a historical accident, not an inevitable condition. The 'outsiders' must snap out of their mood of nostalgic defeat and realize that civilization is their responsibility as much as that of the politicians – far more, perhaps, as civilization owes more to its men of genius than to soldiers and statesmen. As to politics, most successful regimes have been a matter of compromise between freedom and authority. Complete anarchism is as destructive as complete tyranny.

Ayn Rand's work is splendid in its optimism, but its weakness lies in its arbitrariness. One is inclined to ask the same question that one asks of Marxism: But what happens when you achieve your ideal society? In equating business enterprise with artistic creativeness she somehow seems to have taken the point out of art and philosophy. Shaw keeps things in perspective when he declares that the philosopher's brain is the instrument of evolution; therefore, in a sense, the philosopher is the spearhead of the human race. This statement leaves the road to the future open and clearly marked. Shaw writes: 'Our minds are nothing but this knowledge of ourselves, and he who adds a jot to such knowledge creates new mind as surely as any woman creates new men.' It follows that the task of the artist and the philosopher is to go on creating 'new mind', and to avoid too much barren involvement in 'the nets of politics'. Unlike the generation of Joyce and Eliot, the present generation of writers has shown itself only too prone to give up the hard work of creation for the more rewarding labour of political involvement. Sartre is an unfortunate example of a writer who has contributed nothing of importance since he became involved in politics; it looks as though Ayn Rand may be another.

A Personal Note on Ayn Rand

The misgivings expressed in this last sentence have been confirmed by my own experience of Miss Rand's 'organization'. After reading *Atlas Shrugged*, I wrote her a letter expressing my sympathy and stating my points of disagreement. Miss Rand herself did not reply; instead, I received a letter from her second in command, Nathaniel Branden, saying that he would send me his book about her, and continuing: 'It is possible that you do not realize the singular inappropriateness of your letter to the author of *Atlas Shrugged*. Perhaps my book will give you a new perspective on the full context in which your letter was received and appraised – and might suggest to you a new approach'. I had mentioned that I had disliked the work on my first brief acquaintance with it, and had been dismissive when students asked my opinion of it. Branden's letter finished: 'Miss Rand would be very pleased to hear of your interest in her work – when and if you correct your offense against it in the same terms that the offense was committed: that is, publicly.'

I was somewhat staggered by this Messianic tone, and my first reaction was to ignore the whole thing. However, loads of books and pamphlets began to turn up in the mail, so I sent back copies of my own *Age of Defeat* and

The Strength to Dream, together with a letter in which I mentioned that I intended, in any case, to write an essay on Ayn Rand which I would send in due course. The result was a guardedly friendly note of acknowledgment from Branden, and another pile of books and pamphlets. Most of these were denunciations of the Kennedy administration. One of them quoted Kennedy's remark that his father had always told him that businessmen were sons of bitches, but he had never believed it until now, and asked how Kennedy could hope to save the American economy if he slandered the most valuable citizens in this manner. The more I read of these pamphlets, the more clear it became to me that Ayn Rand's capitalism, to say the least, tends to over-simplification of the issues. Some of the views expressed made Goldwater's republicanism seem slightly pink. I joined issue specifically on the question of medical care for the aged and the question of 'State medicine', which Ayn Rand opposed whole-heartedly. In a further letter to Branden I questioned whether extreme right-wing political views were an inevitable consequence of 'heroic humanism', and said that, for my own part, I would remain a socialist and look for the solution of the defeat-problem on another level. This brought no reply at all.

By this time I had written the essay, exactly as it stands above. It seemed to me to be a fair and balanced assessment, recognizing the fundamental soundness of Ayn Rand's instinctive opposition to the 'anti-heroic hypothesis' – the 'fallacy of insignificance' – but questioning her political views. As it was now some weeks since

I had heard from Branden I sent the essay direct to Miss Rand; in a covering letter I explained that it would be printed over here in *The Aylesford Review*,[41] and that she was welcome to print it in her own weekly news-letter, provided it was printed in full. I added that I was somewhat surprised that she had not replied personally before this, that it seemed inconsistent with the courtesy of the heroes of her novels. I sent this care of her publishers, the truth being that I half suspected that my letters and books had never reached her; for Branden's letters gave a distinct impression of a hierophant who is unwilling to allow others to approach his god. The reaction came quickly in the form of another indignant letter from Branden, which stated that 'it is clear that your ideas and ours are opposed in every fundamental respect: in epistemology, metaphysics, ethics, politics, aesthetics and psychology', which was proved, Branden said, since I could offer to allow them to reprint an essay 'which we regard as an irresponsible smear'. The letter ended: 'Miss Rand has asked me to state that you are mistaken in believing that her failure to write to you reflects a lack of courtesy; it is courtesy that has restrained her from writing to you.' I think this letter indicates why Miss Rand is wrong in looking to 'collectivism' as the source of all the evils of society; some of the most ineradicable are a part of human nature.

1963

41 This did not, in fact, appear in *The Aylesford Review* [Ed.]

12

HENRY WILLIAMSON

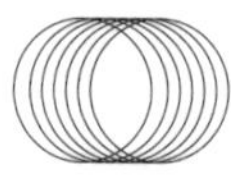

I find it extraordinarily difficult to write about Henry Williamson. Although I have been reading steadily through his books for the past few months, the usual critical methods fail to yield their results. This is because Williamson's life and his work are mixed up together in a curious and complex way. But literary criticism attempts to deal with a book as if it were a pound of cheese. You pay for it, you take it away, you read it. The pleasure you derive from it has nothing to do with the author's private life, any more than your pound of cheese has to do with the life of the man who happened to make it. But with certain authors the reader cannot help feeling an immediate curiosity about the personal background of the book. Who, for example, can read *Le Rouge et le Noir* without wanting to know something about Stendhal? And with other writers, the reader is possessed by a certainty that only a knowledge of the author's background can provide him with a key to the work. Dostoevsky is an example. Henry Williamson is another.

Because Dostoevsky happens to provide the ideal illustration, this is no guarantee that these highly personal writers belong to a superior caste. On the contrary, it is obviously a weakness that a writer should be unable to produce purely 'detached' works of art. Tolstoy would certainly have thought so. But 'personal' writing usually guarantees one thing: the writer is a man who works under a high pressure of inner conflict. He may be a bad artist; but he is unlikely to be trivial or complacent.

It is impossible to read any one of the Willie Maddison or Phillip Maddison novels without becoming instantly aware that their author is a very complex bag of tricks. The reader who knows only Williamson's animal novels – the otter, the salmon, or the peregrine – may think of him as a serene, easy-going man, closely related to Kipling and Richard Jefferies, with perhaps a touch of Lewis Carroll. But half an hour's reading of *The Sun in the Sands*, *The Dream of Fair Women* or *Donkey Boy* will convince him that he is dealing with a temperament that has more in common with a totally different kind of writer: with James Joyce, D. H. Lawrence, or Dostoevsky. Williamson is as irritable as Lawrence, as proud and touchy as Joyce, as highly strung (and sometimes as cruel) as Dostoevsky. There are times when this tormented and explosive man seems to come to terms with himself; then an immense serenity descends; he writes like an angel, or like a prophet. But mostly he is sounding discords, threshing around violently, starting to examine an idea, then forgetting it and shooting off on another tack. First and foremost, he is an egoist. When we speak of artists, this word has neither good nor bad implications; everything depends on the creative force that is mixed with the egoism as potassium nitrate is mixed with sulphur to make gunpowder.

And this is why it is so difficult to write of Williamson. There are times when he stands out as a creative giant; there are also times when he exposes his own weaknesses with masochistic delight and seems to take pleasure in flagellating himself and the whole world. It is like having a best friend who is enchanting and exasperating by turns.

It must be stated then, that Williamson is one of the most difficult and controversial writers of our time. And at the time of writing (1965) he is also surely one of the most undervalued. This is due to a variety of reasons: his confusing fame as a writer of animal books, his advocacy of Hitler and Sir Oswald Mosley before the war, his twenty years' abstention from writing novels (from 1931 until 1951 – not counting a few minor and inferior works). All these will have to be examined more closely in the course of this essay.

There is another difficulty for the critic – and especially for me. We can analyse Dostoevsky's complex relation to his books without restraint; he is dead, and his descendants are not likely to complain, even if someone proved that Dostoevsky had committed the rape on a minor that haunts his work. Henry Williamson is very much alive, and has been completely frank about himself in several autobiographical books as well as in some semi-autobiographical novels. If a critic also happens to be personally acquainted with him, the amount of biographical material at his disposal is enormous. But how far is it permissible to use it? Middleton Murry expressed the same doubts in an excellent essay on Williamson, and replied that it is impossible to write honestly about Williamson without being 'personal'. I find myself faced with the same difficulty, and am inclined to make the same answer. One day perhaps, when the Phillip Maddison saga is at last completed and its celebrity is as great as it deserves (and who can doubt it, remembering the recent parallel case of Durrell's Alexandrian novels?), it will be possible to speak of Williamson as impersonally as of Shakespeare. But I must admit that I am not adequate to that task.

Nothing can be understood about Williamson without first forgetting that he is the man who wrote *Tarka the Otter* and *Salar the Salmon*. These books play their important part, as I shall try to show; but, for the moment, they must be ignored. Second, it must be properly grasped that Williamson sees himself as a prophet, as a man with a message. Although he has never (as far as I know) said so in so many words, he regards himself as a great writer or as nothing. And as his reader, these are the terms on which you must accept him, or totally reject him.

In 1936 Williamson described himself as a 'has-been half-success'. At that time these words might have seemed accurate to many critics; the one-volume edition of the Willie Maddison novels (fourteen hundred pages for twelve shillings and sixpence) had been received with indifference, contrary to the usual rule that trilogies and tetralogies achieve their greatest success in one-volume editions. (Williamson's contemporary, L. H. Myers, achieved his first popular success when his four *Near and the Far* novels appeared in one volume, and won several literary prizes.) And yet today nothing seems more likely than that Williamson will end his days in the hazy aura of literary celebrity and official recognition. The Phillip Maddison saga is nearing completion and there can be no doubt that the completed novel will receive wide attention. Bearing in mind what happened to Lawrence Durrell with the publication of *Clea*, it is possible to gain some idea of the kind of thing that easily could happen to Williamson. What would be its effect on the tense and touchy hermit of Ox's Cross? The question is not as idle as it sounds. For Henry Williamson can be divided into two distinct personalities whose Jekyll and Hyde battle has not always been to the advantage of his creative work. It is of some concern to his admirers which half would be nourished by overwhelming celebrity. It is worth considering this question more closely.

A division into Jekyll and Hyde is, of course, an absurd over-simplification. Nevertheless, it serves its purpose. When Williamson's work is seen in retrospect, the reader is able to feel the presence of an extraordinary creative spirit which bears some resemblance to that of D. H. Lawrence. When this positive side of the balance sheet is added up, we begin to see Henry Williamson as he might appear to some adoring Professor Leavis of the future. The delightful childhood (which, in *The Beautiful Years* and *Dandelion Days*, appears to have been far more fun than Williamson later believed), the violent revelations of the war years and the flowering of a humanitarian idealism following the Christmas Day fraternizing of

1914, the subsequent discovery of Richard Jefferies, the leaving home and living in Skirr Cottage at Georgeham, the years of dedicated work to bring home his idealism to a new world, the fame that followed *Tarka the Otter*, the long years of torment and physical labour, and finally the triumphant *Chronicle of Ancient Sunlight*. One can imagine André Maurois dashing off a sequel to *Ariel*, dealing with Williamson, portraying him as a sensitive but indomitable sun-god of a man who would make a splendid subject for a Hollywood epic (ending, perhaps with a Nobel Prize and knighthood).

I do not suggest that this picture of Williamson is untrue. As far as it goes, it is completely true. But it is only a portrait of Jekyll. We can then imagine another book on Williamson written in the manner of some modern 'biographers'. This one would be a stinker. We would have a morbidly over-sensitive child Williamson, developing an early persecution mania. The war comes and increases his tendency to gloom. After the war comes the quarrel with his father and the retreat to Devon. All the events would be told in an anti-Williamson light; the developing Messianism, the increasing persecution mania; the quarrels with the local gentry; the admitted failure of Williamson's first marriage, due to his irritability and despotism. The admiration for Hitler and the Mosley affiliations would be analysed at length. The failure of the Norfolk farm venture, revealing that Williamson's 'man-of-the-soil' pose is only skin-deep. Finally, the regurgitating of all the old resentments in the Phillip Maddison novels, which would be dismissed as a rewriting of a book he had already written twice in *The Flax of Dream* and *The Gold Falcon*.

I believe there would be far less truth in this Hyde portrait of Williamson than in the Jekyll portrait; but it would have its elements of truth. And this is what makes an assessment of Williamson's work so difficult. It will continue to be so until time gives us the same detachment from Williamson that we have from Dostoevsky and Lawrence. However, I have agreed to attempt it here, and must do my best without detachment.

The chief problem in assessing Williamson's achievement is that he is not a profound thinker; consequently his ideas cannot be neatly isolated and discussed separately. However, the attempt must be made.

When Williamson returned from the 1914 war he was possessed by the conviction that wars are the outcome of miseducation. What exactly did he mean by this? Not, I think, education in the sense of formal schooling, but rather the prejudices we are brought up to believe. Williamson's feeling seems to have been similar to that of Céline who, in *Voyage au Bout de la Nuit*, had written:

> Lie, copulate and die. One wasn't allowed to do anything else. People lied fiercely and beyond belief, ridiculously, beyond the limit of absurdity; lies in the papers, lies on the hoardings, lies on foot, on horseback and on wheels; Everybody was doing it, trying to see who could produce a more fantastic lie than his neighbour. Soon there was no truth left in town. (Céline is also writing about the 1914 war.)

On Christmas Day, 1914, the British and German armies at Ploegsteert Wood fraternized and buried their dead. Williamson was amazed to discover that the Germans also felt they were fighting for truth and homeland, and that they all seemed decent, ordinary men, like his own comrades. Siegfried Sassoon, who tried to protest that the war was being prolonged for political reasons, was interned in a shell-shock hospital as a mental case.

When he came back from the war, Williamson quarrelled with his father on the subject. One day, when he declared that the Germans were not to blame for the war, but that international finance was the real culprit, his father left the room after calling him a traitor to his country.

Shortly after his return in 1918, Williamson discovered Richard Jefferies's book *The Story of My Heart*; he has described its effect on him in the last of the Willie Maddison novels. Apparently it was a revelation. Jefferies immediately became a major influence, with his nature worship (not unlike the spirit of some of Hemingway's stories of the backwoods). Jefferies's *Bevis, the Story of a Boy*, seems to have been the spark that started Williamson writing his first novel, *The Beautiful Years*, the story of the early boyhood of Willie Maddison. Williamson wrote it just before he moved down to Devon with his friend, the Swinburnian poet 'Julian'. It is a curious book in many ways. Williamson apparently began it as the first part of a tetralogy, which he thought of as a new Gospel. Williamson himself had been passionately attached to his mother in childhood, and later portrays her delightfully as Phillip Maddison's mother in *The Dark Lantern*. But in *The Beautiful Years* Willie's mother dies in childbirth. Its effect is to load the balance in favour of self-pity; Willie is the completely lonely and misunderstood little boy. (Williamson makes him an only child; Phillip – the more objective portrait – has two sisters.) The main 'message' of the book is Willie's love of nature. There is also an interesting character called Jim, who seems to symbolize Williamson's Rousseau-like notion of freedom; Jim lives a wild life, sleeping in the fields, and has to give up a gardening job because he cannot bear a roof over his head. But at the end of the book he is killed off arbitrarily – the first of Williamson's sympathetic characters to die. Here one sees the first sign of Williamson's curious obsession about death, which occasionally seems to become a thoroughly unreal, romantic attitude (as when, in *The Golden Virgin*, Phillip sentimentalizes about the war dead who have 'returned to nature' and are therefore, in a Pickwickian sense, not really dead). The final chapter of *The Beautiful Years* is an interesting account of an encounter between Willie and his father – Willie's desire for someone he can love completely, and his father's coldness and embarrassment, united to a desire to be kind.

Where is the 'gospel' in this book? If the intent was didactic this is hardly apparent, except in a fine scene where Willie smashes several bird traps and expresses his sympathy with wild life and nature.

The purpose of *Dandelion Days*, the second Gospel, is more apparent. This is an account of Willie's schooldays, with a distinct flavour of *Stalky and Co*. It is an excellent book, written without the self-pity that often seems dangerously close in *The Beautiful Years*. Its point seems to be that the formal school education is nonsensical; the masters are mostly fools, particularly the head; Willie learns far more from roaming around the countryside. The head loves to quote Latin tags, and inculcates British imperialist principles into the boys. (Williamson records that he was horrified when a war film portrayed the Germans as fat and cowardly and the children in the audience booed.)

The essence of Williamson's mysticism is now becoming apparent. It is based on a Wordsworthian feeling for nature and animals. (In his original cottage in Georgeham, cats, dogs, birds, and otters used to drink out of the same bowl.) Secondly, it is a sense of the brotherhood of all men. It would be hard to say what place God occupies in Williamson's universe, but there are frequent invocations to some 'Great Earth Spirit', and Willie Maddison exclaims, 'The sunlight! Truth pours down in the sunlight'.

Now occurs a strange gap in the four Gospels: Willie Maddison goes to the war, but his experiences are not described. (From the point of view of popular success this was a pity, for Williamson would have caught the market of the mid-twenties for books about the war.) The book has something of the mood of Hemingway's *The Sun Also Rises*, where the hero's war wound has led to an emotional as well as a physical disablement. It is the story of Willie's love affair with Evelyn Fairfax, a married woman. Willie is now writing a book called *The Policy of Reconstruction* which expresses all Williamson's ideas on 'education'. The affair is spoiled by Willie's violent emotional demands, his craving to have the woman all to himself. The reader is inevitably reminded of another autobiographical novelist who was frank about his morbidly affectionate nature and the absolute demands that wrecked his love-life – Marcel Proust. Comparison with Proust, however, makes one aware of a factor that has never been widely noticed – the lack of style in Williamson. He *can* write superbly, as in *Tarka*, but (again one thinks of Lawrence and Dostoevsky) he is too inclined to be careless and colloquial; and just occasionally his stylistic offences are agonizing and embarrassing. He writes rapidly and hastily, like a man talking fast. And even *Tarka*, for all its precision, is full of overblown words and bits of would-be fine writing. There are words like 'sere' and 'a-glimmer'; he never seems to know when to stop so the beautiful sentence: 'At the tail of the pool [the river] quickened smoothly into paws of water' is spoiled by the addition: 'with star-streaming claws'. One can see why T. E. Lawrence admired him, for Lawrence also had his delusions about 'fine writing', as when, at the beginning of *Seven Pillars*, he writes that the heat of Arabia 'came out and struck us like a drawn sword'. Williamson is aware of this and admits it freely, but he has never discarded the fault completely; he has often talked about 'the craft of writing' with the enthusiasm and naïveté of an amateur rather than the cold and precise eye of a professional for whom words are tools and not precious stones.

This amateurishness that often appears in the style would hardly be worth remarking if it were not an indication of a fundamental lack of discipline that seems to be one of Williamson's Hyde qualities. He is a wild-man of literature. It is no use looking to him for the calculated utterance of a Thomas Mann or Joyce, or for the polish and control that seem to be part of the fundamental equipment of most Continental writers. In only one thing does he know precisely what he is doing: in expressing his basic mysticism. This is what makes *Tarka* and *Salar* so excellent; they are Williamson's declarations of the oneness of life. In writing the two Maddison sagas he was attempting to extend this mysticism to the human world with a courage that is not often found among writers. John Steinbeck and Rudyard Kipling also discovered that they were at their best when writing of animals or moronic men, and they have made no real attempt to enter the adult world; James Barrie showed a lifelong reluctance to leave the world of childhood and purity. Williamson knew perfectly well that his animal novels achieved a certain classic perfection, and he has been told frequently enough that his talent vanishes when he tries to write about human beings. He showed nevertheless a determination to develop his creative powers, to bring his mysticism to bear on the complex and twisted world of human emotion. It was not until 1951, with the publication of *The Dark Lantern* – the first volume of the Phillip Maddison saga – that readers understood that the struggle had been won, and that Williamson had achieved a new stature as a creator.

However, we left Willie Maddison at the end of *The Dream of Fair Women*. The last novel of the series, *The*

Pathway, reveals clearly the dangerous romanticism of Williamson's nature. Willie Maddison, now almost a Byronic hero, comes to live at a house in Devon to complete his great work, the allegorical novel *The Star-born*. Mary, the quiet, self-effacing daughter of the house, is in love with him. So is Diana Shelley, a musician, who is loved by Howard the Falconer, who is loved by Jean, Mary's sister. Willie is Jean's confidant. This book is Williamson's *A l'Ombre des Jeunes Filles en Fleur*, with Willie, the dedicated writer with the secret sorrow, the centre of admiration of all the young people in the book. (Mary is the friend of Elsie, the little girl with whom Willie had been in love as a child; she had always ignored him.) For all its excellent writing, I personally found *The Pathway* a little too personal, as if the author were indulging in a thinly disguised burst of self-admiration. In many ways a fine novel, particularly in its descriptions of Devon, it is somehow off-key. The discord lies, I think, in the character of Willie. Williamson wishes to project him as a genius, and his original intention was that Willie should be ultimately triumphant. Willie's great work is *The Star-born*, a semi-mystical fairy-tale that sounds, from the occasional comments in *The Pathway*, like a cross between Exupéry's *Little Prince* and *The Wind in the Willows*. (I am thinking particularly of a curious episode in the latter called 'The Piper at the Gates of Dawn'.) But such a fairy-tale allegory is the very book that neither Williamson nor Willie is qualified to write, lacking the imaginative detachment. If the finally published version of *The Star-born* is anything to judge by, then Willie is certainly no genius.

Willie and Mary finally declare their love, and it looks as if all will be well. Then the devil of perverseness seems to get into the author. Instead of giving his readers the happy end that seems pre-ordained – the genius Willie finally discovering peace in the arms of the gentle Mary – he shows the lovers breaking up when Mary's mother objects to Willie's heterodox opinions; and Willie is accidentally drowned when he is cut off by the tide. He burns *The Star-born* manuscript to try to attract attention to his plight.

Again this death-complex; the character with whom Williamson identifies himself fails and dies. Why? One solution appears in an autobiographical book, *The Children of Shallowford*, in which it appears that Williamson actually married the girl who is portrayed as Mary in *The Pathway*, but found that married life simply failed to work out. His life's serenity irritated him, and he found himself treating her with the same intolerance and irritation with which his father had treated his mother. (All this appears later in the early Phillip novels.) Williamson had married to find a partner to help him in the loneliness of creation; instead, the baby cried continuously; his wife fell ill; *Tarka* was intractable and cost him four years of effort; he had no money and lived in a damp cottage. It is not surprising that the marriage was not a success. Since Williamson was writing *The Pathway* after his marriage there was no solution, except to confess that Willie would have made a mistake in marrying Mary. This may be the reason that their separation is crudely contrived, followed by Willie's death. But this cannot be the whole reason; Williamson's defeat complex was reappearing, the romanticism about death[42] that had been so obvious in the animal sagas and that was now making its way into the human world.

This is perhaps the point to speak about the autobiographical *Sun in the Sands*, one of Williamson's best books, which covers the period during which he wrote the first three volumes of the 'Gospels'. This is an altogether curious work. After *The Beautiful Years* had been accepted Williamson was thrown out of home by his father, and went to Skirr Cottage on his motor-bike. 'Julian' moved down to live with him. Their relationship was not entirely friendly. Julian loved Swinburne, and his relation to Williamson is amusingly similar to that of Buck Mulligan and Stephen Dedalus in *Ulysses*. There is a kind of respect for Williamson's dedication, a lack of belief in his work, and an ironic awareness of his egoism that appear in his habit of addressing Williamson as 'Maître'. In an *Adelphi* article, written in 1948, Williamson quotes his 'Swinburnian guest' as saying, 'By God, Harry, I could write that stuff you're writing – but I don't want to.' The comment must have irritated Williamson, to be brought up a quarter of a century later.

Williamson became acquainted with a married woman whom he calls Irene, and her extremely pretty young daughter, Barleybright. Williamson became Barleybright's tutor. ('Barleybright will learn a great deal from old Harry,' Julian comments typically, 'but only about old Harry.')

42 There is a strong element of this in Jefferies's *Story of My Heart*.

Williamson tells how he joined the local tennis club, but became unpopular with the local gentry because of his 'unconventional reputation' and was finally forced to resign. Here we become aware of the element of undiscipline that is present in the Willie books; he lacks the aloofness of the true artist and the discipline; he wastes time on 'personalities', on petty involvements. The ego is stinging itself like a scorpion.

The incipient love affair with Irene seems to peter out. Williamson falls in love with a beautiful schoolgirl called Annabelle, who seems to be indifferent to him. Julian finally leaves the cottage. Various weird characters drift across the scene. Then, towards the end, there is a curious change of tone in the book, almost as if it has become fiction. One can only say that, if it is not romantic fiction, then it ought to be. He goes to stay with Annabelle, who now declares she is in love with him. But Williamson's heart has turned to stone under the suffering she has inflicted, and he leaves her. He joins Barleybright and Irene in the Pyrenees. Barleybright has turned into a dazzlingly beautiful teenager, who is also frantically in love with the Byronic and misanthropic writer. Williamson is 'filled with a feeling of clear power', but nevertheless leaves the delicious Barley and goes off to try to cross a dangerous mountain pass; Barley follows to try to stop him, falls over a cliff and breaks her back. The book ends on this note of tragedy, with the possible implication that a malign fate has again deprived the author of his chance of a disinterested love and devotion.

How far *The Sun in the Sands* is literal autobiography and how far it is fictionalized it is impossible to say. What is most interesting is that the old death-and-failure complex seems to have disappeared. The book is stimulating to read because it is told in the tone of one who has every intention of not being beaten, and who seems to be highly successful, in a Byronic way, in his love-life.

This is blatantly evident in *The Gold Falcon*. The hero of this novel is actually called Manfred! This is obviously a half-hearted attempt to reconsider the problem of *The Pathway*. Willie could not be married off to Mary so he had to die. But supposing Willie had not died, what then? He would have left Mary and gone off in search of some ideal woman. But the ideal woman, Barbara, escapes him, and like Willie, he is drowned as he is returning to his wife across the Atlantic. The book was published anonymously in 1932, and is generally considered a failure.

The long and bitter period was beginning for Williamson. He seems to have felt that he had achieved nothing as a writer. As a human being he had certainly not achieved serenity and self-confidence – for reasons that are abundantly clear in the novels and autobiographies. A hostile critic might say that the fictional Henry Williamson who emerges from his early books is selfish, neurotic, and self-tormented. As if this was not bad enough, he also became an admirer of Hitler, declaring in the preface to the one-volume *Flax of Dream* (1936): 'I salute the great man across the Rhine, whose life symbol is the happy child'. This admiration for Hitler immediately deprived

Williamson of the support of the new literary cliques, who were left-wing and anti-fascist. Yet it is only a logical outcome of his feeling of the humanity of the Germans that began on the Christmas Day of 1914. It seemed at times that Williamson identified himself with Hitler, seeing Hitler as the successful visionary who could clear away the mess of old ideas with his vitality. No doubt Williamson's own boredom and frustration had something to do with it. But this does not explain why he chose Hitler and fascism rather than, say, Lenin and communism, as a symbol of the brotherhood of man. Even more curious is an article written in the *Adelphi* in 1949, in which he impenitently quotes his earlier high opinion of Hitler as Lucifer the Lightbringer, and ends by adding that Hitler refused to take advantage of England's prostration after Dunkirk because he felt a great affection for the British. Now in this there can be no doubt that Williamson is quite correct; Bormann's records of Hitler's Table Talk make this clear. There can be no doubt that, in some weird, Wagnerian way, Hitler was an authentic visionary and man of genius. But how does Williamson reconcile this with the extermination of the Jews? That England was spared because Hitler wanted us to join him in a crusade against communism may excuse Hitler in the eyes of an English patriot. But Williamson is not an English patriot. Presumably, therefore, Hitler's proposed invasion of Russia is also excusable, like the concentration camps. This may be so; but it is difficult to reconcile it with Williamson's mystical preaching of the brotherhood of man and nature, and the stupidity of war. Presumably his future biographers will gloss over the problem by talking about the 'impractical' and unworldly mind of the great artist.

Williamson's disillusionment with the thirties and with himself led him to leave Devon and to take up farming in Norfolk; the story of a four-year struggle is told in *The Story of a Norfolk Farm*. But in spite of his Tolstoyan theories, he found no real peace in farming, and no particular liking for farm-hands. They seem to have driven him wild with irritation. Then came the war; Williamson was briefly interned under 18B, but was allowed to return to his farm, where he was regarded with suspicion by neighbours who at one point entertained the ambition of shooting him. Fate seemed to be planning to increase the old persecution mania. The next novel, published in 1948, bristles with it. It is called *The Phasian Bird*, and seems to be a record of failure and disaster on the Norfolk farm during the war years. The owner is interned as a spy, the farm becomes a waste, and finally the farmer is killed trying to save the life of a golden pheasant, shot by poachers. The novel is as much a failure as *The Gold Falcon*; it is too obviously an attempt to objectify the miseries of the war years, and to show his hero withdrawing yet again into death.

In 1948 also appeared another edition of Williamson's early fable *The Star-born*. It is obvious from *The Pathway* that Williamson had then a very high regard for this book by 'Willie Maddison'; it was issued in 1932 and again after the war. But although the book has its ardent adherents, it is in my opinion the least successful of Williamson's attempts to express his mysticism. The writing has most of Williamson's faults when he is at his worst: too many overblown adjectives, too many artificial-sounding phrases. It is not surprising if the general opinion in 1950 was that Henry Williamson was a 'has-been half-success'. When the first Phillip Maddison novel appeared in 1951 there were many who thought that, although it showed an altogether new and objective Williamson, he was still burrowing away in the past. Phillip is apparently a carbon-copy of his cousin Willie, another over-sensitive boy with a father who misunderstands him. But the love affair of Phillip's parents was told with a new vigour that had an almost Dickensian ring. Certainly Williamson was now swimming in the deep waters of creation, no longer sticking close to his own life.

There is, unfortunately, no space here to speak about these novels in detail, even to indicate the outline of the plot. Williamson has become objective; he is obviously determined to recreate the early years of this century and the period of the war. It begins to look very much as if his book may well be the most important picture of the 1914 war so far produced. The portrait gallery is enormous. It begins with an altogether sympathetic portrait of Phillip's father, Richard Maddison, and his marriage to the delightful Hetty. The pace is leisurely, and there are some signs at present that the books are not written as separate entities, but as a long continuous novel, which is chopped arbitrarily into volumes by Williamson's publishers. *The Golden Virgin*, the sixth of the series, contains some of Williamson's finest writing in the war scenes.

This time he makes no attempt to evade them, and they are magnificent.

At the time of writing, Williamson is arriving at a most fascinating point in the series. The latest volume, *A Test to Destruction* (the eighth) has brought Phillip to the end of the war. He is therefore where Willie found himself in *The Dream of Fair Women*. Now the problem begins all over again. So far Williamson has shown a tendency to evade the issues of coming to terms with oneself by killing off his hero at the crucial moment. The remaining volumes of the series will show just how far Williamson has advanced – in spiritual maturity – since 1920. It almost seems that the early volumes of the Phillip Maddison series are a *reculer pour mieux sauter*. He has shown himself triumphant in tackling the problem of the war; now we await his solution of the problems of peace-time. If they are as successful as *The Golden Virgin*, Williamson will have accomplished one of the greatest artistic pilgrimages of our time.

1960-1965

Editor's Notes

This essay updated one written for *The Aylesford Review* (no. 4, Autumn 1961, pp. 131-143 (**C34**)). In her book *Henry Williamson: Tarka and the Last Romantic* (Stroud: Alan Sutton, 1995 (**HB34A**)) his daughter, Anne Williamson, explains that some '... quite virulent remarks... ' were cut from this essay at Henry's request to which the editor, Brocard Sewell, reluctantly complied. This goes some way to explain Wilson's rather ambivalent attitude to both Williamson and his work.

He further updated his assessment after Williamson's death in 1977. His essay

'Henry Williamson and his writings: a personal view,' was printed in *The Henry Williamson Society Journal* (no. 2, October 1980, pp. 9-20 (**C298**)). This was reprinted in *The Literary Review* (no. 29, Nov. 14-27, 1980, pp. 16-21 (**E178**)) as a review of the book *Henry Williamson: the Man, the Writings: a Symposium* edited by Brocard Sewell. In this essay, after calling Williamson a 'thin-skinned monomaniac' he wrote: This may sound as if I... dislike Williamson; nothing could be further from the truth. We always got on well together because I took care to tread carefully around his self-esteem. At the same time, I felt an immense sympathy and pity for him. He was an 'outsider' if ever there was one.

He goes on to reveal some very amusing and telling incidents in his 'friendship' with Williamson. This review was further reprinted in *Existential Criticism: selected book reviews* (Nottingham: Paupers' Press, 2009 (**A178**)).

Further anecdotes can be found in Daniel Farson's *Henry: an appreciation of Henry Williamson* (London: Michael Joseph, 1982 (**HB22**)) and the above-mentioned *Henry Williamson: Tarka and the Last Romantic.*

After *A Test to Destruction* Williamson wrote 7 more volumes in the *A Chronicle of Ancient Sunlight* series, concluding in 1969 with *The Gale of the World*, forming an unsurpassed fictional account of life in early twentieth century Britain. He died in 1977.

PART THREE

THE WRITER AND SOCIETY

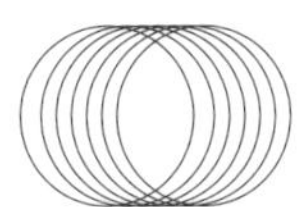

INTRODUCTORY NOTE

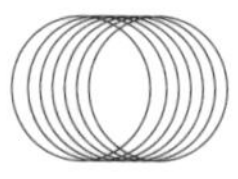

The two articles that follow are occasional journalism. One was written in 1959, the other in 1960. I include them in this volume because they throw some light on the problem of the relation between the writer and the public, particularly in the second half of the fifties. I have made no attempt to bring them up to date – first, because what they say would not be made more or less relevant by so doing; second, because I no longer feel so strongly about the subject, and could only alter them beyond recognition. No doubt further sociological observations could be drawn from the success of the Beatles or the suicide of Marilyn Monroe; but making this kind of change is a self-defeating business, since the new material will be equally outdated in five years' time. So – with some slight misgivings – I leave the articles as they were, complete with acerbities, over-emphases and mistaken judgments. 'The Writer and Publicity' first appeared in *Encounter*, and 'The Success Problem' in *Aswat*, an Arab quarterly. The fact that the second article appeared only in Arabic explains why its general tone is more reckless, and perhaps more didactic, than that of the first. The final essay, 'Influences on My Writing', was also written for *Aswat*.

13

THE WRITER AND PUBLICITY

Kenneth Rexroth, the 'father figure' of the Beat Generation, told me that he bumped into an old friend recently in Provence, and was greeted with the words, 'Hello, Frankenstein, what are you doing in Europe? Trying to hide from your monster?' The joke, Rexroth said, was that that was precisely what he was doing in Europe. He created the monster all right. (His manifesto *Disengagement: The Art of the Beat Generation* was published long before Kerouac's *On the Road.*) But it was the boys on Madison Avenue who galvanized the shambling, half-conscious Petrouchka into its present weird publicity dance. Rexroth fled. Yells and grunts pursued him across the Atlantic.

The other day I came across Edmund Wilson's description of the famous Dada meetings in Paris in the 1920s. It struck me then how much Tristan Tzara and Raymond Duncan missed by not being born thirty years later. I can imagine the *Daily Express*: 'Hello, Mr Tzara, this is Millicent Progworth here. I'm doing William Hickey today. Would you mind giving me your opinion on falsies?' Tzara (gutterally): 'I have ceased to wear falsies since the London Transport claimed they occupied too much room in the rush hour. Try Marlon Brando.' As I write, *Woman's Own* has just rung Bill Hopkins to ask his opinion of seams in lady's stockings, and he replied solemnly, 'Straight seams add allure to lovely legs', and the woman said 'Thank you so much Mr Hopkins', and hung up. And one night the *Evening Standard* woke me up to tell me the Rusian rocket had landed on the moon and had I any comment? My comment was not printed.

All of which leads me to remark that the writer in the fifties ought to be excused for spending a lot of time brooding about the situation of the writer in the fifties. Because there really is a situation, and he is really in it. I sometimes feel a peculiar discomfort in talking to writers of an older generation: a sense of different worlds, different languages, different standards. This disappears when I speak with contemporaries like John Braine, Kingsley Amis, John Osborne. They've been through the same mill-race; we meet like fellow criminals who are introduced to one another at a company directors' dinner at Claridges. We share an insight that would be hard to define in the text-book language, as furtive as a taste for tripe and cowheels.

The present essay is an attempt to give my own version of it. It will be prejudiced, lop-sided, egotistic, and self-explanatory. This is because it is about myself, and I cannot view the subject unemotionally.

A year ago a new advertising magazine sent me a letter asking for a contribution; they remarked that, since I am known as an expert in the art of self-advertisement, they would appreciate a frank account of my publicity methods. I replied that to ask me how to get publicity is like asking a football how to score goals. I went into some detail to explain the analogy. The magazine printed my letter with a headline: 'Colin Wilson Explains his Publicity Methods'. I didn't even get paid for it.

I drew a lesson from this. Obviously, the magazine had nothing to learn from me about the methods of modern journalism. Or maybe they got the idea from my letter. In either case, I should have dropped their letter into the wastepaper basket; nothing can come out of nothing.

To some extent the writer in the Fifties is handling a new medium. His personality and books reach a new audience. And the old audience – the book-buying and library-frequenting public – reacts in a new manner. The very fact that the writer's *personality* is involved is an additional complication. Before television and the gossip columns took an interest in writers, the personality only mattered in so far as it emerged in the books. But anyone who has ever met his favourite author knows that nothing is more disastrous and disillusioning than to allow the personality to become superimposed on the books. Unless the author is an exceptionally unified being, a mutual distortion occurs. There is an effect of double exposure, and both images are reduced to the status of phantoms.

And this cuts both ways. The women who listen to 'Mrs Dale's Diary' are not the only ones who get a weird idea of the author of *Lucky Jim* or *Look Back in Anger*. The serious critics get just as befuddled.

Consider the case-histories of a few of the Angry

Young Men. John Wain's first book *Hurry On Down* received good notices and sold extremely well. (I'm not sure of the figures – probably between 5,000 and 10,000; an excellent sale for a first book). Amis's *Lucky Jim* followed a few months later (in early 1954), and Walter Allen published his *New Statesman* review in which the two were linked as exponents of 'the new hero.' For the next eighteen months, Amis and Wain came in for a great deal of discussion in the literary weeklies, and both expressed themselves a great deal in reviews and articles. Amis insisted on remaining the slightly aloof 'funny man', puzzled by his own success. Wain was less wise; his verdicts tended to be positive and pugnacious.

In the following year both published new novels. Amis's reviews were not bad: lukewarm but not hostile. But Wain's were murderous; *Living in the Present* came up once for air, and disappeared for good. The consequence was that Mr Wain became even more irascible and pugnacious, and developed a complex about critics, his moods of Yeatsian disdain alternating with fits of virulent scorn. Occasionally in recent years this has come to look like a persecution mania. But who can blame Mr Wain? Was it his fault that the critics in 1953 had not ceased to bleat about 'the end of English literature', and that they fell on his novel with sobs of relief? And it was certainly not his fault that, by 1955, everyone was sick of the sound of his name and of chatter about the New Hero. I am not arguing that *Living in the Present* was a masterpiece that received unjust treatment; on the contrary, I tend to agree with those critics who believe that Wain has not yet proved he can write a novel. But Wain is a serious writer, and the spotlight treatment and the chorus of boos and cheers are not the best stimulus to serious writing.

Amis's luck has not been a great deal better in spite of the relatively polite reception of his second novel. Its sales were probably less than a quarter of those of *Lucky Jim* (which ended by selling close on 50,000 in hard covers) and his third book, *I Like It Here*, received such lukewarm notices that its sales could hardly have reached 10,000. As far as the booksellers are concerned, his sales show a steady decline, and Amis is still the author of *Lucky Jim* and nothing else.[43]

In a book on Puccini by Edward Greenfield I find this comment:

> Nothing shows more clearly the jealousy of success among Puccini's close contemporaries than the first performance of *Butterfly*... There can be little doubt that the agitation was organized. Not only that. There is evidence that the organization won sympathy from the ordinary public. They too were glad that Puccini had had a failure...

This was in 1904. But at least Puccini had behind him the success of *Manon Lescaut*, *La Bohème* and *Tosca*. He also had the consolation of seeing *Butterfly* a tremendous success when it was produced two months later in Brescia. And his early success was real success; audiences really applauded *La Bohème* and *Tosca*; he owed nothing to the

43 In 1963, on the tenth anniversary of *Lucky Jim*, Miss Brigid Brophy published a kind of obituary on Amis's talent in the *Sunday Times*, pointing out that his books have grown steadily more fatigued and nihilistic; her remarks verify the above comment.

Observer or the *Sunday Times*. So the anti-success mechanism did not matter much after all. Wain and Amis have not that consolation.

Neither, of course, has Osborne. In this case the rôle of the gossip columns and literary weeklies became more obvious. *Look Back in Anger* was virtually made by Kenneth Tynan's rave review in the *Observer*; the daily papers had treated it with complete indifference, but after Tynan the rest of the posh weeklies hastened to follow suit. (Kenneth Allsop gives more detail of its reception in his *The Angry Decade*.) It happened that Osborne's success came at the same time that Michael Hastings's play *Don't Destroy Me* was produced (he wrote it at seventeen and was nineteen when it was produced), and the week before my own book *The Outsider* came out. *The Daily Mail* immediately asked Hastings, Osborne, and myself to contribute to a series of articles called 'Angry Young Men' in which we were required to explain 'what we were angry about'.[44] The craze was launched. The 'new hero' of Amis and Wain had never got beyond the confines of the *New Statesman* and *Spectator*, but Osborne's Angry Young Man reached the *Daily Mirror* and the *Sunday Pictorial*.

When his second play, *The Entertainer*, was produced a year later, there was a general feeling of bewilderment. I went to the first night of the play to review it for *Reynolds News*. I was rather disappointed and bored, and most of the critics I spoke to were bewildered by it. I got a feeling that some of them were wondering: 'Is it really as bad

44 I explained that I was not angry about anything, but they offered me £100, so I quickly found something to be angry about.

as we think, or is there something wrong with us?' The problem was that the play was so totally defeated, as if the authors of *Love on the Dole* and *Waiting for Godot* had collaborated. Everyone expected another refreshing blast of anger and establishment-baiting, and got a long-drawn-out cry of despair and self-pity. The next day most of the dailies carried pictures of Olivier dressed as Archie Rice. But the reviews confined themselves to the plot of the play, and such neutral comments as 'Not very angry any more'. No one seemed quite to know whether the play was a success or a failure. Finally it was transferred to the West End, and the spectacle of Olivier dressed as a fourth-rate comedian continued to draw large audiences, rather as if one of those dubious Berlin night clubs were advertising Sir Winston Churchill wrestling in mud with Doctor Edith Summerskill. It ran. Pictures of Olivier as Archie Rice continued to appear in glossy magazines. Therefore, in some Pickwickian sense, it must be a success. But one perceptive critic wrote that Mr Osborne should go on his knees and thank Olivier for making a very bad play seem to be a very good one.

Unfortunately Osborne's third work, *The World of Paul Slickey*, was presented without the protection of Sir Laurence Olivier or any other major name, and the result was inevitable; the jeers and catcalls are too recent to need recalling. Osborne was rash enough to state publicly that no English critic had the intellectual equipment to deal with his plays – a curious comment in view of his repeated declaration that his main aim is to make people feel – and the play was finally withdrawn after staggering along for a month with half-empty houses. It was the story of Wain's second novel repeated, but in front of a far bigger audience – the audience of the *Daily Mirror* and *Express* instead of the *Observer* and *New Statesman*, a multiplication by many thousands.

At least Osborne has one important consolation. The theatre is a world in which money can be made quickly and in fabulous quantities, and he has made it. He likes to quote Liberace's reply when someone asked if a particularly harsh criticism had upset him: 'I cried all the way to the bank'. This is another consolation that neither Wain nor Amis had.

The financial question is worth mentioning. In the year of *Look Back in Anger*, Osborne is reported to have made towards £20,000. This means nothing; it is easy to spend that much money when one achieves success suddenly (as I discovered in the same year). But he has stayed in the high-income bracket ever since. Wain, on the other hand, admits that he makes very little money from his novels and lives mainly by reviewing. Amis was at that time a university lecturer, but has since retired. Their immense success has not been a financial success, and they are rather in the position of a man with a title and no money to keep it up.

In the same way, John Braine's first novel *Room at the Top* sold nearly 40,000 copies in its hard-cover edition. This large figure actually represents only about £5,000 in royalties. (The usual royalty terms on a book costing a pound are between two and three shillings per copy.) His immense sales in Penguins – around a million copies

– only represent a *penny* or so a copy. (I have not asked Mr Braine any questions, about his royalties, and am only quoting general figures.) The film rights of the book were sold outright for a sum that the *Sunday Dispatch* quoted as £5,000, so that the author has gained no advantage from the film's extraordinary success. Since this sum (say £12,000 in all) was made in one year, the income tax would decimate it by about a half. From my own experience, I know that nothing is easier than to spend a great deal more than £6,000 in one year when one makes it quickly and makes a sudden alteration in one's way of life. So Mr Braine's fabulous success is by no means a financial success as far as this first novel goes.

Equally interesting are the cases of Bill Hopkins and Stuart Holroyd. These two writers had been close friends of mine for many years when the publicity wave hit *The Outsider*. Holroyd was engaged on a book called *Emergence from Chaos*, whose theme was similar to that of *The Outsider*. After the success of *The Outsider* my publisher quickly accepted *Emergence from Chaos*, and issued it in an edition whose binding and general presentation were very similar to that of *The Outsider*; the dust jacket declared that readers who had enjoyed my book would be equally excited by this one. The result was inevitable, for the reaction against *The Outsider* had been going strong for nearly a year by that time. One of the two newspapers that had hailed *The Outsider* ignored the book; the other sneered at Mr Gollancz's habit of looking in cradles for his philosophical prodigies. The book very quickly disappeared. Holroyd was already engaged on his second book, a kind of autobiographical credo called *Flight and Pursuit*, which its publisher expected to be one of his most important books of the year. This fared even worse; a short burst of machine-gun fire from one literary weekly, and there was no longer any question of it being a 'book of the year', or even of the week. That was in 1958; Mr Holroyd has published nothing since.[45]

Both Stuart Holroyd and Bill Hopkins had been associated with me a great deal in public: for example, both of them contributed to an anthology called *Declaration* before either had published their first books, and their views obviously had much in common with my own. This meant that before either of them published a book, both were frequently grouped with me in newspaper comments, as if we were the three musketeers. One critic had gone so far as to warn his readers about Holroyd, referring to him as a 'new Messiah of the coffee bars', before his book appeared. I have said that Holroyd's first book was largely ignored; but for some reason Bill Hopkins's novel *The Divine and the Decay* roused everyone to fury. In *The Angry Decade* Kenneth Allsop has remarked that it is almost unprecedented for a first novel to receive this kind of universal hatcheting treatment. Not surprisingly, Bill Hopkins has also published nothing since then.[46]

I could labour this point a great deal longer and produce more instances, but it would be pointless. A citation of my own experience, however, might reinforce and clarify my argument.

45 This is still true in 1965.

46 Also true in 1965.

I have always worked upon the assumption that I have something important to communicate. In my teens, most modern writers depressed me because their world was so dull, so devoid of romantic idealism. I was also irritated by the kind of weakness and self-depreciation that led to the defeat of so many writers of the nineties – Dowson and Johnson, for example. In the writers I loved, I found a lack of this crippling self-depreciation, a lack of neuroses. Dante, Goethe, Shakespeare, Nietzsche, Shaw, all worked with an assumption of genius, a tendency to take it for granted that they were the favourites of the gods. It seemed to me that the main difference between the great writers of the past and the defeated figures of our own time is not so much a difference of talent or genius, but the failure of modern writers *to make this assumption*: a lack of self-confidence.

In this spirit I worked upon an assumption of my own genius, always bearing in mind the reservation that I might be mistaken. Keats's friend Haydon was mistaken; Blake's friend Fuseli was mistaken; the Victorian poets Alfred Austin and Lewis Morris and Bailey (who wrote *Festus*) were mistaken. But better a thousand Haydons and Baileys who produce grandiose rubbish than one T. E. Lawrence or Van Gogh who died because they could never believe in their own genius. Thomas Mann expressed his admiration for the vast cyclic works of the nineteenth century, the *Comédie Humaine*, the *Rougon-Macquart*, the *Ring*, and quoted the chapter of Seville cathedral, who said to the architect, 'Build me such a cathedral that future generations will say the chapter must have been insane to undertake anything so immense'.

When I was about nineteen I got used to my manuscripts being returned promptly and decided not to send them out again. I decided that if I had to wait until I was fifty before I published my first book, the intervening years might provide me with a vast amount to say. So many writers of my acquaintance let rejection discourage them and stopped making the effort. To me this was stupidity; the effort and the genius were almost synonymous. So I wrote like mad, filling note-book after note-book, revising and re-revising my novel, cheering myself with the thought of Seville cathedral.

Success came abruptly and shatteringly. I never doubted for a moment that it was my due, but it unbalanced me. To begin with, I regarded myself as the only real psychologist in European history since Goethe and Nietzsche; but Goethe and the *Daily Express* made a disconcerting contrast.

I tried hard to communicate my ideas, and reporters – on the whole – tended to be sympathetic. But I soon saw that they were inclined to take a note of the surprising things I said, and then to quote them in isolation to produce an effect of zany irresponsibility or outright insanity. To illustrate this I have to look no further than a recent *Daily Mail*. I had spent a whole day with the reporter, who turned out to be exceptionally cultured and intelligent; we discussed Mahler, Bruckner, Wedekind, and Heinrich Mann. The article, when it appeared, took occasional sentences (which I had certainly said) out of context, and made a most extraordinary farrago of them.

I am quoted as saying that I intend to live to be 300 (I actually stated that I admired Shaw's proposal in *Back to Methuselah*). I quote: 'I want to write the best book that has ever been written by a man of eighty. I want to demonstrate the supremacy of the human spirit. Even if somebody were to drop the A-bomb, that still wouldn't stop me. I'd still believe in human progress. But I haven't the faintest intention of being killed by a bomb or run over by a car. I'm far too valuable. I'm quite certain I can reach the age of 110. Only the pointless are killed pointlessly… ' And so on. It would be futile to correct the occasional word that makes all the difference, to add the qualification, to point out that at a certain juncture the reporter interrupted to ask a question of his own, and mixed in his question with my reply.

This is one of those 'insights' that I mentioned earlier – the ones I share with other 'Angry Young Men' when we meet. But there are too many to detail.

A few months after *The Outsider* had been published, I noticed that the tone of my press cuttings was changing; they were becoming noticeably unpleasant; in some cases stupidly spiteful. I began to understand Wain's outbursts of baited fury about his critics; it was difficult to carry on working quietly with so much bitchery flying around. The reason, of course, was partly the appearance of such articles as the one I have quoted above, and partly the ordinary anti-success mechanism. In fact its success had been staggering. To begin with, it had sold as many copies in America as in England. (English best sellers tend to be flops in America, and vice versa), and quickly sold translation rights into a dozen languages. In England alone it sold 40,000 copies, at a guinea a copy. I accepted every offer to lecture, write articles, or appear on the radio or television. In some way that I still do not understand I spent £2,000 in two months, and had nothing to show for it except a few books and records.

The amount of enmity I aroused worried me. On the whole I tend to like people; I have very seldom made enemies through personal contact, except by misunderstanding. I was often startled by the violence of the reactions produced. When I wrote an article denouncing D. H. Lawrence in the *Listener*, the editor received dozens of letters filled with rage and indignation. On another occasion I turned up at the BBC to take part in a recorded Third Programme discussion and was immediately handed my postcard on which I had accepted the engagement. I had mentioned on the card that I was very busy; some BBC official had scrawled on it, 'It is very condescending of Mr Wilson to come', and had made sure that the card was handed back to me. The discussion itself was a flop; I found that I disagreed with everyone else on the panel, and that they all seemed to take it personally. (They were mostly of my own age, young men just down from the universities.) The discussion was never broadcast; probably the underlying animosity came over too clearly. One of these young men has since become a critic upon whom I can always rely for a murderous review of any of my books.

My first response to the slaughter of my next book was one of relief. I was sick of being a 'public figure' and not recognizing myself in the reactions I aroused. It was a sensation like being lifted from a high and dangerous pinnacle and replaced on the ground. By this time I had moved out of London. I had given too many lectures, met too many people, attended too many parties, and I was tired. Cornwall was soothing: only the weekly press cuttings revived the sensation of being sniped at. And after *Religion and the Rebel* had been murdered by all the critics, the tone of the Press became almost imperceptibly kinder. At the PEN congress, Vera Brittain referred to me as 'that unfortunate young man whose career has been laid in ruins', and Alec Waugh pointed out that writers are not as delicate as all that, in spite of Keats and the *Quarterly*. On the whole, I felt a lot better. I had returned to the kind of life I prefer: listening to records for hours of every day, buying all the books I wanted, and seeing very few people. I played darts in the local fishermen's pub to avoid visitors who might recognize me or budding writers who wanted advice, and made a point of avoiding any 'intellectual' conversation, even with friends. I went to Norway, then to Hamburg, giving some lectures to university audiences, and was surprised that reporters asked me about my ideas and not about my private life. Bill Hopkins had also gone to Hamburg – largely, I think, as a result of the murderous reviews of his novel. We agreed that a foreign country is an immense relief when one has had a book panned. (Stuart Holroyd had fled to Munich after his first book came out.) The foreign city was like being in Paris again in 1953 when we were both working on our first novels. It was strange to realize that success can be such an ordeal.

I wrote my third critical book out of pure cussedness. It was intended as an anthology piece, to be published with a long essay by Bill Hopkins and one by Stuart Holroyd. In writing it I felt a perverse desire to provoke the people who had praised *The Outsider* and then attacked *Religion and the Rebel*, and to appear as a completely impenitent quoter of other writers. I had the consolation of knowing that it could never meet a worse reception than *Religion and the Rebel*. In any case I had nothing to lose. Besides, I had finally brought my long novel about a sex maniac, *Ritual in the Dark*, near to completion. Since I began this at the age of nineteen it had been through a great many metamorphoses, and Gollancz's had turned down an earlier version on the grounds that 'no printer would dare to set it up'. It seemed to me to express my feelings far better than the critical books. A clever critical book can impress with a façade of opinions, but a good novel can't be faked: it has no opinions. It can only show, with complete accuracy, what it is actually like to be the writer. So I wrote *The Age of Defeat* without many misgivings; nothing very bad could happen to it.

And in fact nothing very bad did happen to it. My publisher decided that it had better be published on its own; it was too long to be one-third of an anthology. Most of the reviews lacked the maniacal fury I expected; many of them leaned over backwards to say something nice, even when the reviewer plainly disagreed with the book. Professor Ayer did not assail the book. (I had attacked him in both my previous books, and he responded with shattering reviews of them both.) Philip Toynbee, who launched *The Outsider* with an enthusiastic review and then retracted it all when he reviewed *Religion and the Rebel*, also made no comment. And the comment that I most expected was not made at all: that I had stated that *Religion and the Rebel* would be my last critical book, and had not kept my promise. Any reviewer would have been justified in demanding, 'When is he going to stop telling everybody how to write creative literature and produce some himself?' The query would have been relevant because it is the logical conclusion of my existentialism: intellectual discussion becomes a bore; only some form of action can redeem the 'existential thinker'. And the only form of action that is meaningful is creative. For this reason I have always preferred music to literature, and would rather be a composer than a writer.

When I look back on the years since *The Outsider* I haven't many regrets. Certainly the personal publicity was a mistake. It always is a mistake. Shaw is still largely unread because most people are more aware of the legendary Shaw created by the newspapers than of the man who wrote *Major Barbara*. Mr Priestley's name is still a dirty word in the mouth of many intellectuals because they remember his broadcasts during the war and the 'Jolly Jack' legends; his fine novels and penetrating criticisms are forgotten. Even Mr Eliot's prestige has been sinking steadily since the widespread publicity given to his plays and to his second marriage. The anti-success mechanism starts. And because each of his plays is received with funereal respect, there is a powerful but suppressed resistance to his ideas.

He was better off as the violently attacked author of *The Waste Land*.

But, the modern world being what it is, personal publicity is not always avoidable. In this case, there is only one antidote to it: to produce good work. The greatest danger for the writer is to cease to work. The only ultimately effective form of publicity is a body of major work. In so far as the modern literary climate distracts writers, or drugs them with immoderate praise or goads them with stupid blame, it is working towards the death of literature. In many ways the writer was better off when he read his poetry to a clique, and was contented if he sold 500 copies. It was easier to be subjective. But these are the conditions under which we must learn to work. Reviewers who detest the very idea of a writer becoming involved in the publicity machine should realize that it is a machine, and that the writer *is* caught up in it. The writer may be too stupid or too naïve to realize quite what is happening, but to blame him for this is to expect him to possess something beside literary talent – and this is to cease to judge him purely as a writer. The main danger is that he should cease to work out of sheer disgust with the absurd see-saw of literary judgement and gossip-column broadsides.

1959

Editor's Notes:

This essay was first published as 'The Writer and Publicity: a reply to critics' in *Encounter*, no. 13, November 1959, pp. 8-13 (**C18**). In it, Wilson mistakenly wrote 'Woman's Hour' instead of *Woman's Own* when recounting the seams in lady's stockings conversation. This caused much consternation at the BBC and helped to blacken his relationship with them somewhat.

John Wain wrote a reply to this essay in *The Guardian*, October 20, 1961: 'On reputations, publicity, middlemen etc'.

Bill Hopkins did not produce another novel; the manuscript of his second, *Time of Totality*, was apparently destroyed in a house fire and not rewritten. He became an art dealer. *The Divine and the Decay* was reprinted as *The Leap* in 1984 and now enjoys a moderate cult status. He died in 2011.

Stuart Holroyd *did* continue to write intermittently. A memoir *Contraries: A Personal Progression* appeared in 1975 (London: The Bodley Head). This was expanded as *His Dear Time's Waste: A 1950s Literary and Love Life Memoir* (Manchester: Pronoia Books, 2013). At time of writing, 2017, Holroyd is the last surviving 'Angry Young Man'. For more details on Holroyd's life and work see *Stuart Holroyd: Years of Anger and Beyond* by Antoni Diller (Nottingham: Paupers' Press, 2012).

Wilson, Hopkins and Holroyd, along with John Braine and the journalist Tom Greenwell all shared a *pied e terre* at 25 Chepstow Road, London in the late 1950s. Greenwell subsequently wrote a play about the experience: *Chepstow Road: A Literary Comedy in Two Acts* (Nottingham: Paupers' Press, 2002) for which Wilson wrote an Introduction. Upon leaving, in 1960, Hopkins commissioned sculptor Lawrence Bradshaw (1899-1978) to produce a blue plaque which was placed on the wall outside the front door. It read: 'In this house lived, 1955-1960, Colin Wilson, John Braine, Stuart Holroyd, Tom Greenwell, Greta Detloff, Bill Hopkins. Hallowed be these precincts.' The plaque disappeared soon after and has never since come to light. There is, however, a picture of it on the back cover of Greenwell's play.

14

THE SUCCESS PROBLEM

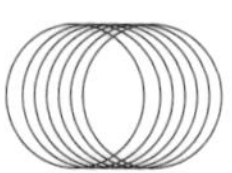

I have in front of me as I write a popular daily newspaper which carries a front page headline: SHELAGH DELANEY'S NEW PLAY A FLOP. Shelagh Delaney was the young Salford girl whose first play, *A Taste of Honey*, brought her sudden fame. A few weeks after its success, Miss Delaney explained how she had decided to write it after seeing John Osborne's *Look Back in Anger*; she thought this 'awful crap' (in her own words) and decided she could write something better. Within a year, her faith in herself was justified to the extent of £30,000.

An interesting success story, but why should a daily newspaper with a huge circulation take pleasure in proclaiming her second play a flop? Has the editor a grudge against her? Or has one of the gossip-column writers particular reason to dislike her?

I doubt it. The truth is simpler. The newspaper's readers have been hearing a great deal about Miss Delaney, England's Françoise Sagan. They have read about her clothes, her new car, her home in Salford. They are naturally curious to know whether she can sustain her success.

If a writer of the early thirties spent the next thirty years in some remote part of Africa where he never saw a newspaper, and then came back to London to take up his literary life again, how would he feel about this strange situation that has developed in England? He might well be totally bewildered. He would, of course, remember the newspaper publicity received by men like Shaw, Wells, and Chesterton. But this was in the 'respectable' newspapers, led by *The Times* and *Manchester Guardian*. Shaw's controversies were carried on in the *New Statesman* and *The Times*. He would also remember that Eliot's *Waste Land* had caused a furore in 1922, that Joyce's *Ulysses* had been attacked in the *Pink 'un* (a newspaper devoted to racing), and that Aldous Huxley's *Antic Hay* had been labelled 'the spirit of a new generation' by the 'respectable' newspapers.

But he would have been startled to see the *Daily Mirror* on the day after Dylan Thomas's death, when a whole page was devoted to a huge photograph of the poet, together with a story about his famous drunken orgies. He would undoubtedly have found it strange to see the endless gossip-column references to the 'Angry Young Men' – John Osborne, John Braine, myself, Kingsley Amis, etc. – in 1957 and 1958. If he took the *Daily Express* recently, he would have been even more startled to see the announcement that a novel by 'the Voice of the Sixties', a young man named Auberon Waugh, is to be serialized daily. Mr Waugh's first novel was published the week before, and received the usual kind reviews accorded to a first novel together with one or two rather guarded reviews that obviously felt that Mr Waugh had a certain unfair disadvantage in being the son of Evelyn Waugh.

Mr Waugh's first novel – as far as I can judge from the extracts in the *Express* – is a work that shows talent and an ability to write well. But this does not stop me from realizing that thirty years ago it would have received its share of good reviews in the 'respectable' weeklies, sold 5,000 copies, and been forgotten until its author had proved whether he had any staying power. As it is, it may sell 25,000 copies and make several thousands of pounds; and long before he has published his next book the author will be feeling a terrifying sense of being in the public eye. And if his next book (as often happens) is not as good as his first, he can expect the headlines: AUBERON WAUGH'S NEW BOOK A FLOP.

It is a terrifying situation. We live in an aura of publicity. John Wain recently pointed out to me an interview in *The Times* in which a young poet declares: 'Anger is out of date. That was for the generation of the fifties. The new generation will have more sense... ' etc. I published my first book *The Outsider* at the same time that Osborne's *Look Back in Anger* was produced. Four years later, we are already out of date! A truly astounding situation!

Scott Fitzgerald once said about writing: 'You would never be as famous as a film star, but what fame you had would last longer'. Well, the first part of that statement is untrue today. I believe that Osborne and myself were the first writers in England to get the full publicity treatment in mid-1956; before that, it had been reserved for names like James Dean, Elvis Presley, and Marilyn Monroe. But how about the second part of Fitzgerald's statement – that what fame you had would last longer? I think it unpleasantly possible that the publicity will throw writers off their balance to such an extent that their work will not deserve to be remembered. One has only to recall the name of Michael Arlen, the most feted author of the twenties, whose *Green Hat* brought him a fortune, and who then wrote nothing worthwhile for the rest of his life. Some of his later books are so bad and cheap as to be unreadable.

The effect of publicity is something that any good and serious writer can learn to combat. But what about its effect on other people, on the critics and journalists? Although Mr Auberon Waugh's name has been 'famous' only for a fortnight as I write this, I have already read some very harsh comments about him. It is natural that many journalists – particularly the ones who write books themselves – should feel some jealousy.

At this point I should like to tell a story that illustrates my argument. Some years ago a new magazine published an interview with me that was written in a rather cheap and journalistic manner. This was largely the fault of the editor, who had cut out all but sensational matter. It was headed 'Colin Wilson talks about MY GENIUS' and quoted me as saying that my main ambition was for my name to become a household word like that of Dickens or Shaw. About two weeks after this appeared, I received a letter enclosing the carbon copy of another article about me. It was an extremely bitter and violent article, and ended, 'Your name is a household word, Mr Wilson, and the word is PHONEY'. The writer explained to me that he had written this article for the same magazine but they had rejected it; however, he wanted me to know his opinion of me, and so sent me his article.

I replied, thanking him for the article, and pointing out that the publicity I received was really not my fault, and that it had many disadvantages for me. As a result of this I got an immensely long letter from him – about five foolscap sheets of single-space typing – in which he said that he had been angry because he had fought on the beaches of Dunkirk with many young lads who aspired to be writers, many of whom had died in the war, and here were we young upstarts getting all the publicity, etc. He went on to explain that he was a literary agent, and to tell me about his own disappointments in the world of writing, Again I wrote a sympathetic reply; again I received a gigantic letter, full of confidences. We corresponded for some time, and his letters must have amounted to a hundred or so pages. It soon became obvious that the violence of the original article was simply a protest at the neglect he felt his generation was being accorded.

This, then, will account for much of the hostility that Mr Waugh is now provoking. For my own part, I sympathize with him. Success is pleasant, but he didn't ask to be lionized in the Press; and if he hopes to express some quite individual viewpoint in his books, he will no doubt be puzzled and hurt when he discovers that criticisms of his future work seem to have little reference to what the books are about. The very young writer reads about the 'great unrecognized' writers, and hopes he will never be a Ronald Firbank or L. H. Myers. Only experience can teach him that there is a far greater danger in too much recognition. The example of Bernard Shaw should prove this; throughout the early years of this century he was one of the most famous writers the world has ever known (in his own lifetime, that is). Yet his influence was infinitesimal, and it will be another hundred years before he can be read without memories of his publicity interfering.

The case of John Osborne is also instructive. I first met Osborne when a 'respectable' Sunday newspaper had run pictures of us both in the gossip column, and Mr J. B. Priestley had written an article on us in the *New Statesman*. His *Look Back in Anger* had not then made much money, but it had made him an immense reputation. By the time his second play, *The Entertainer*, was presented, there was a great deal of hostility to him in the Press – it had increased in proportion to the number of times his name was mentioned by the gossip columns. But in some amazing way his second play was not attacked. This was almost undoubtedly due to the presence of Sir Laurence Olivier in the lead, for the play is not a good one, and its film version has more recently received extremely bad notices. But Osborne's third work, *The World of Paul Slickey*, had no important names to protect it, and the critics had a field day. The author was even booed outside the theatre. The reviews were harsher than any I have ever seen in the British Press. It is true that *Slickey* was an extremely poor work; but half a dozen equally poor plays are presented for the first time every week without arousing such fury.

It will be interesting to see how far Mr Osborne can survive the slaughter of his play, the inflating of his reputation, and become a good dramatist. Because there is no precedent for the sort of problem he has to face. Other playwrights have had overnight success – from Gay's *Beggar's Opera* to Kurt Weill's later version of it; but success is one thing: to be regarded as 'the voice of a generation' – especially in the gossip columns – is quite another.

The Psychology of Fame

There is a quite special relation between the general public and its idols. It is a relation that is growing steadily more complicated. Two centuries ago, an actress or an admiral might become popular overnight; but neither actresses nor admirals are likely to be unbalanced by popularity, for success makes a man more forthcoming, more of an extrovert, so to speak. And success can only be increased when the object of universal adoration seems to feel an equal affection for his (or her) public. (We might recall the example of Gracie Fields, who was probably the most popular woman in England ten years ago; or Wilfred Pickles, with his 'Have a Go' radio programme.)

But a writer is a different matter. The first writer to be considerably affected by success was Charles Dickens. In his day, he was one of the most loved figures in England. There is a story of a railway accident when Dickens played a creditable part as a rescuer. He clambered off the derailed train, walked up to the engine driver, and said, 'My man, do you know who I am?' The driver replied, 'Yes sir, you're Mr Dickens'. 'Then do as I tell you', said Dickens. This was in the days before the newspapers printed photographs. When Dickens went to America, cheering crowds lined the streets of every city he visited. Nowadays, only a famous rock-and-roll star or a popular politician would receive the same acclaim. But Dickens came to lust for acclaim; when some of his books failed to sell as many copies as *Nicholas Nickleby* he was deeply depressed. Finally he enjoyed reading aloud to large audiences, for they cheered him and he could bask in the acclaim he was used to. He used to read the murder scene from *Oliver Twist*, although it often made ladies in his audience faint with horror. The effect was the important thing.

In the days before education was general, it was natural that the extraordinary men should receive this awe-stricken acclaim. It was also the 'right' of the aristocracy. Both the aristocracy of wealth and the aristocracy of talent were like gods from Olympus. There is still this relation between a great section of the general public and its idols. The scenes of hysterical mourning caused by the death of Rudolph Valentino have been repeated in recent years when James Dean killed himself in a racing car. The ju-ju of fame is still powerful. But there are also increasing numbers of men and women with enough education to reject the idea that Marilyn Monroe and Elvis Presley are the most enviable of human beings, while still finding themselves oppressed by the general acceptance of the 'idols'. The result is a feeling of active hostility towards the idols. I expect that any day now, some irritated idealist will make an attempt on the life of Liberace. (This is always a possibility; one only has to read the life of, say, Charles Guiteau who murdered President Garfield, to realize that the assassin is often protesting at his own 'undeserved failure' rather than at another man's success.)

One might say that the relations between the public figure and the public are becoming at once much closer and much more hostile. It is rather on the same principle that family quarrels are always the most bitter. The modern writer might well be 'spoilt' by too much attention; it is equally likely that he will be suffocated by it.

A certain detachment has always been necessary to great achievement. Beethoven was known to all cultured Europe as a man of genius, but his private life was so withdrawn that a policeman once arrested him as a tramp and put him in jail. Can one imagine this happening to Stravinsky today? James Joyce wrote his *Ulysses* in a long and poverty-stricken exile, while the Dada movement in Paris, now totally forgotten, was capturing the headlines in much the same way that the Angry Young Men and the Beat Generation captured them in the 1950s. It is hard to think how any good work can be done without this withdrawal. And yet it seems that, whether we like it or not, this withdrawal may be denied to writers of the sixties.

I have so far forborne to speak of myself and my own problems, but at this point they become relevant. Although my notoriety came early – when I was twenty-five – I had been confidently anticipating it since I was sixteen, and preparing to write a great many books. Consequently, although I was thrown badly off balance by the sudden wave of publicity, I was more prepared for it than some of my contemporaries. Besides, I had always been an admirer of T. S. Eliot and T. E. Hulme, and had consequently always had a strong feeling for 'tradition'. So while I was writing my first book, I was also more or less aware of the place I wanted it to occupy in European literature, its position in the history of ideas. I had already, as it were, written my own history of European thought in which a chapter on me followed chapters on Sartre and Camus, Eliot, Shaw, and others. I was acutely aware of the problem of the decay of religion and the collapse of civilization it was likely to bring. And although I was as egoistic as most writers – I wanted fame, money and security – I was also genuinely concerned to avert this collapse by attempting to recreate a new basis for European culture. I was concerned to redefine values.

So it was disconcerting to find myself attacked by many journalists as a publicity-seeking intellectual hooligan (Professor Frank Kermode, for example, dismissed me in *Encounter* as 'an intellectual Tommy Steele'). I think it was not the attack that mattered so much as the total lack of understanding behind it; occasionally, in fact, the undisguised malice behind it. I like to be optimistic about human beings and to assume that, for the most part, they are decent and concerned to make communication possible. Malice is like a deliberate sabotage of the telephone wires between human beings.

Still, I was by no means surprised when my second book was slaughtered unmercifully in the Press. I had got used to a year of various kinds of malice. I had even ceased to resent it. After all, as in the case of Miss Delaney, the Press is only giving its readers 'what they want'; and if its favourite sport is tearing down idols they also, at least, build them up. But I now felt the main problem to be simple enough: how long would it be before the enormous dust-cloud would die down, and my books would be read without any memory of publicity and gossip columns? This, I'm afraid, is a question I have still not answered. Because whether reviews of my books are good or bad, they are still plainly influenced by a picture of me that was projected by the newspapers. This often inspires a strong suspicion that a reviewer has not bothered to read the book, but has simply trotted out his preconceived opinion of the Angry Young Man myth, of which I am, for the moment, one of the chief embodiments.

And this brings me to my final point: the whole problem of the attitude of the critics in this new situation.

Let us be clear about this: malicious and stupid critics have always existed. Very often they belong to the establishment, who resent a younger generation. (The infamous *Edinburgh Review* attack on Keats – which, Byron claimed implausibly, killed him – was attributed to Hazlitt, for example). A murderous review of his violin concerto by the viperish Hanslick 'haunted' Tchaikovsky to his dying day. The same Hanslick helped to drive Hugo Wolf insane. There is an even worse example that dates from pre-revolution Russia: a certain music critic published a virulent review of a new work by Prokoviev; what he did not know was that the performance had been cancelled at the last minute. The result was a famous musical scandal; the critic apparently made a habit of writing reviews without hearing the work. This is a case in which the scandal became open, but it is depressing to think how many pieces of similar critical malpractice never come to light.

Many artists and writers hold an entirely hostile (or indifferent) attitude to their critics, declaring that a critic is a kind of parasite or blood-sucking insect that battens onto creators. But how would many of us come to know a great deal of music and literature without books on the subject? The critic ought, in theory, to serve the same purpose as an amplifier on a gramophone: to make the greatness of works of art more immediately obvious.

It is natural that many critics – especially young ones – should spend a lot of their time attacking the works they are reviewing. (As they get older and make friends in 'the game' they tend to get more tolerant.) At times, this hostility may be so undisguisedly due to envy that the criticism almost becomes a criminal offence. (For example, *John O'London's Weekly* recently printed a letter from a reader about Benjamin Britten in which the reader said sneeringly that he would give every single work by Britten for any two bars of Mozart; one would like to put the reader on trial and subject him to a cross examination on the works of Britten and Mozart and find out how much he really knows about either.)

But for the moment I am not speaking of this type of critic, who has as much relation to a real critic as an abortionist has to a Harley Street surgeon. The real problem arises with our new type of 'single paragraph' criticism.

In the nineteenth century, a critic like Lord Macaulay or Carlyle might produce a 10,000-word essay as a book criticism. Today, thousands of new books are printed every year, and even the respectable newspapers have a habit of reviewing six novels at a time in a 600-word article.

This, then, is the first factor in the new criticism. The other is that tendency I have already mentioned for a few writers to receive overwhelming personal publicity. I could cite a dozen examples in the past few years. Take the case of James Gould Cozzens, a middle-aged American writer who has produced many rather pedestrian novels about the law and professional men. Three years ago he decided it was time to try to treat a more universal subject, and produced *By Love Possessed*, a monstrous, slow-moving book, full of interminable conversations in legal jargon, and dealing, in a very incidental way, with rape and adultery. It is in many ways a worthy and interesting book; but no one will ever know why the American critics all decided to hail it as the latest candidate for the Great American Novel. It shot to the top of the best-seller list (most of its buyers must have been sadly bewildered by it) and was, naturally, bought by the films. A few months later someone realized that it wasn't really so good after all, and the great reaction began. A witty critic altered its title to *By Words Obsessed*; the magazines which had published the original bursts of praise now produced attacks. At the moment, one would need to be very indifferent to the opinion of one's fellow reviewers if one dared to say a word in praise of Cozzens in America. Mr Cozzens, who is apparently a dour and stoical man, must have found his natural pessimism and mistrust fortified by this *volte-face*. It is useless to point out to the critics that it was not Mr Cozzens who wrote the original reviews of his book and so it is hardly fair to be so malicious at his expense when the critics discover they were wrong about it.

The feuds and petty malice involved in criticism would hardly matter if literature and art generally remained a kind of closed shop, where the artist could feel to some extent judged by his equals, even if adversely. This is, after all, what happened in previous ages. And it hardly matters if critics are very unkind to the books and plays of other critics – as they usually are. But we are beginning to face an extremely gloomy situation in which the low standard of general criticism, affected by modern publicity methods, affects in turn the standards of writing. An example is Miss Delaney's reaction to Osborne's play: 'I can do better than that'. A more understandable reaction would be 'I have more to say than that'. If a writer is spurred simply by dislike for the acclaim of another writer, no one can be surprised if the works produced under this stimulus should not seem to be saying much.

What is worse still is that many writers who ought to know better let themselves be completely depressed by the hostility of critics. It is not surprising if Osborne's third play should be a tasteless and pointless social satire, since his critics had given him the feeling that what he had to say was largely a satirical attack on modern society. But I have often been amazed to meet famous and serious writers who seem to give immense weight to what the critics say – particularly when it is unkind. One such author told me that the critics have 'had their knives in him' for the past twenty-five years.

We are living, I think, in one of the most culturally treacherous ages that has ever beset Western civilization. Literature in particular has become a kind of morass that breeds fevers of the judgment. It seems, therefore, to be of particular importance today for a writer to try to think and create oblivious to the ill-judged attacks that appear every week in respectable newspapers and magazines. And if he really has anything to say, he might do worse than make a vow never to look into any of the highbrow literary weeklies – at least until he is so sure of himself that he can remain unaffected.

What it amounts to is that there may be in the world at the moment a dozen or so writers who *could* become serious and important – as serious, let us say, as Eliot or Joyce. Their chances are considerably lessened by the present situation. Unless they are lucky enough to succeed in writing half a dozen books without much publicity or acclaim, they will be deflected by the usual barrage of undesirable attention. (It is interesting to imagine what might have happened to Eliot if he had received the publicity treatment after he published *Prufrock* in 1917.) Great art has to be created in the dark; it thrives best with a certain amount of attention and appreciation, but a flood of undiscerning curiosity can kill it.

Shortly after I published *The Outsider*, T. S. Eliot was kind enough to offer me some advice. The right way to establish a reputation, he said, was to become known to a small circle of discriminating readers, then to a wider circle of people who take the word of the discriminating readers about what is good; finally, *if at all*, to the general public. At the time he said this I was too elated by 'success' to understand what he meant. I have since come to see his point.

As a writer, I have one invariable method for dealing with my problems – to try to drag them into the light of consciousness. Hence the point of the present essay. Besides, I suppose I'm lucky in some respects: being an 'intellectual' rather than a poet, I can resist the pressures better than some of my contemporaries. It is easier to stop a man from feeling than to stop him from thinking.

1960

Editor's Notes:
The article 'Colin Wilson Explains: My Genius' was written by Daniel Farson. It appeared in *Books and Art*, October 1957, pp. 24-25 (**J24**). It was preceded by another article by Farson in the *Daily Mail* 'I Meet a Genius with Indigestion', July 13, 1956, p.4 (**J4**).

J. B. Priestley's article 'Thoughts on The Outsider' appeared in the *New Statesman*, July 7, 1956, pp. 10-11. This was included in his book *Thoughts in the Wilderness* (London: Heinemann, 1957 (**HB1**) and then in *Colin Wilson, A Celebration: Essays and Recollections* edited by Colin Stanley (London: Cecil Woolf, 1988 (**HA8**)).

15

PERSONAL

Influences on my Writing

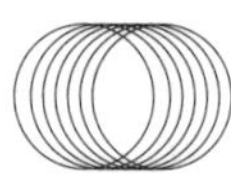

It seems to me that most modern writers – and I am now thinking of writers in Italy, Germany, France, England, and America, which is as far as my knowledge extends – are too provincial in their attitude to writing. They are not conscious enough of the past, of other parts of the world, nor, above all, of the real problems faced by civilization in the twentieth century.

I am aware these are big words, and that they may seem almost meaningless. Sometimes when I read articles that I wrote a few years ago – my contribution to *Declaration*, for example – I feel disgusted with my own writing; it seems too vague and general. And yet if I read it carefully, without worrying about the kind of impression it makes on people who dislike my writing, I can see exactly what I meant, and that what I meant was not just a 'vague generalization'. So let me try to explain what I mean by my statement above. It is an essential preliminary to explaining what I mean to do about it.

For some reason, one of my central psychological drives has been a thirst for knowledge – knowledge in the sense of academic information. When I was ten years old an uncle gave me a book called *The Marvels and Mysteries of Science*, full of photographs of the planets, of prehistoric monsters, of waterfalls, and the patterns made by snowflakes. In a few months I had read it from cover to cover; I then managed to save five shillings, and went to a large bookshop in the town where I searched the science shelves for another book of the same type. Unfortunately, the war was on; the price of books had risen in a few weeks. The only book I could find for five shillings was a cheap reprint of Sir Arthur Eddington's *New Pathways in Science*, and I bought this and took it home. It opens with a quotation from Poincaré: 'Does the harmony which the human intelligence thinks it discovers in Nature exist apart from such intelligence?' I read this sentence a dozen times without being able to fathom its meaning. (I should explain that my brain refuses to work with abstract statements; all my ideas begin as intuitions connected with my feelings and sensations.) I refused to be put off by my inability to understand, and read through the whole volume, determinedly, word by word, like a man who has made up his mind to eat a plate of potatoes when he is not hungry. (After all, I had paid five shillings for it.) I did not learn anything from the book – it was five years or so before I could understand it – but I read it because I felt it contained secrets that I ought to know. I still cannot explain this urge to uncover secrets. Sometimes now, I take a volume on mathematics off a library shelf and see a page full of equations that are meaningless to me; again I am seized with the same hunger to know what it is all about; I may take the book home and read fifty pages before I realize that there is no point in tackling the theory of equations before one even understands how to use the square root of minus one.

A psychologist might explain this urge as a feeling of 'academic underprivilege' or something of the kind. All his life D. H. Lawrence had a feeling of social underprivilege, and this made him write a book in which a lady gives herself to her gamekeeper. John Braine, the Angry Young Man who wrote *Room at the Top*, shows the same tendency. I have never been bothered about my social position in this sense, but no doubt I have other peculiarities, and my obsession about 'knowledge' is one of them.

There is no point here in going deeper into my instinct to find a meaning in life. It may be that this urge is futile, that all men die whether they live like animals or with the passion of a Beethoven. But my need to explore my own life for meanings has led to a quite definite attitude to the writing of my contemporaries, and this, I think, is worth explaining in more detail.

The first very great influence on my work and thinking was Bernard Shaw; the second, T. S. Eliot. It is hard to imagine a couple of more ill-assorted spiritual godfathers. I never met Shaw (who died when I was twenty), but I have had the privilege of Mr Eliot's acquaintance since the publication of my first book. And Mr Eliot still considers my admiration for Shaw wholly ill-advised. (Strangely enough, his friend and contemporary Sir Herbert Read allowed my enthusiasm to persuade him to reread Shaw, and he told me that he felt I was right, and that Shaw is one of the greatest writers of our time.) Mr Eliot, who attacked D. H. Lawrence in the 1930s, has now decided that Lawrence was a very great and important writer; but he refuses to change his mind about Shaw, whom he has always considered shallow and lacking in poetry.

I have written a great deal about Shaw, including an acknowledgment that I borrowed the word 'Outsider' from him. But Mr Eliot's influence on me has never received full acknowledgment, and if I speak of him here it is to repay a debt as well as to open a way into the subject of my contemporary writers.

The first thing about Mr Eliot's writing that impressed me was his sense of the past. This seems to me to be very like my own thirst for any kind of knowledge. He obviously feels a certain contempt for writers who write simply about their backgrounds, and make no attempt to assess that background in terms of the whole of literature. It is almost as if Mr Eliot said, 'To be great, a modern writer must *know* a lot more than his colleagues of a hundred years ago'. In fact, I believe he does say something of the sort in one of his critical essays. But it is not merely his insistence on knowledge and discipline that has always appealed to me. When I compare him with the great English writers of the last century – Jane Austen, Dickens, Wordsworth, even Coleridge – they seem amazingly innocent by comparison, like children. Dickens, with his innocently good characters and his unbelievably sinister or brutal villains, Wordsworth with his optimistic nature worship, Trollope with his country parsons and demure spinsters – all these seem one-dimensional when compared with Eliot and his complex sense of the human predicament. It is not simply that Eliot has a more sophisticated sense of evil than these writers; so has Mr Graham Greene, who seems to me a complete theatrical fake as a writer. It is that Eliot seems free from the emotions and delusions that made these writers self-satisfied; that he realizes that human salvation and damnation are matters of immense difficulty; yet he also knows that men are capable of a depth of horror and a height of mystical ecstasy that makes human life something far greater and deeper than Dickens or Wordsworth realized. Eliot looked to the past for a kindred sense of good and evil, and found it in Dante, in certain saints and mystics of the Middle Ages, in the *Bhagavad Gita*, and (in brief flashes) in stories like Conrad's *Heart of Darkness* and Hawthorne's *Ethan Brand*.

Hence the first and most basic cause for the tremendous attraction that Eliot exercised over me. He made human life seem something of far greater dignity and depth than any other writer I had read. He began by sweeping the board clean of illusions with a great wet sponge of despair:

> Our dried voices when
> We whisper together
> Are quiet and meaningless
> As wind in dry grass...

It seemed as if all previous experiences of the human reality had been observed by schoolboys. 'Literature' in the nineteenth-century sense was a different art; it was the mere telling of stories to amuse one another. Only towards the end of the century had a few writers felt the same fatigue as Eliot, men like Dowson and Verlaine. Admittedly, Dowson's poetry is mostly sentimental day-dreaming; but its weariness is the fatigue of a man who has grown up and finds the world a brutal and confused place. His best poetry has the same ring of honesty as Eliot at his best.

This honesty seemed to me the only thing worth aiming at in literature. Story-telling is all very well, but real literature is something different. It is like man creating for himself a pair of spectacles so that he can at last take a good look at the world; real literature is a revolt against human myopia.

Eliot's immense erudition for me was another proof of his total sincerity and the seriousness of his approach to writing. Most of his contemporaries seemed, by comparison, ignoramuses, men with no real intention of using literature to recreate a spiritual oasis in the confusion of the twentieth century. Such American writers as Dos Passos and James T. Farrell may possess some of the same sort of story-telling genius as Dickens, if in a lesser degree but a badly confused man who read Dos Passos would end even more badly confused. In all the writing of Dos Passos, there is not a single invocation of a modern city as clear and powerful as the one in Eliot's short poems, *Preludes*. A sensitive youth who found the modern world stupid and confused and shallow – a world that only apes could accept without protest – might read Eliot's poetry and find his own diffused and splintered rejection canalized suddenly into a positive revolt.

> ... the light crept up between the shutters
> And you heard the sparrows in the gutters,
> You had such a vision of the streets
> As the street hardly understands...

This is the power of poetry: to create a vision of the confusion that the confusion would not understand. Again and again Eliot's poetry begins from images of the complex, factory-dominated civilization, and ends with a strange and beautiful reconciliation. 'This music is successful with a dying fall now that we talk of dying', he says in 'Portrait of a Lady. In Rhapsody on a Windy Night' the beating, incantatory rhythms of the poetry dissolve the harsh material – the 'broken spring in a factory yard', the prostitute in the doorway, the starved cat eating rancid butter – and the poet is strangely reconciled to his world. But he is reconciled because it is night, the factories are silent, the ageless wind tears through the streets where earlier there were pedestrians and automobiles. In the same way in *The Waste Land* the complexity of modern civilization – and its stupidity – are first of all focused into a mood of despair and rejection; the world is seen as a desert without water. Then an increasing violence enters the poetry, with:

> A woman drew her long black hair out tight
> And fiddled whisper music on those strings

and the poem ends in a mood of prophetic denunciation – falling towers, the end of the world.

Eliot gives a sense of being one of the most responsible writers since the prophets of the Old Testament. None of his admirers or imitators have given anything approaching the same impression of quiet authority, sensitivity, penetrating intelligence. Mr Auden has, indeed, taken a leaf out of Eliot's book: he speaks of the need for discipline and austerity; but I know of no single poem of his that shows anything more than a man who wants to be an accepted poet, a modern oracle. There is never the same note of authority. But, above all, Auden gives no sense of having a unifying vision of the modern chaos; he has not, like Eliot, experienced it to the point of suffering, and finally overcome it by the strange alchemy of creation.

The question of Eliot's erudition is perhaps worth further comment. I am not attempting to argue that erudition and good literature necessarily go together, but only that Eliot seemed to me one of the few writers who have made an attempt to understand and master their own age. When I was fourteen I had an unconquerable revulsion for a certain type of modern novel. Ever since I was ten I had read my mother's library books: volumes with titles like *I Carried a Gun for Al Capone*, *Don't Call Me a Crook*, cheap paperbacks about American gangsters and novels about life in slum districts in England and America. (D. H. Lawrence's *Sons and Lovers* was one of my mother's favourite books). Then, when I was thirteen, I discovered English literature – Chaucer and Spenser and Ben Jonson and Milton and Charles Lamb and Palgrave's *Golden Treasury of Songs and Poems*. Here was an orderly universe where great passions could work themselves out in an atmosphere of predestination. Instead of the brutal and stupid deaths, and even more brutal and stupid lives, I had read about in my mother's *True Detective* magazines or gangster novelettes, here was a world where human beings approached the dignity of gods. Consequently I rejected wholesale all the novels and poetry written after the year 1900. All modern writing seemed too superficial; it lacked that sense of deep tragedy and meaning that both the Greeks and the Elizabethans possessed in abundance. Only in the writing of Shaw and H. G. Wells – and the early writing of G. K. Chesterton – did I find the same underlying feeling that the world ought to be meaningful, ought to be controlled by men with ideals. After them, the world seemed to go to pieces. I remember hearing a radio performance of Noël Coward's *Cavalcade* with its final cry 'The world's gone mad'. This seemed to me the underlying message of both the serious and the cheap literature of the twentieth century, of Hemingway's novels as well as the trashy gangster novelettes of James Hadley Chase that were so popular at the beginning of the war.

This, then, defines the reason that I found Eliot's erudition such an important part of his attitude to literature. Men like Hemingway and James Hadley Chase seemed unaware of anything but the brutal and meaningless present. Other writers, like J. B. Priestley, seemed simply to be writing slightly above the standard of sentimental women's magazines. Even Joyce's *Ulysses* revolted me as another chronicle of futility. Eliot seemed to me one of the few men who had a right to pass judgment on his own age because of his sense of the past.

Strangely enough, I very seldom read Eliot nowadays. This is not because I have in any way ceased to feel immense respect for what he has done. (Although there is a strong reaction against Eliot in England and America today, it springs from a revolt against thirty years of his 'cultural dictatorship'.) Perhaps – I hope – it is because I have absorbed Eliot so completely into my way of thinking that it is superfluous to reread him.

But what continues to astonish me is how little influence Eliot seems to have had on other young writers. With the exception of my friend Stuart Holroyd, I can think of no writer of the past ten years who shows any sign of ever having read Eliot (if one excepts John Osborne's satirical references in *Look Back in Anger*). It is chiefly for this reason that I feel alienated from the other young writers of England and America. Not, I hasten to add, simply because they are uninfluenced by Eliot, but because they seem to possess none of his god's-eye view of the present. It seems to me that Eliot has demonstrated that a man who wants to be a significant writer in the twentieth century must have certain basic equipment – and this includes a sense of tradition and a sense of man's paradoxical position in the universe, poised between animal and god.

This is not wholly true of the rest of Europe, where a few writers like Thomas Mann, Albert Camus, Jean Paul Sartre and (more recently) Friedrich Dürrenmatt have continued to write with a deep sense of man's predicament. But Thomas Mann belongs to an older generation than Eliot, and I have always found Camus and Sartre strangely unsatisfactory when compared with Eliot. In fact Camus has always seemed to me a kind of lesser T. S. Eliot, while Sartre often has a cheapness and superficiality that is too reminiscent of the American writers who have influenced him. For all his apparent intelligence, for example, Sartre fails to see the absurdity and immaturity of declaring himself an atheist. I am not now arguing as a convinced 'believer'. But any great artist knows that the springs of his inspiration are incomprehensible, beyond the reach of his daylight personality. He experiences depths of emotional violence that defy expression in the language of logic or the newspapers. Consequently, no great artist dares to say, 'There is no God'. He is far more likely, like Nijinsky, to preserve the concept of God to describe his deepest intuitions: 'God is fire in the head'. (See for example how Shelley, who began as a militant atheist, ended by frequently referring to 'God' in his poetry because he needed a concept that would embody the greatest ideals he could conceive.) Even Nietzsche, who declared 'God is dead', had to use the word 'life' or 'eternity' to describe otherwise inexpressible sensations. (His use of eternity is, of course, completely out of keeping with the rest of his philosophy; in *Zarathustra*, where he advises men not to bury their heads in nonsensical concepts like 'heaven' and speaks defiantly of eternal recurrence, he nevertheless makes Zarathustra say, 'For I love thee, oh eternity'.) Sartre's continual declarations of atheism immediately place him on a lower plane than the great poets – they establish his level among argumentative communists and anarchists and members of the flat earth society.

The work of Friedrich Dürrenmatt is, at the time of writing, hardly known to a large audience outside his own country – Switzerland. His play *The Visit* had considerable success on Broadway and in London. But it is on the evidence of two very short novels that I consider him one of the most important writers of present-day Europe. One of these is called *The Pledge*, and deals with a police officer who sets out to catch a sex maniac killer, using a small girl as 'bait' to lure the killer into the open. The trap almost works, but the killer dies in a road accident on his way to commit his last murder. The question Dürrenmatt poses is: Was the police officer's use of the child as 'bait' justified? In the modern world we tend to judge an act by its consequences. If the sex maniac had been caught as he was about to murder the child, we should believe his action was wholly justified. But if morality has a meaning, it is connected with a set of values that has no relation to the consequences of an action; the action is judged before its consequence happens. Dürrenmatt is trying to speak of our complete lack of standards and – worse still – our tendency to feel that common-sense pragmatic judgments make it unnecessary to speak of the 'supernatural'. What Dürrenmatt is trying to show is not that the supernatural is the real basis of all value judgments (this would place him in line with Graham Greene and François Mauriac – a position I am sure he would hate), but that the value problem refuses to be fitted into the world of communist pragmatism or into the world of the Catholic Church. Man lives in a world of values which have nothing to do with the consequences of actions. It is, as it were, a religious world without any religious dogmas.

This appears even more clearly in his other short novel, *A Dangerous Game*. In this novel, a travelling salesman stops in a small Swiss village when his car breaks down, and accepts the hospitality of an old gentleman who used to be a judge. The old gentleman has three other friends who were also involved in the law – two lawyers and a hangman! To amuse themselves in their retirement they play a game of 'mock trials'. Their guests are placed on trial, their lives are examined, and they are found guilty or innocent. It is, of course, only a game, not, as in Kafka, a nightmarish reality. The travelling salesman is made to confess that he slept with his boss's wife and then made sure that the boss found out; the boss died of heart failure and the salesman stepped into his shoes. And yet it was not a planned murder; in fact the salesman does not even think of himself as particularly guilty, for 'business is business' and one has to do many dubiously ethical things... As the prosecuting counsel denounces his guilt, the travelling salesman begins to feel pleased with himself. Formerly he felt himself to be a very ordinary, dull little man, whose worst crime is to commit adultery whenever he gets the chance. Now he is revealed as one of the most cunning murderers of the age; his meaningless life is given depth and dignity. When his 'defending counsel' pleads that his client is not really guilty of a crime but only of a thoughtless misdemeanour, the salesman protests violently. No, it is not true; he is actually a master-criminal... He begs to be regarded as a master-criminal and sentenced to death. His host obligingly sentences him to death, and the party breaks up with hilarity and mutual good will. But when the travelling salesman reaches his bedroom, he is so delighted and relieved to find that his life has actually been far more meaningful than he ever suspected that he carries the story to its logical conclusion and hangs himself.

The end of the story seems to me somewhat weak and contrived, but its meaning is very clear. We are living messy, pointless lives, and if we commit crimes they are often not crimes because they are committed out of pointlessness, not out of calculated defiance of moral values. But even the most pointless of us still longs secretly for values, for good and evil.

Dürrenmatt's importance seems to me to be simply this: he has found a language for speaking of the need for good and evil that owes nothing to Eliot or D. H. Lawrence or Sartre or Camus. And he is working 'at a depth' in a way that no other writer in Europe or America can be said to do.

To conclude this essay, I want to speak of my own attitude to writing and of what I would like to do in modern literature. Unfortunately for myself, I possess a stronger analytical faculty than a 'creative intuition'. A book like

The Outsider was much easier for me to write than my novel *Ritual in the Dark* or the four plays that I have written in the past two years. Nevertheless I feel that this is as it should be. The age of men who created freely and un-analytically is past. The creator of the future must learn to bear an altogether heavier burden of self-consciousness than his predecessors. This also means of course, that it must cost him an altogether greater effort to embark on creative activity. (As far as I can see Dürrenmatt is extremely lucky; on the evidence of his two novels I would judge that he is a wholly intuitive creator whose intuitions are as deep as Eliot's.) But the need to be analytical as well as creative need not weigh on writers too heavily; after all, we now have a broad Western tradition of 'intellectual creators', from Dostoevsky and Andreyev to Pirandello and Sartre.

My novel *Ritual in the Dark* (which deals with a sadistic killer of women) is my first book which attempts to state a theme that will, I think, be the subject of many more of my works – my attitude to sex. *Ritual* is not by any means a complete statement of my attitude. I would like to try to define it more fully here.

Why, in the first place, attach any great importance to sex? My reason is simple: sex seems to be one of the few clear and definite primeval urges in modern man. The world reveals no motive or significance to our most careful scrutiny; it is like a completely expressionless face. Dr Pangloss declared that he sensed a benevolent deity behind it all; the Manichees sensed an evil demiurge; Thomas Hardy sensed a spirit of irony bent on making men suffer; G. K. Chesterton sensed a God who had created the world as a good-humoured joke. Who is right? Jean Paul Sartre came closest to portraying the world as it seems to modern man in his novel *La Nausée*, where his hero sees everything as totally meaningless, quite absurd. Man, Sartre implies, spends his life projecting his comfortable little emotions on to the world; but the world is neither benevolent nor malevolent: it is completely *alien*, indifferent. In other words, man and the world are like two trains running on wholly different tracks; they may run parallel for a while, but it is pure chance.

This, I admit, seems highly probable. But, for me at least life does occasionally show its hand. The sexual urge, particularly in its purer forms, seems to reveal an underlying purpose. In the light of sex, we can occasionally glimpse the purpose of history. By 'its purer forms' I mean when separated from personality, either by idealism or by physical violence, as in certain sex crimes.

Now all this is not new. As I have summarized it above it might be taken for a précis of the ideas of D. H. Lawrence. And yet, on the contrary, I feel an abyss separating my own intuition of the world from Lawrence's. This is why, in a bedroom scene in my novel, my hero thinks: 'Lawrence was a fool...' Lawrence insisted on separating sex from the other great superhuman drives – the drive of the mathematical intellect, for example. I think they cannot be separated. Consequently I do not find a sense of sex akin to my own in Lawrence. But I *do* find a sense akin to my own in another twentieth-century writer, the German Frank Wedekind, who is hardly known in this country. Wedekind seems to me far more aware than Lawrence of the demoniacal element in sex. For him sex is not something that 'fulfills' Lady Chatterley and her gamekeeper (or any other pair of Lawrence lovers). It can be a terrible and destructive urge, *which is nevertheless greater than anything else that human beings are likely to experience*. For example, in a masterly and terrible short story called 'The Burning of Egliswyl', a young convict describes how he had relations with every girl in the village, until eventually he met a girl who drove him insane with desire. One day, when having intercourse with her, he feels that she is untouchable, that she is permanently beyond him. In a frenzy he sets fire to the village. 'I howled and shrieked like an animal in a slaughter house.' He is driven to a frenzy by the element of the permanently unattainable in sex – what one might call the 'supernatural'.

He sets fire to the village because the flames give him a temporary illusion of having achieved that heart of the fire of life. In the same way, Zola's 'human beast' Claude Lantier feels an urge to kill women because he wants to 'possess them to the point of destroying them.'

I hope that this example has made plain the way in which my own intuition of sex has nothing in common with Lawrence's.

There is another work by Wedekind in which he approaches even closer to this intuition: the two plays that make up his *Lulu*. Lulu is a street urchin who is picked up by a newspaper editor who makes her his mistress. (She is already the mistress of a sinister old man whom everyone thinks to be her father.) The editor wants to marry an innocent young girl, and for this purpose marries off Lulu to an old man. Lulu is unfaithful with a young painter, and the old man dies of heart failure; Lulu then marries the painter. But he finds out that she is the mistress of the newspaper editor, and commits suicide. The editor determines to go through with his marriage to the young girl, but at the last moment Lulu's fascination proves too great, and he marries her. He now becomes her victim, like all the other men; in a jealous frenzy he tries to shoot her, and is himself shot dead. His son now becomes Lulu's lover, possessing her for the first time on the very divan on which his father's body had lain.

The rest of the story is too complex to detail (Alban Berg used it for his opera *Lulu*). It ends with Lulu as a prostitute in the East End of London, where she is murdered by Jack the Ripper. A mere plot summary of the plays makes them sound absurdly complicated; in fact, they produce one single overwhelming impression: the terrible sexual magnetism that emanates from Lulu *and over which she has no control*. She is not a *femme fatale*, one of those evil sirens made popular on the silent screen by pale-faced Hollywood actresses. On the contrary, although she victimizes men, she is also the victim. At the end, she is exploited by everyone; the editor's son lives off her immoral earnings, after spending all her money. She embodies the innocent, destructive, unconscious, and irresistible force of life. She burns through Wedekind's play like a torch.

A study of Berg's opera based on Wedekind has determined me to use the idea of 'Lulu', at least partially, as a basis for a novel, a long *Bildungsroman* told in the first person by a young man who undergoes various forms of education. I expect this novel to produce a far clearer impression of my concept of sex than I was able to achieve in *Ritual in the Dark*.

My own vision of the future of literature is optimistic. There was a brief time during the thirties and forties when critics declared that the novel had come to an end after *Ulysses*, and that perhaps all English literature had come to an end. The personalities of Eliot and Joyce dominated the literary scene so completely that this view was understandable, for no one could create anything that was not directly or indirectly influenced by them. This seems to me to be no longer true. Admittedly the critics, as usual, are completely blind to what is actually taking place. They believe that the literary revolution of the 1950s was the rise of the Angry Young Men – writers like John Osborne, Kingsley Amis, John Braine (I myself am frequently classified with these writers although, heaven knows, I have nothing in common with them except my age). But the truly cheering thing about modern literature is the revolution that began with Eliot, and that is now continuing with Dürrenmatt. And (if I might say so without immodesty) with myself, Stuart Holroyd, and Bill Hopkins in England. This is the tradition of an intellectual creation with its roots in analysis, and its eventual aim to be a new form of self-consciousness.

1958

Editor's Notes
For the full-story of the so-called 'Angry Young Men' see Wilson's *The Angry Years: The Rise and Fall of the Angry Young Men* (London: Robson Books, 2007 (**A173**)).
Wilson never completed his novel *Lulu* despite it being commissioned for serialisation by BBC2 in 1976. As late as 1983 he wrote: 'For twenty-five years now I have been writing a novel called *Lulu*, and I must have started it a hundred times." In 2016 I found the 176 pages of what remained of the manuscript among Wilson's papers, which I was helping to sort prior to them going into his archive at the University of Nottingham. These were published in 2017, with an Introduction by Wilson-scholar Dr Vaughan Rapatahana, as *Colin Wilson's* Lulu: *An Unfinished Novel* (Nottingham: Paupers' Press (**A184**)) along with some of Wilson's notes and journal entries appertaining to the novel.

ABOUT THE AUTHORS

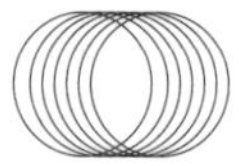

Colin Wilson was born in the East Midlands city of Leicester in 1931. After the phenomenal success of his first book *The Outsider* in 1956, he moved to Cornwall where he pursued a successful career as a writer, producing over 150 titles in fifty-five years. Essentially an existentialist philosopher, he has also written on crime, psychology, sex, the occult, literature, music, unexplained phenomena, history, pre-history and over 20 novels in various genres. He died in December 2013.

Gary Lachman is the author of several books on the meeting ground between consciousness, culture and the western esoteric tradition including *Jung the Mystic: the Esoteric Dimensions of Carl Jung's Life and Teachings*; *The Secret History of Consciousness*; *The Caretakers of the Cosmos* and many others. In 2016 his *Beyond the Robot: the Life and Work of Colin Wilson* was published. As Gary Valentine he was a founding member of the rock group Blondie and was inducted into the Rock and Roll Hall of Fame in 2006.

Colin Stanley was born in Topsham, Devon in 1952 and educated at the Exmouth School. Beginning in 1970, he worked for Devon Library Services, studying for two years in London, before moving to Nottingham where he worked for the University of Nottingham until 2005.

The Managing Editor of Paupers' Press, he is also the author and editor of several books about Colin Wilson including *An Evolutionary Leap: Colin Wilson and Psychology* and *Around the Outsider*, a festschrift for the author's 80th birthday. His collection of Wilson's work now forms *The Colin Wilson Collection* at the University of Nottingham, an archive opened in 2011 and which now contains many of the author's manuscripts and papers.

Dr Todd Swift is the founder of Eyewear Publishing Limited, a small London press. A screenwriter, poet, anthologist, editor and critic, he was Pembroke College (Cambridge) Poet-in-residence 2017-2018. He is married and lives in London with his wife, Sara. He has many nephews and nieces. British now, he was born in Montreal, Quebec, Canada, on Good Friday 1966.

EYEWEAR PUBLISHING

Eyewear publishes fiction,
non-fiction, and poetry.

Recent prose works include:
That Summer in Puglia by Valeria Vescina
Juggling With Turnips by Karl MacDermott
Aliens, Gods & Artists by Sam Eisenstein
Last Performance At The Odeon by Carol Susan Nathanson
The Other Side Of Como by Mara G. Fox

Literary criticism:
This Dialogue Of One by Mark Ford

WWW.EYEWEARPUBLISHING.COM